Without Permission

Conversations, Letters, and Memoirs of
Henry Mandel

Cherry
Orchard
Books

Without Permission

Conversations, Letters, and Memoirs of
Henry Mandel

Edited by
SAMUEL FLAKS

BOSTON
2021

Library of Congress Cataloging-in-Publication Data

Names: Flaks, Samuel, 1984- editor.
Title: Without permission : Conversations, Letters, and Memoirs of Henry Mandel /
   edited by Samuel Flaks.
Other titles: Henry Mandel and the Mercy Ship Ben Hecht
Description: Boston : Academic Studies Press, 2021. | Includes bibliographical
   references and index. | Summary: "A fantastical propaganda play depicting an armed
   revolt financed the purchase of the yacht Abril and its conversion to an "illegal"
   immigrant passenger ship renamed the Ben Hecht. The plan was to evade the
   British naval blockade and bring Holocaust survivor refugees to Palestine. Henry
   Mandel volunteered aboard the Ben Hecht, a converted yacht that challenged the
   British blockade of Jewish immigrants to pre-state Israel. Captured and detained in
   Acre Prison, Mandel aided the efforts of prisoners planning an escape. After release,
   Mandel helped set up a secret bazooka shell plant in New York, which he helped to
   reassemble in Israel during the 1948 Arab-Israeli War. Mandel was an Orthodox Jew
   whose reminiscences provide a uniquely illuminating perspective on the creation of
   the Jewish state. Mandel's story is explicated in a running commentary that includes
   the personal narratives of other members of the Ben Hecht crew as well as historical
   background"-- Provided by publisher.
Identifiers: LCCN 2021041027 (print) | LCCN 2021041028 (ebook) | ISBN
   9781644695944 (paperback) | ISBN 9781644695951 (adobe pdf) | ISBN
   9781644695968 (epub)
Subjects: LCSH: Mandel, Henry, 1920-2015--Interviews. | Ben Hecht (Yacht)--History.
   | Bergson Group. | Jewish refugees--Palestine--History--20th century. | Palestine--
   Emigration and immigration--History--20th century. | Zionists--New York (State)--
   New York--Biography. | Merchant mariners--United States--Biography.
Classification: LCC DS151.M3162 W58 2021 (print) | LCC DS151.M3162 (ebook) |
   DDC 320.54095694/092--dc23
LC record available at https://lccn.loc.gov/2021041027
LC ebook record available at https://lccn.loc.gov/2021041028

ISBN 9781644695944 (paperback)
ISBN 9781644695951 (adobe pdf)
ISBN 9781644695968 (epub)

Book design by Lapiz Digital Services
Cover design by Ivan Grave

Published by Cherry Orchard Books, an imprint of Academic Studies Press
1577 Beacon Street
Brookline, MA 02446, USA
press@academicstudiespress.com
www.academicstudiespress.com

Dedicated to my wife Lauren and our daughter Sarah, with love.

וַיַּעְפִּלוּ לַעֲלוֹת אֶל־רֹאשׁ הָהָר

Yet defiantly [vaya'apliu] *they ascended to the top of the mountain . . .*
—Numbers 14:44

ויעפלו — לשון חוזק וכן (חבקוק ב, ד) הנה עפלה. אינגרי״ש בלע״ז לשון עזות, ומדרש
תנחומא מפרשו לשון אופל, הלכו חשכים שלא ברשות.

Vaya'apliu—*language denoting "strength." And similarly, "Behold, presumptuous" (Hab. 2:4). Engres in Old French, denoting "impudence." . . . And the
Midrash* Tanchuma *interprets it as denoting "darkness" —they went darkly
without permission.*
—Rashi, ad loc.

(Translation adapted from Abraham Ben Isaiah and Benjamin Sharfman, *Pentateuch and
Rashi's Commentary: Numbers* [Brooklyn, NY: S.S. & R. Publishing Company, Inc., 1950]).

Contents

Introduction   xi

Part One. Interviews and Reminiscences of Jewish Illegal Immigrant Ship *Ben Hecht* Crewman Henry Mandel   1

1. Vienna Born, Bronx Bred   3
2. The War Comes Home   14
3. The Merchant Marine   20
4. From Gowanus Canal to Atlantic Crossing   31
5. Final Preparations   42
6. The Irgun Had Other Ideas   48
7. Bazooka Plant   62

Part Two. Letters and Contextual Commentary   71

8. The Bergson Group   73
9. The Mission and the Crew   87
10. Atlantic Crossing to the Mediterranean Sea   103
11. The Palestine Run   115
12. Piracy on the High Seas   125
13. Breakout   155
14. Release   161
15. Machal   171
16. A Mercy Ship's Legacy   179

Part Three. Henry Mandel Reflects   191

17. Family and Brotherly Love   193
18. Civil Servant and Union Activist   201

Epilogue   205
Acknowledgments   209
Selected Bibliography and Works Cited   211
Index   225
Illustrations   231

Introduction

More Ships Are Coming

Your American dollars paid for the Hebrew Repatriation ship, "S.S. Ben Hecht" . . . and for other ships we need. American crews man those ships. American food sustains the passengers. The British try to call it "illegal." But Americans say there is no such thing as an ILLEGAL Hebrew life. If it's legal for the British to live, IT'S LEGAL FOR HEBREWS TO LIVE. In dignity. In safety . . . instead of DP camps. YOUR money does it! . . . THE SHIPS ARE READY . . . THE CREWS ARE READY . . . BUT THE PASSENGERS ARE WAITING . . . WAITING! NOW IS THE TIME TO THROW ANOTHER PUNCH, THE STRONGEST ONE YOU CAN. $250 saves a life —repatriates a Hebrew man, woman, or child on the way to Palestine. Send us $250,—$50—$5 to speed the Hebrews home on an Armada of Mercy Ships. The need is now—the time is now. . . .

—American League for a Free Palestine Advertisement, March 13, 1947[1]

On Saturday night, March 8, 1947, the 8:15 p.m. broadcast of Jerusalem radio broke the news to the people of British Mandatory Palestine that an "illegal" immigrant ship carrying 600 passengers had been boarded, captured, and brought into port without incident by the Royal Navy. The Mandatory Government information office announced that the immigrant ship, named *Abril*, had been seen off the coast of Jaffa at ten in the morning and that Naval Marines had boarded the ship and captured it without opposition.[2] London radio soon broadcast that the ship was outfitted by

---

1   "More Ships Are Coming," American League for a Free Palestine's (ALFP) Advertisement, *New York Post,* Thursday, March 13, 1947, found in Bob Levitan collection, accession number 2010.505.1, United States Holocaust Memorial Museum (USHMM).

2   "Immigrant Ship Captured and Brought to Haifa," *Al Hamishmar,* Sunday, March 9, front page, dateline Haifa (Hebrew); "Arrest of Illegal Immigrant Ship," Sunday, *Davar,* March 9, 1947, front page (Hebrew).

American Zionists at the start of the year.[3] A newspaper reported that "[i]t is thought that the captured ship that had sailed on February 28 from France under the Honduran flag was sent by Peter Bergson's group, and its name, apparently, is *Ben Hecht*."[4]

The yacht, propelled by diesel engines, had been renamed in transit as the *Ben Hecht* in honor of the author whose play *A Flag is Born* helped finance its mission,[5] though the name on the bow still read *Abril* when it was captured.[6] The 600 passengers had in their possession identification and travel papers issued in Paris on February 28, 1947 by the Hebrew Committee for National Liberation (HCNL), purporting to act on a provisional basis until the establishment of a Hebrew government in a free Land of Israel, and signed by Eri Jabotinsky, the son of the late Revisionist Zionism founder Ze'ev (Vladimir) Jabotinsky.[7]

Along the stranger-than-fiction journey of the *Abril / Ben Hecht,* a fantastical propaganda play depicting an armed revolt financed the purchase of a yacht and its conversion to an illegal immigrant passenger ship. The plan was to evade the British naval blockade and bring Holocaust survivor refugees to their homeland. If captured by the British, a trial of the crew would expose Britain's arguably illegal and indubitably cruel anti-Jewish immigration policy. Although the Royal Navy apprehended the *Ben Hecht* and took the refugees to camps on Cyprus, the refugees were released within two years and did in fact immigrate into Israel. The imprisoned American crew aided an Irgun and Lechi fighter breakout from Acre Prison that shook the British Empire and was a factor in leading Britain to abandon its rule of Palestine. Subsequently, the charmed vessel played a key role in a naval battle that secured the nascent state of Israel's access to the sea.[8]

---

3   "Illegal Immigrant Ship Arrested near Haifa," *Hasapha,* Sunday, March 9, 1947, front page (Hebrew).

4   "599 *Abril* Immigrants Sent to Island of Deportation," *Al Hamishmar,* Monday, March 10, 1947, 2, dateline Haifa, Sunday, March 9, 1947 (Hebrew).

5   I. F. Stone, "Refugees Driven on Cyprus-Bound Ships like Cattle," *PM,* March 10, 1947, 1, 2, 7, *PM* reel 53, 3/2–4/30/47, NYPL.

6   Oral history of Robert Levitan, accession number 2010.505.2, RG Number: RG-50.932.0001, USHMM.

7   "The Immigrants Expelled from the Land of Israel," *Haaretz,* front page, March 10, 1947 (Hebrew); Chaim Lazar, *Immigration Ship "Ben Hecht"* (n.p.: Museum of Combatants and Partisans, 1995/1996), 5–17 (Hebrew).

8   Natanel Lorch, *The Edge of the Sword: Israel's War of Independence 1947–1949* (New York / London: G. P. Putnam's Sons, 1961), 329; J. Wandres, *The Ablest Navigator:*

My grandfather Henry Mandel (1920–2015), an American Merchant Marine sailor during World War II, a crewman aboard the *Abril / Ben Hecht*, a prisoner in Acre Fortress, and a volunteer for the Israeli Army during the 1948 Israeli War of Independence, was an Orthodox Jew whose reminiscences provide a unique illuminating perspective on the redemption of captives and the creation of a Jewish homeland in the late 1940s. Henry— called Hymie by his family, Hank by his crewmates on the MS (Motor Ship) *Abril / Ben Hecht*, and Chaim by his comrades in the Israeli Army—was a member of the Greatest Generation of Americans who struggled in the Great Depression and then triumphed in an all-consuming World War.[9] He was born in Vienna on September 6, 1920, and came to the United States as a toddler in 1923. Mandel worked at the Brooklyn Navy Yard from January 1940 until 1945 as a civilian machinist and then served aboard United States Merchant Marine ships.

Mandel volunteered for several activities between 1946 and 1949 in the fight to establish Israel. A Mr. Green, a neighbor of his family in the Bronx whose daughters were friendly with Mandel's sisters, told Mandel about the *Ben Hecht*, and he unhesitatingly volunteered.[10] Mandel served as second engineer and oiler in the engine room as well as an electrician and plumber aboard the undermanned ship. En route to Palestine, its engine was damaged, probably due to British sabotage. Mandel and his fellow crewmen in the engine room expeditiously and skillfully rigged a patch repair, which enabled the voyage to continue. Mandel, along with the rest of the crew of the *Ben Hecht*, spent a little less than a month as a remanded prisoner in Acre Prison in March 1947. During his imprisonment he and his crewmates smuggled in a camera and electric batteries to prisoners before they were released by the British, due to their status as American citizens.

Mandel was approached to join the *Altalena* after returning to New York, but he declined because he was engaged in assembling a secret bazooka shell plant with machinery that had been sold by the US government as surplus, and he could not leave to join the crew as his skills as a trained machinist were sorely needed at the covert operation on Greene

---

 Lieutenant Paul N. Shulman USN, Israel's Volunteer Admiral (Annapolis: Naval Institute Press, 2013), 1–2.

9 Tom Brokaw, *The Greatest Generation* (New York: Random House, 1998), 4–5, 7–8.

10 Henry Mandel interview by Alyssa Goldschmidt Magid, December 1, 2006 (audio recording in possession of the editor); Henry Mandel interview by Esther Mandel, Aaron Mandel, and Chana Liba Mandel, circa 2012.

Street in Manhattan. Mandel was organizing the dismantling and labeling of the plant and its machinery, which he thereafter helped reassemble in Israel as a foreign volunteer in the new Israeli Defense Forces.[11]

In a letter to the Israeli Defense Ministry dated February 25, 1998, Mandel described his involvement with the *Ben Hecht*:

> Shalom Chaverim [comrades],
>
> I must apologize for writing in English but my *Ivrit* [Hebrew] is not good enough for expressing myself properly. I have filled out the forms that you have forwarded to me, but I cannot fill out Paragraph *Vov* [6] [which asked for verification from Mandel's commander] as requested. In 1946 I was in the United States Merchant Marines and my ship returned to New York where I lived. A neighbor told me that an organization was looking for seamen. He sent me to the American League for a Free Palestine. The Chairman of the League was Senator Guy Gillette, but it was actually run by an Israeli Irgunist, Peter Bergson. I was told that this was not his real name, but I do not know if this is so. The purpose of the League was to raise funds for the Irgun and to influence the American public, and particularly the American Congress. Mr. Bergson spent much of his time in Washington. Ben Hecht, the writer, was very active in the organization. He published full page advertisements, and he wrote and produced the play *A Flag is Born* on Broadway to raise funds.[12]
>
> I was interviewed by someone, I do not recall his name. He wanted me to speak to Avraham Stavsky who was out of the country but would be back in a few days. In the meantime, I signed off of my ship. I spoke to Mr. Stavsky who said he was looking for an American crew to man their ship the *MS Abril* (which was later changed to *MS Ben Hecht*). Up until that time the crew of Aliyah Bet ships, when captured, would mingle with the passengers and the British would not arrest any crewman. The intention with the *MS Ben Hecht* was that if the ship was captured the American crew would remain to be arrested by the British. Because of the publicity they could not intern Americans in Cyprus or Eritrea. There would have to be a public trial where the Americans involved would be charged with "Aiding and Abetting Illegal Immigration." The defense would be that the immigration was legal and that

---

11   Henry Mandel letter to the Israeli Defense Ministry, February 25, 1998 (in possession of the editor).

12   Julien Gorbach, *The Notorious Ben Hecht: Iconoclastic Writer and Militant Zionist* (West Lafayette, IN: Purdue University Press, 2019), 236–237.

the British were given the Mandate to make Palestine a homeland for the Jewish people. This would show the English in a very unfavorable light before the entire world and would hasten the exit of the British from Palestine.

***

The Bergson Group, known after its leader Peter Bergson (whose real identity was Hillel Kook, a nephew of Abraham Isaac Kook, the first Ashkenazi Chief Rabbi of British Mandatory Palestine), was a committee of members of the Irgun Tzva'i Le'umi (in Hebrew, the "National Military Organization," variously referred to herein as the "Irgun" or by its Hebrew initials "ITzL" or "Etzel") who arrived in the United States in 1939 and 1940. The Irgun was an underground military resistance organization in British Mandatory Palestine that rejected the mainstream Haganah's self-restraint policy and performed violent retaliatory operations after Arab attacks in the 1930s.[13] For the Irgun, "[t]he enemy was British imperialism, not the British people."[14] Many liberal intellectuals supported the Bergson Group. Bergson Group members joined the Irgun, explained the son of a member who himself eventually founded a pro-peace and pro-Israel advocacy group, "to actively pursue national independence and to organize Aliyah Bet . . . to save lives, not to advance a political agenda. Their immigration work in particular was neither rightwing nor leftwing."[15] Bergson Group member Samuel Merlin explained that the Bergson Group believed "that a military force fighting to liberate the country from colonial rule could succeed only if accompanied by a vigorous propaganda and diplomatic campaign to explain and back up the military activities."[16] The Bergson Group's underlying strategy with the illegal immigrant ship *Ben Hecht*, similar to its

---

13 Aaron Rakeffet-Rothkoff, *The Silver Era in American Jewish Orthodoxy: Rabbi Eliezer Silver and His Generation* (Jerusalem / New York: Yeshiva University Press / Feldheim, 1981), 218.

14 Yitshaq Ben-Ami, *Years of Wrath, Days of Glory* (New York: Robert Speller & Sons, 1982), 394.

15 Jeremy Ben-Ami, Afterword, in Samuel Merlin, *Millions of Jews to Rescue: A Bergson Group Leader's Account of the Campaign to Save Jews from the Holocaust*, ed. and annotated Rafael Medoff, Foreword Seymour D. Reich (Washington, D.C.: David S. Wyman Institute for Holocaust Studies, 2011), 196, 206.

16 Merlin, *Millions of Jews to Rescue*, 15.

earlier attempts to stop the Holocaust, was to take bold public humanitarian action and publicize that action.[17]

The MV *Ben Hecht* was the only Jewish ship to transport illegal immigrants to Palestine, from the end of World War II until the establishment of the State of Israel, which was not sponsored by the Mossad L'Aliyah Bet ("Organization for Plan B Immigration"). The Mossad L'Aliyah Bet was associated with the Haganah, the establishment Jewish Agency's pre-state secret army. Mossad L'Aliyah Bet almost totally dominated illegal immigration after the war, though the Zionist Revisionist movement, inspired by Vladimir Jabotinsky, had been very active in organizing illegal immigration to Palestine before World War II and during the war's early years. In 1946, the Mossad L'Aliyah Bet purchased the *Josiah Wedgewood* and the *Haganah*, two former Canadian corvettes manned by American volunteer crews. This was the beginning of an expansion of the scope of Jewish illegal immigration to Palestine through the use of larger vessels and American crews. Though each of these larger vessels hardly stood a chance of sneaking through the British naval blockade, the Mossad L'Aliyah Bet's large-scale operations and the ever increasing numbers of interned illegal immigrants who refused to be returned to Europe increased political pressure that contributed to the British decision to abandon its Palestine Mandate. Ultimately, as one scholar observed, "[i]t was the quantity that produced the quality."[18] Illegal immigration, as another scholar has surmised, "served the purpose of founding a Jewish state by political means"; the Haganah's Aliyah Bet operation "was meant to keep the headlines and world public opinion busy with the problem of the Jewish DPs who were rotting away in Europe many months after the war was over" and to "exploit the moral advantage of the Zionist cause" over England's barring "the way of Holocaust survivors to their homeland."[19]

Scholars of the struggle for a Jewish state have studied the *Ben Hecht* because it was unique as the only post-war Jewish illegal immigration ship not organized by the Haganah. It was the policy of the Aliyah Bet organization to facilitate unauthorized immigration covertly, up to the point ships

---

17   Adina Hoffman, *Ben Hecht: Fighting Words, Moving Pictures* (New Haven, CT / London: Yale University Press, 2019), 173.

18   Mordechai Naor, *Haapala: Clandestine Immigration 1931–1948* (Tel Aviv: Ministry of Defense Publishing House and IDF Museum, 1987), 51, 32.

19   Aviva Halamish, *The Exodus Affair: Holocaust Survivors and the Struggle for Palestine*, trans. Ora Cummings, (Syracuse, NY: Syracuse University Press, 1998), 267, 265.

were intercepted by the Royal Navy. The voyage of immigration refugee ship *Ben Hecht* to Palestine, sponsored by the Bergson Group entity, the American League for a Free Palestine (AFLP)—a lobbying and public relations organization which supported the Hebrew Committee for National Liberation (HCNL)—was very different.[20] The *Ben Hecht* received a great deal of contemporary press, mostly courted by AFLP itself, during several events, including its semi-secret outfitting during the winter of 1946 on the Brooklyn waterfront, its journey to the French harbor of Port-de-Bouc to embark Jewish displaced persons, its capture by the Royal Navy on March 8, 1947, the detention of its passengers in Cyprus, the short imprisonment of the crew in Acre Prison, and the subsequent exile of the crew to America from Palestine on March 30, 1947. In recent decades its story has received significant scholarly attention.[21] The ship's voyage remains controversial and subject to aspersions in statements of British officers that participated in the vessel's arrest, criticism by non-Revisionist Zionists, and jaundiced published accounts by some disaffected crewmembers. However, Henry Mandel's eyewitness narrative, buttressed by the weight of the evidence, paints a very different picture, in which the American crew and refugee passengers of the *Ben Hecht*, with common sense and uncommon daring, struck a significant blow against the British Empire and its imperialist policy of denying the Holocaust survivors of Europe a permanent home and national self-determination.

---

20 The David S. Wyman Institute for Holocaust Studies, "The Bergson Group, Voyage of the Ben Hecht," part of "The Bergson Group, A History in Photographs," http://new.wymaninstitute.org/2017/01/the-bergson-group-voyage-of-the-ben-hecht/; Tzvi Ben-Tzur, "The Voyage of the 'Ben Hecht,'" http://www.palyam.org/English/Hahapala/hf/hf_Ben-Hecht; "Voyage of the S.S. Abril, alias the Ben Hecht," http://cosmos.ucc.ie/cs1064/jabowen/IPSC/php/event.php?eid=855.

21 Rafael Medoff, "Special Feature: Ben Hecht's a 'Flag is Born': A Play that Changed History," April 2004, http://new.wymaninstitute.org/2004/04/special-feature-ben-hechts-a-flag-is-born-a-play-that-changed-history/; Wandres, *Ablest Navigator*, 119–123; Judith Rice, "Ben Hecht, An Obscured Tale of Zionist Heroism—The S.S. Ben Hecht, 'The Mandate of Conscience,'" *Jewish Magazine* (June 2010), http://www.jewishmag.com/144mag/ben_hecht/ben_hecht.htm; Alan Swarc, "Illegal Immigration to Palestine 1945–1948: The French Connection" (PhD diss., University College London, 2006), 159, https://discovery.ucl.ac.uk/id/eprint/1445118/1/U592432.pdf; Jeffrey Weiss and Craig Weiss, *I Am My Brother's Keeper: American Volunteers in Israel's War of Independence 1947–1949*, Foreword Prime Minister of Israel Benjamin Netanyahu (Algen, PA: Schiffer Military History, 1998), 24–37; Lazar, *Immigration Ship "Ben Hecht,"* 9.

The Jewish immigrants who attempted to enter into Palestine in the 1930s and 1940s, despite British prohibitions, in the Aliyah Bet unauthorized immigration movement, were called *ma'apilim*, a reference to the biblical Israelites who attempted to force their entry into the Land of Canaan.[22] These original illegal immigrants are described in Numbers 14:44 as "Yet defiantly [*vaya'apliu*] they ascended to the top of the mountain." Rabbi Shlomo Yitzchaki-Yarchi (Rashi, 1040–1105),[23] the most influential medieval Jewish biblical commentator, glosses the verse thusly: "*Vaya'apliu*—language denoting 'strength.' And similarly, 'Behold, presumptuous' (Hab. 2:4). *Engres* in Old French, denoting 'impudence.' . . . And the Midrash *Tanchuma* interprets it as denoting 'darkness'—they walked darkly, [that is,] without permission."[24] According to Rabbi Naftali Zvi Yehuda Berlin (1816–1893), who, as Mandel liked to note, was the father of both Chaim Berlin, for whom the ultra-Orthodox Brooklyn yeshiva was named, and Meir Bar-Ilan, whose namesake is the Religious Zionist Israeli university, the intent of that medieval gloss is that there "were many of those who went up who believed and knew they would not succeed and would fall in war, but nevertheless they considered it worthwhile to be killed in the Land of Israel and be buried there and not in the desert."[25] However, that is not the end of the story. According to one Talmudic opinion, decades later the daughters of Zelophehad, one of the defiant failed ascenders to the Land, successively petitioned that they inherit their deceased father's portion of the Land.[26] Rabbi Tzadok ha-Kohen Rabinowitz of Lublin (1823–1900) hypothesized that the impudence—*chutzpah*—of the *ma'apilim* did change the divine decree, though they were premature, and that they would ultimately ascend to the Land when messianic times approach.[27]

The crew and passengers of the *Ben Hecht* were participants in a great Exodus from Europe. Like their biblical forerunners, the passengers of the *Ben Hecht* did not initially succeed in entering into the Land. Their bold

---

22 Numbers 14:39–45. See Rabbi Julian Sinclair, "Ma'apilim," December 4, 2008, https://www.thejc.com/judaism/jewish-words/ma-apilim-1.6533.

23 Aryeh Kaplan, *Meditation and Kabbalah* (York Beach, ME: Samuel Weiser, 1982), 24.

24 Numbers 14:44, Ben Isaiah & Sharfman, *Pentateuch and Rashi's Commentary: Numbers*, 149 (with minor alterations).

25 *Haamek HaDavar* on Numbers 14:44, Sefaria.org (English translation).

26 Numbers 36:1–12; Talmud Bavli *Shabbat* 96b.

27 Tzidkat HaTzadik 46:1. Rabbi Daniel Eisenbach brought this idea to my family's attention.

semi-secret attempt to enter the Promised Land initially appeared to be self-defeating and to have failed. But shortly thereafter the State of Israel was born and they were able to immigrate to Israel.

Previous accounts of the *Ben Hecht* have not explored certain heretofore inaccessible documents and reminiscences that explain the motivations of key participants in the ship's story scattered in archives in both the United States and Israel. These are now much easier to access than in the past. The sources reveal that neither the ship's crew nor the members of the Betar Revisionist youth group who escorted the passengers attempted to violently resist the British—who anticipated a firefight upon boarding the ship—because of the risk of bloodshed. The crew, under the direction of their Bergson Group American League for a Free Palestine recruiters, did not evade arrest. Instead, they sought to present a test case in which American citizens, in an open trial, would challenge the legality of the British prohibition of Jewish immigration to Palestine outside of the miserly constraints of the 1939 White Paper quotas. The relationship between the Bergson Group and the Irgun after World War II was fraught. The Bergson Group's AFLP had undertaken the venture on its own initiative; if they had been consulted, Irgun leaders would have directed the funds raised by the League's successful campaign to finance their underground armed revolt against British rule in Palestine. By restudying the familiar small-scale story of the *Ben Hecht* with fresh eyes, we can better appreciate how the determination of working-class sailors and Holocaust refugees in situation-specific and complicated circumstances contributed to the establishment of the State of Israel.[28] Throughout the text, the ship is referred to as both *Abril* and *Ben Hecht*, which reflects the varying preferences and rhetorical orientations of its crew and chroniclers.

***

The first part of this book will present edited transcripts of interviews given by Mandel. The second part contains materials that provide historical context, other recollections by Mandel, and the viewpoints of other participants of the *Ben Hecht*'s journey. The third part presents significant letters and speeches by Mandel about his life after that adventure, which

---

28   See Eliana Hadjisavvas, "Journey through the 'Gate of Zion': British policy, Jewish refugees and the La Spezia Affair, 1946," *Social History* 44, no. 4 (2019): 469–493.

was committed to religion, public service, and unionism. Mandel did not record his underground activities in contemporaneous letters, nor did he write a comprehensive memoir. However, this book preserves his unique eyewitness accounts and fair-minded perspective of critical episodes in the founding of Israel. His story focuses on the often overlooked question of how the victims of the Holocaust rebuilt their lives in the post-World War II period, a subject that has great relevance to present debates on unauthorized immigration and refugee migration.

This volume is organized around interviews conducted with Henry Mandel, his letters, and the stories, anecdotes, and sayings he often told his family, so that his voice can be heard as clearly as possible without intermediary summarizing. Those materials were admittedly edited and annotated by a grandchild of the subject, not a disinterested neutral party, which comes with inherent disadvantages from a scholarly perspective. However, my passion for discovering the truth about my grandfather's story, and sympathetic understanding of his viewpoint, hopefully have advantages too. Mandel's interviews are presented verbatim with only minor adaptations to improve readability. Like Boswell, "for this almost superstitious reverence" for preserving seemingly casual conversation, and preservation of Mandel's pattern of speech and thought despite some repetition and rough patches inherent in informal verbal remarks, we can rely on the authority of medieval Rabbi David Kimchi, who in his commentary on the first chapter of Psalms, wrote that "even the idle talk . . . of a good man ought to be regarded."[29]

Grandson Benjamin Leinwand has observed that many of the experiences that Mandel related in oral history interviews, such as his father's ill health, deprivation during the Great Depression, and imprisonment for aiding illegal immigration to British Mandatory Palestine, could have been experienced as traumas. However, Mandel had both the disposition and the wisdom to believe and narrate his life as a series of challenges overcome for a higher purpose. He believed in telling stories that were factually true as well as embodying his own subjective narrative truth that the historic events he participated in served a great purpose. Stories that perceive the subjective meaning of the events of a person's life can inherently

---

29 James Boswell, *Life of Johnson, Complete and Unabridged in One Volume* (New York: Modern Library, 1955), 12; see Solomon Schechter, *Studies in Judaism* (Philadelphia: Jewish Publication Society of America, 1905 [1896]), 145.

be positively transformative.[30] All can learn from Henry Mandel's honest, humble, bemused, and optimistic self-reckoning of how one person's self-sacrifice and courage helped defeat the Nazis, bring Holocaust refugees to their homeland, and win Israel's War of Independence.

***

We are fortunate to have a video of an interview of Henry Mandel (denoted by HM in interview excerpts) by Florence Shuster (FS), which was conducted on June 5, 2000 at the Museum of Jewish Heritage in New York under the auspices of its project to interview American Jewish veterans of World War II. Alyssa Goldschmidt Magid (AGM) conducted a telephone interview of Mandel on December 1, 2006, which is recorded on audio tape. Additionally, Esther Mandel, Aaron Mandel, and Chana Liba Mandel took detailed notes while conducting an interview with Henry Mandel in 2012 for a school project. Memories of discussions with Henry Mandel held by other members of his family are a less exact resource, but nonetheless preserve many of the stories that he felt were important and are of continuing significance. The following accounts are drawn in large part from these interviews and conversations. Hopefully, they convey his character, which was as inspiring as his deeds.

---

30 Eugenio M. Rothe, "A Psychotherapy Model for Treating Refugee Children Caught in the Midst of Catastrophic Situations," *The Journal of the American Academy of Psychoanalysis and Dynamic Psychiatry* 36, no. 4 (Winter 2008): 625–642.

Part One

Interviews and Reminiscences of Jewish Illegal Immigrant Ship *Ben Hecht* Crewman Henry Mandel

I went out to sea, I joined up with Aliyah Bet. Alas, I ended up in jail, with no one around to put up the bail. The Jews returned to the land of the Fathers, a great nation, so the people could gather, to build a place to replace the strife. With World War II and all it took, and now the refugees could return to the Land of the People of the Book. He came back when the job was done, to the Navy Yard where it had all begun, and then Libby's hand he sought and won. His marriage on 6 [June] 29, 1952 united us too.

—Libby Dershowitz Mandel[1]

1   Henry Mandel seventieth birthday party, September 19, 1990 (videotape in possession of the editor).

Chapter 1.

Vienna Born, Bronx Bred

God that is dear and great, redeem your oppressed from the mouths of lions, and bring out your people from exile, your people which you have chosen from all nations, to sanctify you again in the Holy of Holies, the place where we will gladden our spirits and souls, and sing to you songs and whispered prayers, in Jerusalem the beautiful city.

—"Koh Ribon," Sabbath evening song

FS: Today is June 5, 2000. My name is Florence Shuster and we are with Mr. Henry Mandel in New York and this interview is in English.

FS: Could you tell me your name, please?

[A seated Henry Mandel wears a yarmulke, black and white striped tie, and dark suit with an Israeli Fighter of the War of Independence pin.]

HM: My name is Henry Mandel. Sometimes called Chaim Mandel in Jewish [Yiddish].

Henry Mandel's parents were born in different parts of what was then the Austro-Hungarian Empire. His mother was born in Bratislava (Pressburg) province in 1894; his father in Poland in 1888. His parents were Orthodox, but not affiliated with any Zionist organization prior to Mandel's service in Israel.

HM: I was born in Vienna, Austria in 1920; September 6, 1920, and I came to the United States with my mother in 1923. And my father came with my older brother to the United States in 1922. My mother had heard stories about husbands coming to the United States and abandoning their family and getting a new wife and so on. So, my mother took no chances. [*HM smiles.*] She sent my older brother with my father so that everybody would be aware that he was a married man. [*Mandel's grin widens.*]

FS: Could you please spell your name for me, please?

HM: M-A-N-D-E-L.

FS: And how old does this make you now?

HM: At the moment, I am seventy-nine. I'll be eighty in September.

FS: And what was your father's name?

HM: My father's name was [Alter] Abraham.

***

(Alter) Avrohom HaLevi Mandel was born in Ulanów (Ulonov) in Galicia in Poland in 1888. A Levite, his last name, Yiddish for "almond," was a reference to the almonds that sprouted from the staff of Aaron, representing the tribe of Levi.[2] He traveled from his home town to study Talmud in the yeshiva of Galante, where he met fellow student Leo Jung, future Rabbi of the Jewish Center in New York.[3] Avrohom then studied in Chust (Khust) in the Carpathian region. Lipot (Schmalhausen) Steinmetz, the father of his future son-in-law, Sol Steinmetz, studied in Chust too.[4] Henry described his father as a "very learned man." He received his *kabala* (authorization to be a ritual slaughterer) from Rabbi Yosef Zvi Dushinsky.[5] Rabbi Dushinsky had headed the yeshiva in Galante and then led the yeshiva in Chust, and Avrohom Mandel followed him. Ultimately his parents left Ulonov too after a pogrom. Later, Rabbi Dushinsky moved to Palestine in 1930 and became head of the separatist Orthodox "anti-Zionist" community in Jerusalem.[6]

---

2   See Numbers 17:8.
3   Editor's recollection of Henry Mandel reminiscence. See Victor B. Geller, *Orthodoxy Awakens: The Belkin Era and Yeshiva University* (Brooklyn, NY: Urim Publications, 2003), 65; Maxine Jacobson, *Modern Orthodoxy in American Judaism: The Era of Rabbi Leo Jung* (Boston: Academic Studies Press, 2016), 14.
4   Sol Steinmetz, *The Little Refugees* (New York: S. Steinmetz, 2011), 18.
5   Mandel interview by Aaron Mandel, Esther Mandel, and Chana Liba Mandel, circa 2012.
6   "Ulanów," https://kehilalinks.jewishgen.org/kolbuszowa/ulanow/history.html; Rakeffet-Rothkoff, *Silver Era*, 245; David Tidhar, "Rabbi Yosef Tzvi Dushinsky,"

Avrohom's father Jacob (Yaakov Tzvi) Mandel was extremely well-versed in the Hebrew Bible, and could list from memory wherever a particular Hebrew word appears in Scripture as if he were a human Biblical concordance. Avrohom Mandel told his son that Jacob Mandel was not as well-versed in the Talmud. Yaakov Tzvi had initially immigrated to the United States earlier than his son. Yaakov Tzvi's brothers, who had established themselves in the United States earlier, had a shop in Los Angeles where Yaakov Tzvi worked. His brothers told Yaakov Tzvi that he had to work on Shabbos. Henry used to exclaim, "Can you imagine, their own brother!" Instead, Yaakov Tzvi went back to Europe, only to return to the United States years later. Yaakov Tzvi was naturalized, under the name Jacob Mandel, as an American citizen on December 27, 1929 when he was sixty-seven years old.

Sol Steinmetz married Avrohom's youngest child, Tziporah Malka (Tzippie). Steinmetz described his father-in-law Avrohom in 1954 as "a very *balabastisher* Yid with beard and all," who owned a Hebrew bookstore, and appreciated traditional formalities.[7] Avrohom Mandel's brothers, Henoch, Binyamin, and Moshe, and his sister Rosie also immigrated to the United States. Moshe served in the US Army in World War I and endured poison gas attacks. Sent to recover in an Army sanatorium in upstate New York, officials claimed he jumped out a window, though the family believed that he was killed by antisemitic fellow former soldiers.

Near the end of his life Avrohom attended a Shabbat HaGadol Talmud lecture without having had the opportunity to prepare the sources beforehand. At the end of the lecture, he congratulated the rabbi on an excellent lecture, but said that there is a small Tosfot (medieval commentary) on a page of the Talmud that knocked the rabbi's whole theory down. The rabbi asked the president of the synagogue to look up the reference. Upon seeing that Avrohom was correct, the rabbi exclaimed that this was a Jew who knew how to learn (*Is a Yid vos veyst vi tsu lernen*), which was among the highest compliments a rabbi could give.

***

FS: And your mother's name?

Encyclopedia of the Founders and Builders of Israel, vol. 4 (Tel Aviv: Rishonim Library, 1950) (Hebrew).

7   Steinmetz, *Little Refugees*, 119–121.

HM: Hedwig [Chana].

FS: And her maiden name?

HM: Reisner.

The Reisners came from Senec, also known as Jempt, in Bratislava.[8] They were not a Hasidic family. Hedwig (Chana) Reisner lost her father Avraham in the 1918 flu epidemic. He was a cattle broker for kosher butchers.

During World War I, over 100,000 Galician Jews came to Vienna as refugees.[9] Avrohom Mandel and Chana Reisner were both living in Vienna after World War I. Chana lived with her mother Rivka on Herminengasse, where many Eastern European Jews lived. Reisner's family could not afford a marriage broker for her. Avrohom Mandel, a divorcee, was sent by a marriage broker to a girl whose family name was Rosner, but received directions to the Reisner family by mistake. As Henry later related, "Someone wanted to introduce him to a girl in Herminengasse, the daughter of the widow Rosner. He asked for the daughter of the widow Rosner. They sent him to the daughter of the widow Reisner. Different apartment. He knocked at the door. Chana Reisner opened the door. She saw a religious young man with a black hat. He had *peyos* and a nice beard. He said, so-and-so sent me here. Her mother said, come in. They hit it off and got married!" The marriage of Avrohom and Chana, who was the younger of the pair, took place in 1918. They soon had children in Vienna: Leo (Yehudah Bezalel) was born in 1919, and then Heinrich (Chaim or Hymie) in 1920. "I wasn't the youngest for long," Henry mused. Daughter Dorie (Devorah) was born in 1921.[10] Henry remembered his parents as being comforting, and fondly remembered his mother singing the Yiddish lullaby "Oyfn Pripetchik." While Chana Mandel's sister Frieda remained in Europe and survived World War II there, Chana was naturalized as an American citizen on March 22, 1937 at the age of forty-two. Her former nationality was listed as "Czechoslovakia-Hungary-Poland-Germany" on her naturalization certificate.

FS: Now you mentioned you had a brother. What was his name?

---

8   Neil Monheit interview by the editor, January 22, 2019.
9   David Rechter, *The Jews of Vienna and the First World War* (London / Portland, OR: The Littman Library of Jewish Civilization, 2001), 72.
10   Mandel interview by Esther Mandel, Aaron Mandel, and Chana Liba Mandel, 2012.

HM: Well, I had a brother, an older brother, at the time, Leo. And I had a younger sister that came with me, Dora. So, the two of us came with my mother in 1923, and Leo came with my father in 1922.

FS: And where were you brought up?

HM: We were brought up in New York City.[11]

***

When Alter Avrohom Mandel arrived in the United States he obtained a job as a *shochet*, a ritual slaughterer, in Gouverneur in upstate New York, ten miles from Canada. When Rivkie (Rivkah Esther) was born, Chana wanted to give birth at home in Gouverneur. A midwife was supposed to come, but she did not arrive in time, and Chana delivered the baby in a bucket. Younger siblings Golda Baila, Moshe, and Tziporah Malka were born in the following years.

Henry's memories of Gouverneur included chicken soup and collecting eggs in the morning. Leo was supposed to go to school, and Henry wanted to go too, even though he was too young to be admitted. Chana solved the problem by telling local public school officials that the boys were twins. That was plausible because at the time Leo was small for his age, so much so that his parents had been concerned about his health when he was born. On his first day of school Henry knew no English, not even enough to ask to go to the bathroom.

In 1925, Avrohom Mandel was called to slaughter an animal in mid-winter in deep snow, and he traveled with a horse and sleigh with a snowplow. The horse was startled and shied. The sled turned over and Avrohom's back was broken. He was hospitalized for months, wore a plaster cast for years, and never completely recovered. Due to this illness, he received the extra name Alter, "Old Man," a traditional way to attempt to improve a person's health.

No longer strong enough to slaughter cattle, Avrohom moved his family to the Bronx where he slaughtered chickens and eventually ran a Jewish bookstore, which were much less remunerative positions. Initially they lived in 1525 Charlotte Street, and then moved to 1035 Kelly Street.

---

11   Henry Mandel interview by Florence Shuster, June 5, 2000, at The Museum of Jewish Heritage—A Living Memorial to the Holocaust in New York.

The family sang *zemirot*, traditional songs, at the Shabbos [Sabbath] table. Henry remembered "Koh Ribon" in particular. His father stood for *kiddush*, on both Friday night and Shabbos day. Alter Avrohom Mandel wore *sefard tefillin* and prayed *Nusach Sefard*, the Hasidic rite, but he always ate *gebrochts* (grain meal with liquid) during Passover because he followed the position of his teacher Rabbi Dushinsky.[12]

The Mandel family struggled through the Depression. In 1932, one-third of the employable workforce in New York was unemployed, and many more were underemployed.[13] Chana often had to split a single hotdog among her children. Occasionally, she would skip a child by accident. When the child complained, she would exclaim "How could I forget my favorite child!" (When he became a father and grandfather, Henry was always quick to add that he loved all his daughters and grandchildren equally and that he had no favorites.)

After many years, a Romanian woman applied a special lotion on Alter Avrohom's legs, which helped him walk. The sight of his father being able to walk brought tears to Henry's eyes. A Holocaust survivor doctor also visited Alter Avrohom at his home every day to massage his legs. Alter Avrohom died in April of 1958; Chana died in December of that year during Chanukah due to colon cancer, though Henry felt she died of a broken heart.

***

FS: And what language did you speak at home?

HM: With my parents, Jewish [Yiddish]. Amongst my siblings . . . I had three more sisters and another brother born here. We all spoke English exclusively amongst ourselves.[14]

At other times Henry told his children that German was the primary language his parents spoke; the children learned English in school.

FS: And what was your education?

HM: My . . . In New York, I went to a grade school. I went to the Salanter yeshiva in the Bronx.

---

12   Ibid.
13   Robert Caro, *The Power Broker: Robert Moses and the Fall of New York* (New York: Alfred A. Knopf, 1974), 323.
14   Mandel interview by Shuster, 2000.

When the Mandel Family moved to the Bronx, Henry attended a public school for first and second grades. The Yeshiva Israel Salanter was being started in the Bronx at that time. Henry remembered that "they asked Father 'give us your boys.' Father said, 'I'll just give you one boy, if he learns I'll give you the second.'" Avrohom Mandel first sent Leo to the yeshiva, and when he saw Leo was being taught well, he sent Henry the next year too. Leo was always one year ahead in Jewish studies, but they were together in secular classes. Salanter was used to students who had transferred from public schools. Salanter was a new kind of Americanized Orthodox school.[15] Mr. Price, who taught in a public school in the morning and early afternoon, was the principal of the Yeshiva Israel Salanter's secular studies department. A Mr. Roe was the principal of Jewish studies department.[16] Today, SAR Academy in Riverdale in the Bronx is the successor school to Yeshiva Israel Salanter.

> HM: And for the high school, I went to the Talmudical Academy High School, which was part of Yeshiva College, which is presently Yeshiva University in upper Manhattan.[17]

Mandel often recounted that Dr. Bernard Revel, the founder of Talmudical Academy High School and Yeshiva College, was referred to as "Roctor Devil" with affection among the yeshiva boys. When he was asked how it was possible that there would be enough rabbinical positions for all the graduates of the schools, Dr. Revel responded that not all of his students would become rabbis, but they would be knowledgeable enough to appreciate a real rabbi. Originally Dr. Revel had planned to build a larger campus, and had purchased the land opposite what is now Zysman Hall for that purpose. Due to the Great Depression and the resulting financial stress that threatened Yeshiva College's existence,[18] this plan had to be abandoned, and the day the land was sold the yeshiva boys could hear Dr. Revel crying in his office. There were also other sacrifices: Mandel often recounted that the reason the ceiling of the Yeshiva University High School for Boys basketball court is so low is because it was designed to be a swimming pool, but out of financial necessity that more ambitious design was abandoned. The unusual

---

15   Rafael Medoff, *The Rabbi of Buchenwald: The Life and Times of Herschel Schacter* (Brooklyn, NY: Ktav, 2021), 111.
16   Mandel interview by Esther Mandel, Aaron Mandel, and Chana Liba Mandel, 2012.
17   Mandel interview by Shuster, 2000.
18   Medoff, *Rabbi of Buchenwald*, 79–80.

dimensions of the court gave Talmudical Academy and Yeshiva College a distinct home court advantage, as opposing teams struggled to adjust the arc of their shots. One of the most exciting moments during Mandel's time at Talmudical Academy was when the Yeshiva College team almost beat one of the best teams in the country, Long Island University, because the visiting team's shots kept hitting the ceiling.

The teacher that Mandel was closest to at the yeshiva was Rabbi Moshe Bick, who was an assistant teacher and worked part-time filling in for the more senior Rabbi Aaron Burack. Rabbi Burack was sometimes absent from class due to his obligations to his congregational pulpit in Brooklyn. A religious Zionist and a leader of the Union of Orthodox Rabbis of the United States and Canada for Eastern European trained rabbis,[19] Rabbi Burack read the English version of the petition of the hundreds of rabbis who marched on Washington on October 6, 1943 to plea for action to help the victims of the then ongoing Holocaust.[20]

Rabbi Bick had himself graduated from Talmudical Academy and was ordained by Rabbi Isaac Elchanan Theological Seminary (REITS) in 1932. Part of his family was Hasidic, which influenced his approach to Judaism.[21] Rabbi Bick became a well-known *posek*, a halakhic decisor, in Borough Park, Brooklyn, after he stopped teaching at Yeshiva University and gave up his *shtiebel* (small congregation) pulpit in the Bronx.[22]

***

> HM: And for college I went to City College in the evening. I began in 1936, and with the war and so on, I did not complete, I did not graduate, until 1948.[23]

Upon graduation from Yeshiva High School, the administration offered Mandel a half-scholarship to Yeshiva College, so that his family would

---

19   "Prof. Burack, Orthodox Leader, Dies during Synagogue Services," *Jewish Telegraphic Agency* (JTA) *Daily Bulletin*, October 10, 1960, https://www.jta.org/1960/10/10/archive/prof-burack-orthodox-leader-dies-during-synagogue-services.

20   Rakeffet-Rothkoff, *Silver Era*, 219–221.

21   Aaron Rakeffet-Rothkoff, *From Washington Avenue to Washington Street* (Jerusalem / New York: Gefen / Oxford University Press, 2001).

22   Jacob Rabinowitz, "Six Decades at Yeshiva," in *My Yeshiva College: 75 Years of Memories*, ed. Menachem Butler and Zev Nagel (New York: Yasher Books, 2006), 86.

23   Mandel interview by Shuster, 2000.

have only had to pay $150 a year. However, Mandel did not even tell his father about the scholarship offer out of concern that the family could not afford the tuition. Avrohom Mandel could not even afford the ten cents to pay for his daily Yiddish newspaper, one of his few pleasures. Mandel said in a profile published in *The Chief-Leader* in 1996 that "I got out of high school in 1936 in the middle of the Depression. . . . There weren't jobs open for kids because there weren't jobs open to adults."[24] In later years, Mandel felt sure that his father would have wanted him to continue to learn in the yeshiva and would have gathered the necessary funds. However, Mandel thought that in that case, like many of his classmates, he probably would have become a rabbi, and would not had the sailing and machinist skills that allowed him to contribute to the struggle for a Jewish state.

FS: Tell me, how did you identify as a Jew growing up?

HM: Well, starting off in the Salanter yeshiva, it was the first yeshiva in New York, and probably in the country, that taught in Hebrew. Whatever yeshivas there were, were all taught in Jewish [Yiddish], and this was the first one that taught in Hebrew, what they called *Ivris b'Ivris*. You took the Hebrew in the Bible and translated it in Hebrew. So in order to get Hebrew-speaking teachers like that, they took Israelis. And they were basically Zionists. And so, I would say that the school was a Zionist school and I was brought up with Zionistic feelings, and that continued. And then when I was a teenager there was a Zionistic group, a youth group, the HaShomer HaDati, which was connected with the Po'alei Mizrachi. Then the name was subsequently changed. Today it is called Bnei Akiva, and it is still an active Zionist youth group in the United States, still connected with the Po'alei Mizrachi.

The Ashkenazi pronunciation of a term that means "Hebrew in Hebrew" is *Ivris b'Ivris*; the Sephardic and Israeli pronunciation of the phrase is *Ivrit b'Ivrit*. It subsequently became very rare to teach Modern Hebrew pronounced in the Ashkenazi dialect. Henry learned *Ivrit b'Ivrit* at Yeshiva Israel Salanter, where he graduated in 1932. During the 1930s at least twenty percent of the Yeshiva College student body affiliated with a Zionist organization, predominantly the Mizrachi youth group HaShomer HaDati.

---

24   "I'd Do It for Free," Henry Mandel interview by Della Monica, circa 1996, *The Chief-Leader* (in possession of the editor).

FS: Just for the record, I want to clarify. You mentioned they had to get Israeli teachers, but Israel wasn't established at that point.

HM: No, but in Israel they would speak in Hebrew, not in Israel but in Palestine. The Jews in Palestine were speaking Hebrew. When they wanted to get teachers that were very fluent in Hebrew, that took people that came from Israel, Palestine. Just like today, you will see the Israelis in the streets and so on, they will be talking to each other in Hebrew because that is their native tongue. So, they basically took teachers from Palestine, which today we know as Israel. And in Jewish [Yiddish] we always knew it as the Land of Israel, *Eretz Yisrael*, so . . . so by calling it Israel I don't think that I was that much out of line. [*HM smiles.*]

FS: What was the ethnic makeup of your neighborhood?

HM: My neighborhood was primarily Jewish, though we had a number of Irish there; we had a number of Blacks . . . not too many. The Blacks in my neighborhood . . . All the buildings in the neighborhood were apartment houses, and most of the apartment houses had Black supers [superintendents]. And as a young child I was under the impression that all the Blacks did in New York was work as supers in apartment houses. And later as I got . . . grew up, got into high school, I realized that it was only a childish impression from the neighborhood, but that they were all over the city and doing all types of work.

***

Migrants from Puerto Rico started to move into the neighborhood as Henry got older. On one memorable occasion, Mandel and his brother Leo tried to sneak into the Polo Grounds, where the New York Baseball Giants played, by following a class of Catholic school students who were on a school trip into the stadium. Horace Charles Stoneham, the son of the owner of the Giants, who later became the owner of the Giants himself, stopped them. Stoneham told them words to the effect of "If you are part of this group then why are your *tsitsis* out?" Mandel attended many other baseball games at the Polo Grounds and Yankee Stadium. Once, in the bleachers at Yankee Stadium, he saw Babe Ruth catch a ball in the outfield, which the overweight Great Bambino then slowly waved in self-mocking triumph to a section of the crowd where most of the African Americans in the stadium were sitting and cheering him on. Mandel was the same age as later Supreme Court Justice John Paul Stevens, who said, perhaps only half-jokingly, that his witnessing of Babe Ruth's "called shot" home run in the 1932 World Series in Chicago was his "most important claim to fame."[25] Mandel's very different anecdote illustrates why the baseball legend was loved, and not merely admired for his record-breaking athletic feats.

---

25   John Paul Stevens, *The Making of a Justice: Reflections on My First 94 Years* (New York: Little, Brown and Company, 2019), 18.

Chapter 2

The War Comes Home

From the one end of the land even to the other end of the land, no flesh hath peace.
—Jeremiah 12:11 (JPS 1917)

FS: How did you come to work in the Navy Yard?

HM: There was a test being given. In the 30s there was a Depression. It was very difficult to get jobs, and a government job was looked on as a sinecure: "Look, oh boy, working for the government;" even someone I knew who was a street cleaner. A relative of my parents was a street cleaner; he was someone everyone looked up to. He had a government job; he had a paycheck coming in regularly. And in the . . . 1938, I believe it was, the end of 38, the federal government gave an exam for apprentices for the Navy Yard. And I took that exam. In 1939, I was called to the interview and I was hired. I started on January 2, 1940. At that time, to give you an idea, I started at thirty-six cents per hour; for a forty-hour week it was $14.40. Took off pension and I had take-home pay of $13.99. And at that time, you did not have free transfers like we have today. It was a double fare from the Bronx to the Brooklyn Navy Yard. And I still feel that was a wonderful opportunity for me and I have never regretted taking that exam.[1]

When Mandel started at a machine shop at the Brooklyn Navy Yard, there was another worker also named Henry. The foreman said that there were not going to be two Henrys in his shop; one would have to be called Hank. "My name is Henry," said the other worker. Mandel said "fine, call me Hank." At work, Mandel went by Hank the rest of his life, among his family

---

1   Mandel interview by Shuster, 2000.

and friends he often was called in Yiddish, Hymie or Hy, and in Israel he used his Hebrew name Chaim. Heinrich, the German name on his birth certificate, was never formally changed but he never used it; he used Henry on official documents.

Mandel's commute from the Bronx to Brooklyn required two tokens. Even after 1940, the year that the City consolidated the IND (Independent Subway System), IRT (Interborough Rapid Transit), and BMT (Brooklyn-Manhattan Transit), there continued to be no free transfers between routes that previously had been operated by independent systems.[2]

Mandel received a draft deferment because he was engaged in defense work. He worked in the Navy Yard on the construction of the Navy battleships *Iowa* and *North Carolina*.[3] The *North Carolina* was launched on June 13, 1940. Construction of the *Iowa* began in the Navy Yard on June 27, 1940, and it was commissioned on August 27, 1942. Both ships would play important roles in defending American aircraft carriers and bombarding Japanese island fortresses during the coming war in the Pacific.[4]

***

FS: Did you know anybody or have any relatives who were still in Europe?

HM: Yes, I had relatives. My . . . Both my parents had relatives in Europe. And my mother had sisters, a sister and brothers. And we were able to get a cousin, my mother's sister's son over and he lived with us. He was at that time, was about fourteen or fifteen, and then when he was eighteen, he joined the Army, the US Army. But when the war broke out, he was in Europe.

FS: Can you tell them [the future audience of the interview] what country he was in?

---

2   See Corey Johnson, "Let's Go: A Case for Municipal Control and a Comprehensive Transportation for the Five Boroughs," March 5, 2019, 22, https://council.nyc.gov/news/2019/03/05/soc2019-report/.

3   "I'd Do It for Free."

4   "Iowa III (BB-61)," Dictionary of American Naval Fighting Ships. Navy Department, Naval History and Heritage Command, July 22, 2015, https://www.history.navy.mil/research/histories/ship-histories/danfs/i/iowa-iii.html; "North Carolina III (BB-55)," ibid., July 1, 2019, https://www.history.navy.mil/content/history/nhhc/research/histories/ship-histories/danfs/n/north-carolina-iii.html.

HM: He was in Austria, but the details are not quite clear because he went, I believe, with some youth group to England [a *Kindertransport*], and then from England he went to the United States. My parents filled out some affidavits and so on and so forth. And he lived with us. Interestingly, when he was in the Army and he was in Europe and he located his mother, and as a veteran of the Army, he was able to bring her to the United States. And his mother lived with us [after the war], until she got her own apartment.

FS: Do you remember everyone's name that you are talking about?

HM: Well, my Aunt was *Tante* ["aunt" in Yiddish] Frieda Monheit, and her son was Freddie Monheit.

Hymie's cousin Freddie Monheit, and his brothers Tuvia and Walter, left with a *Kindertransport* during Hanukkah 1939 from Vienna, ultimately arriving in England. Freddie's aunt Anna, who was not born a Jew, escaped to England using his mother Frieda's identification papers, while Frieda assumed Anna's "Aryan" identity and operated a store in Budapest. Anna's brother Eliazar survived in hiding in the store and went to live in Tel Aviv after the war. Shmuel, Anna's husband and Frieda's other brother, did not survive the war. Frieda's husband died in a Soviet prison camp.

As explained by Freddie's son Neil Naftali Monheit, his father came to the United States in 1943 and lived with Henry Mandel's parents on Kelly Street in the Bronx. He learned in the Chabad yeshiva. Alter Avrohom Mandel thought there was an opportunity to bring Frieda over from Europe during the war, which did not work out. Freddie Monheit started working for a time, which allowed for his draft into the Army in 1944. He had three tours of duty. For his first tour of duty in Italy he was in the Medical Corps because he said he was opposed to violence, then he was retrained for the infantry, and later he was attached to Army intelligence as an interpreter.[5] Freddie Monheit also served as a chaplain's assistant in the US Army.[6]

A brother of Freddie's, Tuvia Monheit, moved to Israel and eventually became mayor of Kiryat Gat. Freddie's other brother, Walter Monheit, became a fixture of the New York celebrity social scene in the 1970s and a beloved avuncular figure at the satirical magazine *Spy*, where he worked as

---

5   Monheit interview by the editor, January 22, 2019.
6   Tziporah Mandel Steinmetz notes to the editor, 2019.

a messenger. *Spy* ran a regular feature under his by-line with mock movie blurbs.[7]

***

FS: What branch of the service did he [Freddie] serve in?

HM: He was in the Army.

FS: Did you hear any stories about what was happening in Europe from him?

HM: No, I didn't because he went into the Army and I was at sea, and we really did not see each other and such, but of course it was known at the time, the stories were getting out. It seemed to have been known to just about everybody but to President Roosevelt.

FS: What types of antisemitic stories did you hear about?

HM: Well, we heard about the concentration camps and about how Germany was killing the Jews, putting them in concentration camps, making slave laborers of them.

FS: Do you remember anything specific that you had heard?

HM: I don't remember anything specific because those things were not that specific at the time; I don't remember specifically.

As Ben Hecht wrote in a book published in 1944, "One million Jews were massacred by the Germans in Poland. Another million were disposed of in Germany, France, Holland, Hungary, Austria, and Roumania [later called Romania in English]. A third million Jews were murdered in Russia, Serbia, and the Slav countries. These three million were not slain obliquely by starvation or overwork or on any battlefront. They were done in according to a plan."[8] Novelist James Jones later observed that "most men had heard of the 'concentration camps' in some form or another. But to see it in the actual process and to realize the magnitude and extent of it, was

---

7   David Kamp, "Monheit Dead! Remembering Spy Magazine's Elegant Blurbist, Messenger, and Nightclubber Extraordinaire," *Vanity Fair*, August 9, 2011, https://www.vanityfair.com/news/2011/08/monheit-dead; "Just Win, Baby . . . ," *Los Angeles Times*, June 26, 2001, https://www.google.com/amp/s/www.latimes.com/archives/la-xpm-2001-jun-26-ca-14669-story.html%3f_amp=true.

8   Ben Hecht, *A Guide for the Bedevilled* (Jerusalem: Mila Press, 1996 [New York: Charles Scribner's Sons, 1944]), 111.

a deep, frightening, psychic shock to the soldiering men of the Western democracies."[9]

FS: As you were growing up, did you encounter any antisemitic experiences?

HM: Well, there was always antisemitism to a certain degree, especially my family was Orthodox, always wore a hat, and sometimes some Gentiles would grab our hat and throw it back and forth and so on. But I would not say overt antisemitism as such.

FS: You mentioned that you were very patriotic. Could you explain a little bit more?

HM: Well, if you as an American, what happened in Japan, or what Japan did in Hawaii. And the fact that there were Americans who were, got killed [*HM clutches a fist to his chest*], I felt that a part of me was killed or chopped off, I felt that I was part of the American body, that part of me had been ravished. So, I felt that I would like to revenge those people. I felt that it was my duty to participate in that endeavor to get the revenge on the Japanese for what they had done.

FS: What did you hear about Hitler?

HM: Of course, we had heard all the stories of his antisemitism. But specifically the details, I did not know so much about them.

FS: Do you remember hearing, among the people you were working with in the Naval Yard, in Brooklyn, do you remember how you got the news with what was happening in the war?

HM: Well, we got the news, we got the radio, and the newspapers, and I worked in the machine shop. And in the machine shop there were a lot of Germans there. And they, they were pro-German. There were a lot of people pro-Germany. And a number of them were removed by the FBI because of they were afraid there might be sabotage. I cannot talk about the other shops, but in the machine shop, there were a lot of German machinists. When I say German, they either came from Germany or they were of German descent. Now, just being of German descent does not of course mean that they were . . . that you were in favor of Germany because our great general Eisenhower

---

9   James Jones, *WWII: A Chronicle of Soldiering* (Chicago: University of Chicago Press, 1975), 210.

was of German descent and no one would ever say that he was pro-German. But there were a number of people that were pro-German in the machine shop.

FS: Do you remember anything specific, anything that they did?

HM: Well, it was just a question of talking. But they did not do anything specifically. But they were always talking in favor of Germany. And they felt that Germany should not have declared war on the United States simply because Japan was at war with the United States. And they felt that we should have just fought Japan, and Germany would be fighting Europe. We would clear up Japan, and Europe, Germany would take care of. And that we wouldn't . . . that there was no need for Germany to be fighting the United States. And they felt that Hitler made a big mistake by declaring war on the United States after Pearl Harbor.

FS: And how did you feel?

HM: The stories that we heard; the antisemitism of Hitler; I was glad we were going against Hitler.

FS: When did you . . . well, actually, tell me a little bit more about what your work as a machinist entailed.

HM: Well, a machinist, in a naval ship yard, what we did is, we built parts to go into the ships, into the engines and so on, and also, we repaired; we overhauled engines, parts of engines, and so on for ships.

Chapter 3

The Merchant Marine

Water, water everywhere / Nor any drop to drink.
—Samuel Taylor Coleridge, "The Rime of the Ancient Mariner"

FS: Did you ever meet anyone in the service that was Jewish, [or] when you were in the Navy Yards?

HM: Well, you know it is an interesting thing. I was on one ship. And it was stationed here in New York. And we, since we were in New York, not eating aboard ship, because I ate kosher as much as I could. So, I would eat breakfast at home, and I would bring a sandwich for lunch, I might go home in the evening and I'd eat supper at home. And one day at work, a fella came over to me and said "I am Henry Chan, I am your new messman. I said "How do you do?" And he says, "You know," he says, "I just got off a ship last week and I planned to stay ashore a few weeks, but I gambled and I lost all my money. Maybe if you could lend me ten dollars, I can pay my landlady and get my luggage out." Now, I thought a messman is always a nice friend to have. So, I lent him the ten dollars and I did not go into mess at all until I went out to sea. And when we went out to sea, we left in the morning, and for lunch I did not go into the mess hall because I still had lunch from home [*Mandel flashes a grin*] that day, but I went in for supper. And I went in and I wore my watch cap because I always ate with a hat, I made the *bracha* [blessing] before I ate and so on, and one of the ABs, that is Able Bodied seaman, said "Hey, take your hat off." He says, "I told you to take your hat off when you are eating." He says, "Where I come from, we take our hats off when we eat." So, I looked at him, I said, "Where I come from we put our hats on when we eat." Just then Henry [Chan] came into the mess hall. And the man said "Henry, don't feed that man until he takes off his cap." Henry looked at me, he looked at the fellow, what dealings he had with the other fellow I don't know. But [*HM smiles*] I had lent him ten dollars. So, he says, "You know, this is my mess hall, and I feed whomever I want to feed. Now, if that man wants to wear his cap, he can wear his cap. If you don't like it, you can leave the mess hall." [*HM smiles.*]

So, now Henry was . . . Henry Chan sounds Chinese, but he wasn't. He was dark, he looked somewhat like an Italian. And when we were shuttling the Mediterranean and Italy, we would get off, he would speak Italian. But next we were in Greece, and in Greece he would speak Greek. [*HM smiles.*] So, I did not know what he was [from]. And I was there for Passover, I was not going to eat their food there during Passover. So, the day before Passover, I said to Henry, "Henry, I am not going to be coming into the mess hall for the next eight days, but what I would like you to do is in the morning I will come by and give me six raw eggs. And that is all, I figured I had a steam line in the engine room, I would boil two for breakfast, two for lunch, and two for supper. And I had picked up some *matzos* in Greece, so I would live off of *matzos* and eggs for a week. And he says, "Well, can't you have anything else?" he says. He says, "How about coffee?" I say "No." "I will give you a brand-new can." I say, "No, I don't want the coffee." He says, "You know, my parents were the most Orthodox people in Turkey," and he says, "We used to drink coffee on Passover." [*HM smiles wide.*] So that was interesting, and Henry, incidentally, I met twice more. I met him on the *Marine Carp* after we were, should I say expelled, or . . . from Palestine. And Henry was on that crew. And then when I was taking a course on Marine electricity at the maritime academy on . . . in Sheepshead Bay, which is today the college . . .

FS: Kingsborough?

HM: Kingsborough College. Henry was taking a course there also. [*HM smiles.*] I met him on two other occasions. But it was interesting . . . I had no idea he was Jewish [*HM smiles*], but it ended up that he was and that he came from a religious family in Turkey.

FS: Do you remember the name of the ship you were on together?

HM: I don't remember the name of that ship. But I know we were together on the *Marine Carp* later. But that particular ship, I don't remember the name.[10]

***

---

10 Mandel interview by Shuster, 2000.

In 1938, Leo Mandel began attending City College by day, which Henry attended through night school. Leo graduated in January 1942. He had a low draft number, and all deferments were limited after the Pearl Harbor attack on December 7, 1941. Leo was supposed to be called up immediately, but there was "a fuss," Henry recalled, about their being inducted a week before the holidays, and the induction was pushed off until after January 1, 1942 so that Leo and his fellow City College students could take their finals and graduate. Leo was a popular guy in basic training; everyone wanted to be the guy behind him in the chow line. But still, he wasn't happy in the Army. Leo had problems due to his observance of the Sabbath and *kashruth*. Chana Mandel, with the help of her daughter Dora (Dore), used to send salami and pumpernickel bread to him; the bread arrived hard as a rock. Leo would bury bread in the ground and built a fire over it, and then it tasted like freshly baked bread, in order to avoid Army bread baked with lard. [11]

***

FS: I just want to go back a little bit. When did you . . . when you were working in the Navy Yards, when did they finally permit you to enter the service, and what branch of the service did you enter?

HM: It was . . . I was supposed to go into the Navy. And I was rejected because I had a hernia. So, I went and I had a hernia operation. Today, I presume that they would have taken . . . they take someone in and operate there, but at that time they didn't. So I went and paid for the hernia operation myself. And then in the winter of 94 . . .

FS: 94?

HM: [*HM smiles*] Excuse me, '44. The winter of 1944 I got a letter . . . I have it somewhere . . . to the Navy to take me into the Navy . . . from a lieutenant commander in the Navy Yard. But when I went there, I failed the eye examination.

Mandel meant to say 1945, not 1944. An "Order to Report for Preinduction Physical Examination" dated June 14, 1945 from the Selective Service System ordered him to report for a physical examination at 9 a.m. on June 21, 1945.

---

11   Mandel interview by Esther Mandel, Aaron Mandel, and Chana Liba Mandel, 2012.

HM: So, I . . . since I could not pass the eye examination, they did not take me into the Navy. I . . . So, I decided that I would use my experience by going into the Merchant Marine. And I came down to get my Merchant Marine papers. It was right here by 42 Broadway, was the headquarters. I remember . . . some things I remember and some things I don't. [*HM smiles.*] I was at 42 Broadway [in downtown Manhattan], and here I also had to pass an eye examination. But after going through . . . and then I also had to take a test to show that I was competent as a machinist. I do have the papers which they gave me that I qualified as a machinist for the Merchant Marine. And I sat down near the people and I waited while several other people had their eyes checked and I memorized the chart backwards and forwards. And then I went and I had no trouble reading that chart. [*HM smiles wide.*] So, I was accepted into the Merchant Marine and then . . . then I went to sea.

FS: And when was that?

HM: That was in May 1945. That was almost at the end of the war. We did not know it yet [*HM smiles*], but it was.

US Merchant Marines are civilians who sail on privately owned ships that are subject to military directives during wartime.[12] Though they were not recognized as military veterans until many years later,[13] Merchant Marines during World War II faced grave perils from German submarine packs that sank many Allied ships.[14]

FS: What was the name of the ship that you shipped out on?

HM: I believe that it was the *Emma Willard*. That was the first ship, the *Emma Willard*. But I sailed on a number of ships. I sailed on the *New Bern Victory*, I sailed on the . . . [*Mandel shakes his head.*] I could remember later, but at the moment . . . I have it somewhere, but its . . .

One of Mandel's Mariner licenses, which was found in his records, lists his service on the following Merchant Marine ships: SS *Emma Willard*, SS *Laconia Victory*, SS *Egg Harbor*, SS *Joel Chandler*, and the SS *New Bern Victory*. A pay stub lists Mandel as a plumber/machinist on the SS *Joel*

---

12   "Military to Mariner," US Department of Transportation, Maritime Administration, https://www.maritime.dot.gov/outreach/military-mariner#My%20title?.

13   "Veterans' Benefits: Eligibility of Merchant Mariners," https://www.everycrsreport.com/reports/R44162.html.

14   Jones, *WWII*, 83.

Chandler as of February 26, 1946, where his total earnings were $653.90, but there was $103 withheld as taxes and "slops." A pay voucher indicates that Mandel served as Engineering Maintainer, second pump on the SS *Egg Harbor*. A pay stub from the SS *New Bern Victory* lists that he was paid a total of $50.75 for 58 days of work from June 24, 1946 to August 20, 1946, which after Social Security and withholding taxes left him a take home pay of $41.61. Another pay stub lists the *New Bern Victory* as having arrived in New York City on September 26, 1946, and that Mandel's earnings for the period from August 21, 1946 to September 26, 1946 were $361.50, but $48.45 was withheld as taxes. The discrepancies in the pay rates listed on these pay stubs may reflect differences between shore and sea pay. A letter dated September 30, 1946 by J. E. Hammer, chief engineer of the SS *New Bern Victory*, and another person whose name is illegible, lists Mandel as serving on that ship as a machinist and plumber from June 24, 1946 to July 23, 1946 and as an assistant electrician from July 23, 1946 to August 26, 1946, and attested that "We found him a person of dependable character and temperate habits, and he left on his own accord." Another pay stub, from the SS *Joel Chandler* is dated October 25, 1946. Mandel's records indicate that he subsequently sailed on the *Marine Carp*, and the SS *Coeur D'Alene Victory*, where he was vaccinated for smallpox on August 6, 1947.

Mandel described sailing in the Merchant Marine as involving long periods of boredom punctuated by moments of abject terror. While steaming off of the coast of Italy, his ship once raced another American Merchant Marine ship all day. As sunlight waned, Mandel's captain decided to cease sailing because the coasts of Italy were still heavily mined in the aftermath of the war, while the other ship went steaming ahead, winning the race, much to the disappointment of Mandel and his crewmates. The next morning Mandel's ship steamed past the debris of the rival ship, which had hit a mine and sunk during the night. It is not surprising that in later years he refused to go on vacation cruises, explaining that he had enough, though once he mused that he was curious to see the engine room of a cruise liner.

FS: Did you meet any other Jewish sailors or servicemen?

HM: Well . . .

FS: When you were in the Merchant Marine?

HM: I met them . . . I met while I was on troop carriers, I met a number of Jewish servicemen.

FS: Did you have services together?

HM: On occasion, when we had a . . . troops aboard . . . we had, we usually had enough Jews for a *minyan* and we had services. And the ship that I was on with David Kaplan, I remember we had services, and on several other ships when we had troops aboard we did have services. However, I never was on a ship with a Jewish chaplain. [*HM grins.*] So we had our own services, which of course, if you want services you can make services. [*HM flashes a slight smile.*]

FS: Did you have your own services, or did . . .

HM: No, we ran our own services.

FS: Were you provided with . . . I know you mentioned you got *matzos* on Crete, in Greece, were you ever provided with any *matzos* or any . . .

HM: No, no. The closest I came to being provided was that we were in Italy, and I went to a *seder* that was being held in an Army base in Italy. And I got some wine from the rabbi who was a Jewish chaplain so that when we . . . That was for the first *seder*, and for the second *seder* I was with myself, so I had one of these little bottles of wine. [*HM smiles.*]

FS: And you used that for the Passover *seder*?

HM: I used that, and we had been in Greece. We were shuttling in the Mediterranean, we had been in Greece, and I had gone to the Joint, and had gotten some *matzos* there.

FS: Could you please describe what Joint is?

HM: That is the Joint Distribution Committee, which was the forerunner of the UJA, or actually the United Palestine Appeal and the Joint Distribution Committee, which was helping the Jewish refugees, was funded by American Jews primarily. And I was able to get *matzos* there. [*HM smiles.*]

FS: I would like to go back and clarify a couple of things. When you went into the service, did you take any personal items with you from home?

HM: [*HM smiles.*] Well, I took my *tallis*, not my *tallis*, my *tefillin* [phylacteries] and a *siddur* [prayer book]. And I took one or two Jewish books aside; I took some clothing. I mean, the Merchant Marine did not provide you with uniforms. So I had to have my own clothing. And the . . . so that was the personal things I took with me. But other than that, not really.

FS: Did you get any reaction from any people you served with because you had these personal religious items with you?

HM: Well, I would get reactions. Two of my roommates, the first couple of times they saw my *tefillin* in the morning and they wanted to know what was going on, and I explained to them, but there was no problem with that at any time.[15]

Rabbi Chaim ibn Attar suggests that wearing *tefillin* while traveling fulfills the biblical command to "go with my [unexplained] statutes."[16]

***

FS: Did you at any time get any antisemitic reaction to, by somebody you served with?

HM: No, I didn't have that problem in the service, thank G-d. Had enough problems. [*HM flashes a full smile.*]

FS: What kind of problems did you have?

HM: Not having enough food. Because I tried to eat kosher. And I did not eat any of the meat. I would not say that the vegetables that I ate were kosher because they were all cooked in *trefe* [non-kosher] pots and so on, but I did not eat any meat. So that was a . . . you know, not having . . . And of course, I had to eat around what they served.

Henry used to cut off the crusts of bread baked on ship, reasoning "You do what you can."[17] In contrast, his brother Leo, who had to use a similar practice at some points of his Army service while in the field, when told later in a synagogue class that the bread had not been kosher, insisted that under the extenuating circumstances, "the bread was kosher, Rabbi!"[18]

HM: Because, I mean there is a meal, you have to eat it. You were . . . Like, for example, Sunday afternoon was the big day aboard the ship. They used

---

15   Mandel interview by Shuster, 2000.

16   *Or HaChaim* on Leviticus 25:3.

17   Mandel interview by Esther Mandel, Aaron Mandel, and Chana Liba Mandel, 2012.

18   Recollection of Brian J. Burstin. See Talmud Bavli *Pesachim* 76a.

to serve . . . have steaks and French fries, and of course I could not eat the steaks, and the French fries were fried in lard. So I had nothing. Of course, the one saving thing was they always had Boston Cream pie. So I ate two, three portions of Boston Cream Pie and milk or coffee. And that was my meal. So that was the main hardship. I really don't consider that a hardship. But that was the only problem there.

FS: Did you find that the lack of protein in your diet that you were deprived, that you were not feeling well?

HM: No, I did not feel . . . not find that at all. I was young then and that did not bother me. But to be honest, I used to take from home some cans of sardines and salmon. Tuna was very rare and expensive at that time, and salmon was much cheaper. Today I think it is just the opposite. But I would take sardines and salmon with me so I was able to get proteins in.

FS: And I guess the milk, probably . . .

HM: The milk helped too.

Henry often bemoaned that when his father sought to train him as a kosher slaughterer, he had not taken up the offer; otherwise he would have been able to supplement his diet with chickens bought at ports of call. Until the end of Henry's life, one of the first things he would do when entering his or his children's homes was to check what food was available in the refrigerator. And he plied his daughters with plenty of milk when they were children.

***

FS: I want to clarify. You shipped out from New York. Where did you go to first?

HM: The first trip . . . I believe that we went to Belgium.

FS: And exactly when was this? In '45?

HM: Right.

FS: In the spring?

HM: In the spring of '45. And we went to Belgium, went to northern Germany, Bremerhaven, went to France, went to Italy, to Greece. As a matter of fact, we were heading for the Pacific. We were just about at the Panama

Canal, when the atom bomb was dropped in Japan, and we got orders to turn around to go home. We had GIs aboard. At that time, they were releasing . . . they gave points for the service, they got one point for every month of service, for action in battles, for wounds, and so on, and over a certain number of points they were discharged, the soldiers, even though it was during the war, once they reached a certain amount of points, they discharged the soldiers. So we had the people with low points, a ship full of soldiers with low points, and we were heading to the Pacific, we were going for the Panama Canal when they dropped the atom bomb, we turned around and went home. And these young soldiers, most of them teenagers, who had been drafted recently, and they came back to the States, while the veterans who had put three or four years in Europe were stranded in Europe because of lack of shipping. [*Mandel grins.*] And the young soldiers were going to be discharged ahead of the veterans.

Mandel often recounted that on the way to the Panama Canal, the ship's captain had sailed by the coast of Florida to signal to his wife at the captain's family home.

FS: What kinds of things did you do on the ship?

HM: Well, on a ship, I presume that you are talking about the free time? And that was primarily reading. There was a lot of card playing going on, which I did not particularly care for. So I did a lot of reading.

FS: Did you receive any mail?

HM: No. No, I never received any mail when I was aboard ship.

FS: So you were in the Merchant Marine. And they were under the auspices of who?

HM: They were under the Coast Guard. But, it is . . . theoretically, they were under the Coast Guard. But for example, when we were taking troops back and forth. When we carried troops, we were in the Army. The Army gave orders. The ships were run by private shipping companies. But they received orders, where to go, what to do, from [*FS sneezes*], G-d bless you [*HM smiles*], the Army if we were carrying troops, or from the Coast Guard if we were carrying supplies. But I presume that most of it was military supplies it would be under the control of the Army, and if it was civilian supplies it was under the Coast Guard.

FS: What specifically was your job, what was your function?

HM: Well, I was in the engine room. And I sailed as a plumber, I sailed as a machinist, I sailed as a combination plumber/machinist, I sailed as an electrician. I sailed as a second plumber in an oil tanker, I was mainly in the engine room . . .

FS: In the course of all of your service in the Merchant Marine what was your rank?

HM: Well, the Merchant Marine does not have rank like the Army does, or even the Navy. I served as an electrician, I have papers as an electrician and as a machinist. Though, as I say, I also served as a plumber, I served in engine maintenance, I served as a second plumber. All of my service was in the engine room, what we called the black gang. I was strictly engine room. I never did any work in the deck gang.

FS: I would like to ask you how your experiences during World War II affected your life?

HM: Well, I would say that I became more worldly. Until then, I was very insular. I was a New York boy and as far as I know I went away a couple of times for a week in the summer to a hotel or something. When I was a child two or three times I went to a summer camp for two weeks. [The camp was located in Lakewood, New Jersey.] I only knew New York, I was strictly . . . to me New York was the whole world. But when I went there, it has nothing to do with my being Jewish, but I got a much wider viewpoint. I saw so much more that the world is more than my own small little town, though it is hard to call New York City a little town. [*HM smiles.*] As a matter of fact, even Brooklyn was a stranger to me because I lived in the Bronx, and between the Bronx, Manhattan, and Brooklyn, I very rarely even had reason to go to Brooklyn, except when I was working in the Brooklyn Navy Yard. That was in and out, to go there for work and leave there and come back to the City, because that was not even considered the City, I mean. So I had a very insular outlook. Very . . . but once going there and being all over the world, I got a much broader outlook. I realized that there is more to the world than New York City.

FS: Was there any time that you felt especially proud to be a Jew in your service?

HM: Well, I would say when we were running these refugees to Palestine, I felt that pride in being Jewish in that we were able to do something like that.[19]

***

Mandel was a member of the HaPo'el HaMizrachi and its youth group.[20] HaPo'el HaMizrachi was a Zionist party in favor of *halakha* (rules of religious observance), as well as physical labor in the pioneering of settlements.[21] Mandel considered himself a Zionist and an Orthodox Jew.[22]

FS: When did your service end again?

HM: In about June 1947. And that's . . . and that's when I went back to the Navy Yard for a year.

---

19   Mandel interview by Shuster, 2000.

20   Henry Mandel Machal questionnaire, Mandel file, Machal [Mitnadvei Hutz LaAretz] and Aliyah Bet Records, undated, 1930–2010, I-501, American Jewish Historical Society (AJHS), Center for Jewish History, New York, NY.

21   Israel Kolatt, "Religion, Society, and the State during the Period of the National Home," in *Zionism and Religion*, eds. Shmuel Almog, Jehuda Reinharz, and Anita Shapira (Hanover, NH: University Press of New England, 1998), 292.

22   Mandel Machal questionnaire, AJHS.

Chapter 4

From Gowanus Canal to Atlantic Crossing

Is such the fast I desire, A day for men to starve their bodies? Is it bowing the head like a bulrush, And lying in sackcloth and ashes? Do you call that a fast, A day when the LORD is favorable? No, this is the fast that I desire: To unlock the fetters of wickedness, To untie the cords of the yoke, To let the oppressed go free, To break off every yoke.

—Isaiah 58:5–6[1]

When asked about his role in bringing refugee Jews to Israel, Henry liked to joke: "How did the Jews get to Israel? *Yiddel* by *yiddel.*" The full story was a bit more complicated.

> HM: I sailed with one Jewish sailor. He was a radioman. Dave, David Kaplan, who subsequently . . . he became a dentist and took a degree at NYU Dental School; he retired recently. But anyway, I sailed with him on one ship, and I really don't recall which one. But then when I was on the *Ben Hecht* looking for a radioman. And when he came into port he then joined me in the *Ben Hecht.*[2]

Dr. David Kaplan wrote in a memoir of the *Ben Hecht*[3] that "[i]n early 1946 I was the radio officer on a troopship bringing home US Army soldiers stationed in Germany. The ship's electrician was Henry (Hank) Mandel and

---

1   *The Tanakh*, New Jewish Publication Society (1985).
2   Mandel interview by Shuster, 2000.
3   Dr. David Kaplan, "Volunteer from the USA on the 'Ben Hecht': 'This Is the Way It Was,'" http://www.palyam.org/English/Volunteers/13570533.pdf.

we were probably the only Jews in the crew. News from Palestine was the daily subject of our discussions, especially the news of *Aliya[h] Bet* ships caught by the British Navy. We decided that whichever of us heard of a ship needing crew would notify the other. Henry and I separated after the troop-ship voyage, leaving our addresses with each other." Based on Mandel's payroll records, the Merchant Marine vessel that Mandel and Kaplan initially met aboard was probably the SS *New Bern Victory*.

Kaplan was on a Gulf Oil Company tanker with a regular route between Philadelphia and Venezuela when he "received a message from Hank saying that he'd found a ship," whereupon Kaplan came home to New York and contacted Mandel, who had been recruiting crew members for the *Ben Hecht*. Mandel brought Kaplan to the offices of the American League for a Free Palestine, where Kaplan presented his credentials to Lieutenant Commander Yehudah Finkelstein and was signed on as radio officer. He was then sent to the Gowanus Canal docks in Brooklyn, where he joined the *Ben Hecht*.[4] *Ben Hecht* was the semi-clandestine name of the vessel; the official registered name of the ship was the *Abril*, and it had formerly borne the names the *Artheus* and the *Argosy*.[5]

FS: Where did you get financing from?

HM: This was financed by the American League for a Free Palestine. And the . . . which got most . . . much of its financing from Ben Hecht, who at that time wrote a play for them, *A Flag is Born*, which was shown on Broadway. It raised a lot of money. And as a matter of fact, the ship was named after him, the *Ben Hecht*. The American League for a Free Palestine was connected with the Irgun.[6]

***

AGM: This is Alyssa Goldschmidt on December 1, 2006, interviewing Henry Mandel at 1 p.m. Mr. Mandel, is it okay if I interview you?

HM: Yes, that is quite all right.

---

4   David Kaplan letter to the Israeli Defense Ministry, April 3, 1998; Mandel file, Machal [Mitnadvei Hutz LaAretz] and Aliyah Bet Records, undated, 1930–2010, I-501, AJHS, Center for Jewish History, New York, NY.
5   Kaplan, "This Is the Way It Was."
6   Mandel interview by Shuster, 2000.

AGM: Thank you. So Sammy told me that you were involved in the Irgun in America. I was wondering if you could just tell me about those experiences, how you got involved, and what you were doing.

HM: I was not really involved with the Irgun in America. I had been in the Merchant Marines in World War II, and I had just come back from a trip, and one of my neighbors, Mr. Green, his daughters were friends with my sisters, I think he had two girls. He came in, and he said to me that there is a ship that is looking for a crew. And would I be interested? Mr. Green, incidentally, was born somewhere in Russia in the same town as his cousin David Green, who later changed his name to Ben-Gurion. He was a first cousin of Ben-Gurion, and they grew up together.[7]

David Ben-Gurion, whose birth name was David Gruen, alternatively spelled Grien, was born in the Polish town of Plonsk, then part of the Russian Empire. Plonsk is about forty-five miles northwest from Warsaw.[8] Mandel underlined the sentence with the information regarding Ben-Gurion's original name and birthplace in his personal copy of Amos Elon's *The Israelis: Founders and Sons*, and put a scrap of newspaper as a bookmark when the information was repeated. Green and Gurion are spelled similarly in Hebrew, which is why the future prime minister chose the Hebraized name Ben-Gurion.

HM: But anyway, when I went down there, it was an Irgun ship. And I had at that time been a member of HaPo'el HaMizrachi, but this was not a question of ideological differences, this was a question of trying to save Jews and trying to get them to Palestine. And so, I went and joined that ship.

AGM: You just joined, not for ideological reasons, but just to help out in Palestine?

HM: Not for Irgun ideological reasons.

AGM: But were you aware of the Irgun?

[*Cross talk, the start of Mandel's answer is indecipherable.*]

7   Mandel interview by Goldschmidt Magid, 2006.
8   "David Ben-Gurion," *Encyclopedia Britannica*, https://www.britannica.com/biography/David-Ben-Gurion; Amos Elon, *The Israelis: Founders and Sons* (New York: Holt, Rinehart, and Winston, 1971), 25, 86.

AGM: Did you associate with them? Did you agree with what they were doing?

HM: I was aware of Betar, which was the Revisionist group in the United States. The Irgun was part of the Revisionists. They were called the Revisionists here.

AGM: And were you aware of the work of the members of the Bergson Group, Peter Bergson, and Ben Hecht, and the Committee for the Jewish Army?

HM: Well, I was on the *Ben Hecht*. I went to the Americans for a Free Palestine, which was run by Peter Bergson.

AGM: Yes.

HM: And there was, the nominal head was Senator Guy Gillette, I think he was chairman.

AGM: Yes, he was.

Guy M. Gillette served as President of the American League for a Free Palestine.[9] He had previously served as a senator from Iowa, and notably opposed FDR's plan to pack the Supreme Court.[10]

HM: And at the time they are running on Broadway a play that Ben Hecht wrote, *A Flag is Born*.

AGM: Yes, yes.

HM: Which and [indecipherable word] I got there and at the time there was not much of a crew. And I had sailed on an American ship with Dave Kaplan on board as the radioman. And I called his home. He was at sea. And they called the ship from shore. And when he reached his folks they told him that I had called and to make him aware that we were recruiting a crew for a ship to run refugees to Palestine. And when the ship came back he got off the ship and joined. So I also was responsible for another member of the crew. I was a member of the National Maritime Union. I went down to the union hall there. I met a fellow there, and we got to talking. I had at the time . . .

---

9 Isaac Zaar, *Rescue and Liberation: America's Part in the Birth of Israel* (New York: Bloch Publication House, 1954), 299.

10 Mark R. Finlay, "Gillette, Guy Mark," in *The Biographical Dictionary of Iowa*, ed. David Hudson, Marvin Bergman, and Loren Horton (Iowa City: University of Iowa Press, 2008), 188; "Iowa's Microcosm," *Time Magazine*, June 13, 1938.

I also had electrician papers. There was a boat, a ship there that needed an electrician. So we checked the dates on our cards and I had the older date. So I said to him that you can't have that ship because I had precedence over you.

AGM: [*AGM laughs.*]

HM: So when they called the other ship and I did not answer, he said "Aren't you going to take the ship," and I said, "No, no, I have another ship."

AGM: [*AGM laughs.*]

HM: "I am already signed up. Are you interested?" So I told him about the *Ben Hecht* and he was interested. And he came. He came with us, with me, we both went down, to the offices of the American League for a Free Palestine.

AGM: And when you went to the offices, what did they tell you about the ship, what was their plan for the ship, what did they expect of you? Can you just tell me of your experiences there?

HM: Well, the plan was to try to get the Jewish refugees into Palestine despite the British blockade. And it was owned by some Germans and it happened to be in a United States port when Germany declared war on the United States. So the American government took it and during the war it was used as a mine layer in the Atlantic Ocean.

***

FS: So, how did this work? This was all a clandestine operation?

HM: And, but, that is what they called Aliyah Bet. The underground immigration into Israel. And until we came along, what would happen is that the crews, and incidentally, most of the ships had American crews. And the crews . . . would melt in with the passengers. And the British would not find any crewmen.

FS: So these Americans . . .

HM: Right.

FS: Were they Jewish or non-Jews as well?

HM: My ship had a substantial number of non-Jews. But on our ship, we felt that it was not sufficient to just try to get the refugees into Palestine. But we wanted to show more. We wanted to show that the British had no right to prevent Jews from coming into Palestine. We felt that they had a Mandate to create a Jewish homeland in Palestine from the League of Nations. That was their Mandate and they should have done that and not prevented Jews from coming in. So in all of the other ships the crews melted in with the passengers and they came back to the United States. We did not. We stayed as a crew. And the British rubbing their hands with glee. Ah, they finally got some people they could . . . and they charged us with illegally aiding and abetting illegal immigration.[11]

**

AGM: Okay. So could you just tell me about your experiences on the ship itself?

HM: Well, we started . . . the ship had just been purchased as surplus from the US government. It had been . . . was being auctioned off . . . and somehow, through some contact I believe, the proper papers were made because they bought it for $36,400 I believe, and the next bid was $36,000, so it seems, but anyway it was picked up in Baltimore and brought up to Brooklyn to . . . it was in the Gowanus Canal and it was being overhauled there while they were trying to get a crew together. It was an interesting thing that there were a half-a-dozen crew-members who had claimed that they were members in the Spanish brigade, what did they call themselves . . . The Lincoln Brigade. The Lincoln Brigade, if you are not aware of it, was a unit of American volunteers there, and they were aboard the ship and were given a stipend and they stayed aboard the ship and they brought their meals and so on. I was going home. I would come in the morning and I would come, go home in the evening and I didn't need a stipend. And…so anyway, but the day we were going to leave, they vanished, they evaporated, they disappeared.

AGM: Really.

HM: And we were short-handed.[12]

**

---

11   Mandel interview by Shuster, 2000.
12   Mandel interview by Goldschmidt Magid, 2006.

"Everybody had more than one job," remembered Kaplan. "I was a radio operator for twelve hours. Then, the other man took over, Eddie Styrak, took over for twelve hours. And then, I was the ship's doctor. Then, I had to go down to the engine room for about two hours to pump oil through the lube oil from the tanks—everybody had more than one job."[13]

HM: We had picked up some young . . . I am trying to remember the name of the youth group, the revisionist youth group [Betar]. We picked up three young fellas from there. There was Eli . . . I am trying to remember his name . . . Lou Binder, Eli Freundlich, and the third fellow was a . . .

[*Libby Mandel, heard faintly in the background*]: [Not clear, but perhaps "She is taking all these notes down?"]

HM: It is on tape. And the third fella was a Polish refugee. His parents had escaped from Poland and they went to Cuba. He did not know any English; he knew Spanish, and we used to call him Spanish John.

AGM: [*AGM laughs.*]

HM: To be honest, I don't even know his name.

AGM: [*AGM laughs.*]

HM: It was an interesting thing about that. Once a week we used to get cigarette rations. And, what-you-call-it, the purser, who used to distribute it, used to write down the names as he distributed it. And he wrote Spanish John.

AGM: [*AGM laughs.*]

HM: And when the British picked us up, they must have come across that particular listing, and they said, "Where is John Spanish? Where is John Spanish?" which, of course, they could not locate John Spanish.

AGM: [*AGM laughs.*]

HM: And Spanish John and Eli Freundlich mixed in with the passengers who were taken to Cyprus. And from Cyprus they eventually got into Palestine. Whatever happened to Spanish John, I don't know, but Eli Freundlich, he

---

13   David Kaplan Oral History, interview by Eliyahu Lankin, July 17, 1987, Jabotinsky Institute, part 1, tape CS-0327, Metzudat Ze'ev (MZ) (Jabotinsky Institute), Tel Aviv, Israel.

was in the Israeli Army. After the War of Independence, he came back, I would see him occasionally. He got married, and his wife became a doctor somewhere in New Jersey but I have not seen him lately. But then again, we have to do it. [Perhaps meaning see each other.] Lou Binder, he married Hutchins' . . . I don't know if you know about Hutchins, he was the President of the University of Chicago, he was the youngest President ever at that time, about twenty-nine when he became President,[14] but he married his daughter, who had converted for the marriage.[15]

HM: They [Louis and Franja Binder] had one child. And they both died from cancer. And we have an organization, American Veterans of Israel, and a couple from that there adopted their child. But Lou, I believe, sailed on a Haganah ship later. [*Ben Hecht* crewmember] Lou Brettschneider[16] that I had recruited, he sailed on a Haganah ship later, our bosun . . . I think the four of them. The bosun, "Heavy" [Walter Greaves], I am trying to remember his name, was a heavyset fella, he was called "Heavy," obviously. I don't remember his name, "Heavy," Dave [Leo] Gutmann,[17] who was a . . . in the engine room and Lou Brettschneider and Lou Binder then went . . . they signed up on a Haganah ship [the *Paducah*].[18] Because the crew was not . . . They were not members of the Irgun, as such. They were all interested in helping fellow Jews. And the politics of it was not their concern. So as I said, four of our crew signed up after that with the Haganah ship. So when you are talking about beliefs of the Irgun and so on, it wasn't. And we had a number of Gentiles there. . . . I am trying to remember their names. So it was a long time ago, I forget things.

AGM: It's okay [*laughing*], . . . you seem to remember a lot. [*Cross talk.*]

HM: My wife writes me a note when I forget things. When I come back from the shopping with half the items I was supposed to . . . She lets me know I forget things.

AGM: [*AGM laughs.*]

---

14 "Robert Maynard Hutchins," https://president.uchicago.edu/directory/robert-maynard-hutchins.
15 Mandel interview by Goldschmidt Magid, 2006.
16 Joseph Hochstein and Murray S. Greenfield, *The Jews' Secret Fleet: Untold Story of North American Volunteers Who Smashed the British Blockade* (New York: Gefen, 1993), 175.
17 Ibid., 176.
18 See Rudolph W. Patzert, *Running the Palestine Blockade: The Last Voyage of the Paducah* (Annapolis: Naval Institute Press, 1994).

HM: And the messman was not Jewish. Actually, we had two messmen, we had Spanish John and another Messman. Our bosun . . . not the bosun, our . . . I forget plain words . . . what do you call him, the person I told you who distributed the cigarettes . . .

AGM: The cigarette distributor?

HM: What?

AGM: The cigarette distributor?

HM: No . . . the purser . . . purser.

AGM: Oh, Okay.[19]

***

Crewmember Marvin Liebman, after decades as an activist and fundraiser for conservative causes, including public relations for Chiang Kai-Shek's regime in Taiwan, held various posts in the Federal government during the Reagan Administration. In his memoir, *Coming Out Conservative*, Liebman chronicles his work as a conservative publicist, his conversion to Catholicism under the influence of his friend William Buckley, and his 1990 public letter to Buckley published in the *National Review* in which he came out as gay and decried homophobia, racism, and antisemitism in the American political right wing.[20]

HM: I am [unintelligible, but perhaps "groaning"] because I am trying to remember his name. But anyway, he later became Chiang Kai-Shek's speaker, [unintelligible, but perhaps "let me qualify that what I mean by that"]; his mouthpiece here in the United States.[21] And he converted to Christianity, and he wrote a book and he happened to have been gay and wrote a book *Coming*

---

19   Mandel interview by Goldschmidt Magid, 2006.
20   "Marvin Liebman, 73, Dies; Conservative for Gay Rights," *New York Times*, Obituary, April 3, 1997; Phil McCombs, "Revelation from a Right Winger," *Washington Post*, July 9, 1990, https://www.washingtonpost.com/archive/lifestyle/1990/07/09/revelation-from-a-right_winger/f06ffc3c-bf95-4f14-8bf8-905435ca8062/; "Marvin Liebman," in Hochstein and Greenfield, *The Jews' Secret Fleet*, 176.
21   See Robert Gould and Thomas Bodenheimer, *Rollback! Right-Wing Power in U.S. Foreign Policy* (Boston, MA: South End Press, 1989), 68.

Out Republican, which was published.[22] No, he had a rather interesting life, among other things. In the book he mentions that when he was on our ship, he didn't . . . nobody knew he was gay, but that was only in his own mind. We were all aware of it, but it did not bother us. I am trying to remember his name . . . All right. And the bosun, "Heavy," was Walter Greaves, that was the bosun's name.[23] And the purser, I am trying to remember his name . . .

AGM: That's all right.

HM: All right, it's a matter of record, I mean . . . And we had a captain that, a Texan, that came, that started with us, but he was a drunk. And we dropped him. When I say we, I was not one of the people involved in sending him home from France, where we landed. And our first mate became the captain. Bernstein . . . what was his first name.

Captain Clay was known to the British "to be a tough customer." Upon capturing the ship, according to a British account, British military intelligence claimed to have discovered that "Clay had found a French girl on whom to spend the crew's payroll, with which he absconded."[24] Jack Bernstein was a crew member of the *Ben Hecht*, though Mandel is actually referring to Hyman Robert (Bob) Levitan.[25]

***

HM: So even in the deck department we were short-handed. As I said before, we sailed with not a full crew and we did what we could. And we went to Port-de-Bouc, in France.[26] That is a small town not far from Marseille, and we were refitted there to pick up the passengers. There were, like, shelves put in. It was originally a yacht. The name was the "Abril": A–B–R–I–L.[27]

The *Abril* / *Ben Hecht* left New York on December 27, 1947.[28] Levitan summarized the first stage of the *Ben Hecht*'s journey as follows: "And I worked

22   Marvin Liebman, *Coming out Conservative: An Autobiography* (San Francisco: Chronicle Books, 1992).

23   Hochstein and Greenfield, *The Jews' Secret Fleet*, 176.

24   Ninian Stewart, *The Royal Navy and the Palestine Patrol* (London: Routledge, 2002), 97.

25   Hochstein and Greenfield, *The Jews' Secret Fleet*, 175.

26   "Port-de-Bouc," Wikipedia, https://en.wikipedia.org/wiki/Port-de-Bouc.

27   Mandel interview by Goldschmidt Magid, 2006.

28   Ronnie Halkenhauser, "Ben Hecht Seamen Tell of Seizure," found in Newspaper Clippings file, 15, Bob Levitan collection, USHMM.

on the ship all of December and then we left for Europe. We left for the Azores, where we refueled, and then we went to Port de Bouc, France and waited there."[29] "In the Atlantic," Kaplan noted of the rough seas the ship encountered, "I never saw a ship take a forty-nine-degree roll and come back. At forty-nine degrees, you were finished. You'd hang there, and then come back. The inclinometer was right over my bed."[30] Levitan remarked that "[i]t was easier for twenty men and a ship to wait for six hundred people than for six hundred people to come down and wait for the ship. So we went to Port de Bouc and waited a couple of weeks. And finally, the people came down. And we loaded them on the ship and we took off for Palestine."[31]

Yehudah Lev, a US Army Air Forces correspondent for *Stars and Stripes* (the Air Force only became a separate uniformed service late in 1947), volunteered for Bricha, the underground railroad that brought Jews out of Eastern Europe with the ultimate goal of entering Palestine. He continued to do so after leaving the Army and becoming an employee in a Jewish welfare organization. "The problem for the Bricha posed by the *Ben Hecht* was that secrecy was essential to an underground railroad smuggling refugees out of Europe. . . . Day after day it [the *Ben Hecht*] sailed across the Atlantic, its location marked on maps that appeared on the front pages of American and European newspapers . . . when it entered Palestinian waters, it [the *Ben Hecht*] cooperated with the Navy in its interception . . . After the summer of 1947 no government could say that they knew nothing of such going ons in their borders; the British had the public information they required to compel other nations to intervene in slowing down the flow of Jewish refugees bound to Palestine." In December 1947, Lev was threatened with arrest and forced to leave Europe.[32]

---

29 Hyman Robert Levitan Oral History, USHMM, RG-50.932*0001, accession number 2010.505.2, https://collections.ushmm.org/search/catalog/irn531076.
30 Kaplan Oral History, part 1, MZ.
31 Levitan Oral History, USHMM.
32 Yehudah Lev, "The Worm's Eye View," *Direction* (January/February 1987): 5, found in Bob Levitan collection, folder 5, USHMM.

Chapter 5

Final Preparations

Rabbi Yoḥanan says: If you see a generation whose troubles flood it like a river, await him [the redeemer].

—Talmud Bavli *Sanhedrin* 98a

HM: And after the war, so we took it the way it was conveyanced that in advance we built basically shelves so the people could sleep on shelves in the hold and so on. We had about five hundred and eighty-five passengers on board, something like that. It was a small boat. It was a smuggling gun ship. And even though it was rebuilt there. Not rebuilt . . . And we all . . . while we were there in France retrofitting, the ship was being gotten ready for the passengers. The crew took turns going on leave. We . . . I know we took a trip to Paris for three days and a trip to Nice for three days while I was there. Because they had at that time carpenters in there rebuilding it.

AGM: Could you just tell me when you were on the ship, you said you went to Paris and to Nice, is that where the ship docked to pick up Jews from Europe?

HM: No, No. Okay, all right. No, the ship was in Port-de-Bouc being worked on, so the crew, so the crew did not have anything to do, so they gave the crew members, they alternated letting them have three days' leave. And in my three days, once I went to Paris, once I went to Nice. The ship was being worked on all the time in Port-de Bouc, which is in France.

AGM: So the Jewish passengers from Europe, where did you pick them up from?

HM: We picked them up from . . . right in Port-de Bouc. They were brought into Port-de Bouc.

AGM: Were these passengers, people who were, had escaped concentration camps or had not yet been brought to the camps?

HM: They . . . some of them were in concentration camps, some were not. There was a number of Moroccans amongst them and so on.[1]

In Shepard Rifkin's novel based on his *Ben Hecht* experiences, Rifkin generalized that "most of the passengers had been in concentration camps. Smells and vomit meant nothing to them, especially with Palestine at the end of the journey."[2]

FS: Is there any other outstanding experience from this time, in terms of being a Jewish experience that you can remember?

HM: [*HM shakes his head.*] No, I don't think that anything special that was a Jewish experience.

FS: How was this . . . I am sorry.

HM: Though when we took on the refugees, in France in Port-de-Bouc, we took on the refugees, we felt . . . it was a very touching moment. When these people were removed . . . they came out of Europe, which to them was a slaughterhouse, and these people had lived to see many of the members of their family slaughtered, some of them actually saw them, others it was they just disappeared. And here they were being on a ship to go to the Land of Israel.[3]

In port in Port-de-Bouc, during the course of seven weeks, "local carpenters ripped out all the fancy trimmings of the yacht and built in four-high bunks to accommodate 625 passengers and crew."[4] "Now, this ship was built originally as a pleasure craft," Kaplan later explained. "There were six staterooms. So, it had twelve people and a crew of about six or eight. The Navy, when they took it over as a picket patrol boat, they put sixty men on it. And we took it, we put 628 people on it all together. It was a little crowded."[5] Levitan later described that "there were six rooms on the ship which had been used for other purposes and we had built these shelves,

1   Mandel interview by Goldschmidt Magid, 2006.
2   Shepard Rifkin, *What Ship? Where Bound?* (New York: Knopf, 1961), 216.
3   Mandel interview by Shuster, 2000.
4   Robert O'Donnell Nicolai, as told to Harry Rauch, "I ran Britain's Palestine Blockade," *Pageant Magazine* 3, no. 7 (August 1947): 25.
5   Kaplan Oral History, part 1, MZ.

which resembled the shelving which they had in concentration camps."
One hundred people were placed in each of the six rooms, for a total of 600
passengers.[6] A fictionalized account of the ship's journey described that the
ship's "officers were to sleep doubled up. Every inch, except for the galley,
the engine room, the storerooms, the crew quarters, and the space necessary for navigation, has been layered in bunks that ran in tiers, bulkhead to
bulkhead. Every suitcase and bundle was to be piled on to the stern in one
huge pile. There was no room whatsoever for luggage in the bunks."[7] Men's
and women's privies were built on the fantail deck.[8]

***

The Hebrew Committee for National Liberation (HCNL), led by Kook,
Merlin, Eri Jabotinsky, Albert Stara, Reuben Hecht, and Abrasha Stvasky
were working in Paris in early 1947 based in the Kutetia Hotel, and calling for the declaration of a provisional government, which Begin opposed,
because he feared it would ignite a civil war with the mainstream Jewish
leadership.[9] In January 1947, American League for a Free Palestine (AFLP)
leader Mike Ben-Ami visited Begin and other Irgun leaders in Tel Aviv.
Throughout 1946, Begin had written to the AFLP/HCNL leaders, and in
the meetings in Tel Aviv he repeated, that all resources were necessary
for an armed resistance to end the British control of Palestine. Ben-Ami
reports that Begin said "We are not interested in gestures but in facts, in
deeds."[10] Begin demanded that all funds be sent to the Irgun, but Ben-Ami
said that most funds in recent months had been for immigration and that
the purchase and equipping of the *Abril* had made the HCNL destitute.
Ben-Ami promised that funds raised by the AFLP would, in the future, be
sent directly to the Irgun. Ben-Ami agreed with Begin that going forward
illegal immigration would be left to the Haganah, due to lack of resources;
the *Ben Hecht* project had rendered the HCNL bankrupt. Any future ships
purchased would be used for the armed struggle. Future plans would be

---

6   Levitan Oral History, USHMM.
7   Rifkin, *What Ship*, 193.
8   Levitan Oral History, USHMM; Rifkin, *What Ship*, 193.
9   Ben-Ami, *Years of Wrath*, 389, 395–396.
10   Ibid., 390.

coordinated with Eliyahu Lankin, the newly appointed Irgun commander in the diaspora.[11]

Eliyahu Lankin recalled that

> I was on the way to Paris after I escaped from [a British prison camp in] Eritrea. When I arrived in Paris in January '47 it became known to me that the *Ben Hecht* was ready to sail, and she sailed a few weeks later to the coast of the Land. It was full of people and so on. I accepted it as a fact. But if they had asked me—I was expressly opposed to it. What did they do this for? To immigrate 500 to 600 young Jews on that ship, which was sent to Cyprus, in practice. That is to say, the British arrested her and brought her there, and the people were concentrated in camps in Cyprus and the ship was confiscated. And thus went down the drain many tens of thousands of dollars that we needed for purchasing arms and things that were much more important, in my opinion. I do not want to say that ship was not important—heaven forbid. But in that era, when they sent that single ship *Ben Hecht*, of 500 to 600 immigrants, in that era the Haganah brought thousands! In many ships. In that era there was the *Exodus* Affair and all the famous ships and the demonstration in the terms of bringing illegal immigration was at its height. The political, diplomatic, propaganda, and psychological effect achieved by the Haganah was above all suppositions. There was no need to add a drop in the sea with that *Ben Hecht*. In my opinion that was just a waste of money. And therefore, I opposed a repeat of that experience. . . . I want to tell you that Hillel Kook bought another ship. And that was the ship *Altalena*, that they bought wanting to send it as a refugee ship. I was opposed. And I stopped that ship in Europe. And I wanted to send that ship with arms to the Land, and not with refugees to Cyprus. So you need to understand our psychology in relation to Aliyah Bet in the years after the War.[12]

***

Levitan later described that "[t]hen we were told that the people would be in the next day. That morning we moved up to the dock and here came an almost endless line of men, women and children with their life's possessions in a sack or in a suitcase by their side. It was an underground

---

11   Ibid., 388–391.
12   Eliyahu Lankin interview by Natan Cohen, October 30, 1964, Sudat Shlishit Radio program transcript, reference code: TS12-20/1, Jabotinsky Institute (MZ) (Hebrew).

operation from country to country over mountains."[13] Liebman explained that "[t]he 'passengers' were separated from the crew so we could get on with our work"; the passengers wore multiple layers of clothing "because they wore everything they owned."[14] Rifkin's novelized account of the voyage described how the passengers slept both below and "on deck, anywhere they could find room. It was jammed solid with bodies . . . They were permitted to sleep anywhere except the crew's quarters, the galley, the bridge, and the engine room. The salon was to be used as a hospital."[15]

FS: You were an American Navy ship and the British arrested you? An American vessel, I mean.

HM: I won't say it was an American vessel because we were flying the Honduran flag. But it was an American crew. The crew was all American. [Honduras was among the countries that allowed Jewish illegal immigrant ships to register, as a flag of convenience.][16]

FS: When did you do that to bring these refugees to Palestine?

HM: That was in 1947. About . . . in February of 1947.

FS: Could you describe that? Was that only one time that . . .

HM: That was the one time. We had hoped to be able to do it more, but we were not able to. We were ready, we were going to these refugees and some of them were in a very pitiful state. They had not recovered from the concentration camps and the work camps which they had been in during the war. And they were a few Russians who had been in the Russian Army. And they were big, strong, compared to the others because in the Russian Army they had been fed the same as the other soldiers. Of course [*HM smiles*], obviously things were not so good either or they would not have wanted to leave and go to Palestine.

FS: Were these Jews?

HM: Yeah, I'm talking about Jews. They were all Jews that we picked up. I'm talking about Russian Jews that had been in the Russian Army.

---

13   Levitan collection, folder 5, lecture notes, 4A, USHMM.
14   Liebman, *Coming Out*, 61.
15   Rifkin, *What Ship*, 199.
16   Wandres, *The Ablest Navigator*, 43.

FS: Did you talk to these people?

HM: I did not have much chance to talk to them because I was doing double duty. I was . . . served as the third assistant engineer, and I was handling the electricity because . . . , and I was also an oiler, because we were short an oiler. So I was standing my regular watches as an oiler, and I also was doing the third assistant engineer work and the electrical work that had to be done aboard ship. [*HM shakes his head.*] I did not have time . . . it was . . . I was working sixteen hours a day. It was . . . and I did not have much time to really talk to the passengers. [*HM smiles ruefully.*][17]

Another crew member, Robert Nicolai, who served on deck, recalled that "[t]he happiest memory I have of the whole episode was getting to know these splendid Jews [the refugees]. They had guts."[18] Kaplan, a future dentist, recalled that aboard the *Ben Hecht*

I did my first extraction. Remember, I of course had nothing then. Hadn't finished college. I hadn't been to dental school yet. But I did my first extraction on a small, short fellow who came in. His face was swollen. And they brought him to me as the ship's doctor. And he wanted *sam*. You know, [poison]. That's the cyanide, that's arsenic. And arsenic, they put in . . . to kill the pain. Obviously, I didn't have any. I had an idea that the tooth should be removed, and we had no anesthetic. So, they held him down. Four men held him down. With a pair of electrician's pliers. I figured, which is the tooth, because I tracked alongside and all the pus came out. I figured that had to be the tooth, I didn't know. And with a pair of pliers, I took out this man's tooth. And the only thing he had to rinse with was grapefruit juice. And only grapefruit juice. He was on top of the wound. But he was very thankful, appreciative. He kissed me. And, you know. If I knew then what I know now, I wouldn't have touched him . . . But, like I said, the good Lord smiles on idiots. And you know, they say the good Lord takes care of idiots and seamen.[19]

---

17 Mandel interview by Shuster, 2000.
18 Nicolai, "I ran Britain's Palestine Blockade," 26.
19 Kaplan Oral History, part 1, MZ.

Chapter 6

The Irgun Had Other Ideas

If one joins redemption to prayer, no mishap will befall him all day.
—Talmud Bavli *Brachot* 9b

HM: When we left from Port-de-Bouc in the Mediterranean we had a problem. The engine went . . . one of the solders went through the casing and we had to remove that solder. And we were going one solder short. So we were slow. We were supposed to land on Friday night. [This schedule is also depicted in Rifkin's novel.][1]

HM: And that Friday night which we were supposed to land, the Irgun took over the city of Tel Aviv. They took over the power plants. They made a blackout there and so on. But we had been under radio silence at the time. And we couldn't . . . and we were not aware of what they were doing; they were not aware that we were behind schedule. And we arrived Saturday night. And the British, they picked us up, as a matter of fact they picked us up twenty-five miles out. And not . . . they picked us up in international waters. Which the British weren't too worried about . . . international law. But the whole matter of about how the Irgun or the American League for a Free Palestine, whichever aspect you want, they knew if we did not get caught this time, we would get caught next time, or the time after. It happened we got caught the first time, unfortunately. But their plan was . . . the Haganah had a system that when a ship was caught by the British the crew melded into the passengers. They had not caught the crew, and wherever they put the passengers in Cyprus for example, they would release them gradually into Palestine, the crew . . . the Haganah that was in charge there would release

---

1   Rifkin, *What Ship*, 229.

the crew first and send them back. But the Irgun had other ideas. They made a point. That they wanted an American crew. And we were arrested for aiding and abetting illegal immigration. We were charged with aiding and abetting illegal immigration. And the Irgun said *no*. [*Emphatic.*] They . . . We could not be guilty of aiding and abetting illegal immigration because the immigration is not illegal. Because under the terms of the League of Nations, Britain first was given the Mandate over Palestine, it was to make a home for the Jews in Palestine. So therefore, it was not illegal. And they were going to have this . . . They were going to fight the cases to say no, these people are not aiding and abetting illegal immigration because the immigration is legal. The prohibition is illegal. And being that we were Americans they couldn't just lock us up and throw away the key. There would be all kinds of American newspapers, American diplomats, all watching what was going on. So . . . and Britain was well aware of it. That they would have a donnybrook on hand if they tried to try Americans on that charge, so after a little over a month we were expelled, we will put it that way, we were expelled from Palestine, we were never tried.[2]

***

FS: We skipped a couple of things, so I want to try to go back chronologically and then continue with this. While you were still in the Merchant Marines, were you able to get any Jewish refugees to Palestine?

HM: Well, I was on one ship, the *Ben Hecht*. And we took Jewish refugees. Unfortunately, we . . . the British captured us, as a matter of fact, they captured us outside of the twenty-mile limit, the twelve mile limit of Palestine. We were on, technically, the high seas. And they stopped us. And they locked us up.[3]

***

---

2   Mandel interview by Goldschmidt Magid, 2006.
3   Mandel interview by Shuster, 2000.

HM: To us, the criminals were the British who were ignoring the League of Nations Mandate for a Jewish state by turning back boatloads of Jewish immigrants.[4]

***

FS: I want to get this clear. You were an American ship and the British charged you? . . .

HM: We were American sailors. The ship had . . . was flying the Honduran flag. But we were American; the crew was American. And the British locked us up. They charged us with the technical crime of aiding and abetting illegal immigration. And we were prepared to fight, saying that the immigration was not illegal because that was part of the Mandate; and if the Mandate was not illegal then we were not aiding or abetting anything illegal. So, we had committed no crime. But they . . . the British realized that and after a month; a little over a month, they released us without bringing us to trial.[5]

A Bergson Group leader later explained that:

[O]ur idea was to force the British to arrest United States citizens, then challenge their actions in the courts in Palestine, and if that failed, in the United States courts and Congress as well. We had apprehensions about the British treating *Irgun*-related passengers more harshly than other *ma'apilim*, so both we in the United States and Lankin in Europe issued instructions for only passive resistance if the vessel were captured. Possibly for this reason, the ultimate boarding and arrests took place without untoward incidents.[6]

Over forty years after the journey of the *Ben Hecht*, Captain Rudolph Patzert, under whom *Ben Hecht* bosun Walter Greaves sailed on the *Paducah / Ge'ula*, a second Jewish illegal immigrant ship, relayed to a researcher that Greaves told him the *Ben Hecht*'s voyage was "A lousy trip. The whole thing was loused up. And when we did get there we had only 600 people aboard. When the British grabbed us, the skipper invited them into his cabin for a drink and the crew surrendered to them. It was a bum deal all around."[7]

---

4   Henry Mandel *Jewish Week* interview, May 22, 1998.
5   Mandel interview by Shuster, 2000.
6   Ben-Ami, *Years of Wrath*, 403.
7   Mike Finegood, "Walter 'Heavy' Greaves," *American Veterans of Israel Newsletter* (April 1993), http://www.machal.org.il/index.php?option=com_content&view=article&id= 607&Itemid=980&lang=en.

There was no captain's cabin on the *Ben Hecht*, as Levitan wrote to the researcher decades later, because all the officers were sharing space to make room for more passengers,[8] so Greaves's reported comment could not be literally true. Perhaps Greaves had in mind the *Paducah / Ge'ula*'s later more significant physical resistance, though that also was called off quickly due to the danger to the lives of the passengers, especially to infants. One suspects that Greaves's evaluation of his trip on the *Ben Hecht* had become garbled through third-hand accounts. After the *Paducah / Ge'ula* was captured, Greaves's patriotic and lewd tattoos betrayed his identity as an American sailor to the British Army on Cyprus, where he was imprisoned under harsh conditions for close to two years.[9]

FS: And where were you being held?

HM: In the Acre Prison in Palestine. That is the old Crusader castle.[10]

Acre Prison, originally a Crusader fortress, was considered immune from break-ins or breakouts due to its seventy-foot high walls of stone and a surrounding moat. The *Ben Hecht* crew were kept in two cells in an enclosure separated from the main prison by barbed wire, where Jewish political prisoners were housed along with Arab prisoners.[11] Mandel put a blanket over some of the barbed wire and used it as bedding, a surreal sight which was captured in a photograph he carefully saved (see bottom image on page 234).

HM: This is when I was a prisoner in Palestine held by the British. I was reading a book. To make myself comfortable I put a blanket over the barbed wire. Sitting in the upper corner is Dave Gutmann, who was an oiler. And you can barely see a piece of Schatz, who also was an oiler. We were all locked up by the British for aiding and abetting illegal immigration.

FS: How did you get this picture?

HM: There was a news service, I believe that it was the Acme news service [actually the Metropolitan Group][12] that one of our crew members, Wallace

---

8   Robert Levitan letter to Mike Finegood, Bob Levitan collection, folder 5, USHMM.
9   Jeffrey Weiss and Craig Weiss, *I Am My Brother's Keeper*, 37–38; 51; Finegood, "Greaves."
10   Mandel interview by Shuster, 2000.
11   Bob Levitan collection, folder 5, USHMM; Levitan Oral History, USHMM.
12   "In the News 1952," part 43, Saturday Night Uforia, https://www.saturdaynightuforia.com/html/articles/articlehtml/itn52part43.html.

Litwin, took this picture and he was connected to the Acme news service. Someone I knew that worked at that service gave me the picture.[13]

Dr. Stanley Burns, an expert on the story of the *Ben Hecht*, describes Litwin's involvement in the *Ben Hecht* and subsequent life and success as follows:

Wallace Litwin (1914–2006) [was a] correspondent and photographer on the *Ben Hecht*. The SS *Ben Hecht* was unlike any other Palestine Blockade runner. It was the first refugee ship sponsored by the Irgun prior to Israeli independence. Unlike the Haganah refugee ships, whose crew blended into the passengers so as not to be discovered, the Irgun planned, if captured by the British, for the crew to be arrested. They hired a professional photographer to document the exodus and in the event they were caught, the photographs could be used as propaganda. Wallace Litwin, a newly minted photojournalist, produced a series of over 250 images of all aspects of the voyage. Litwin took photographs of the ship in Brooklyn being refitted from a twelve-cabin private yacht to a 625-plus-person refugee ship. He then traveled to Grenoble to join the six hundred Jewish passengers and record their journey to Marseille, where they boarded the ship.

During the voyage, he took poignant photographs of life on board, from the crowded sleeping conditions to the makeshift religious services. The boat was captured by British destroyers, the crew was arrested and sent to Acre prison and the refugees were sent to detention centers in Cyprus. It was the only clandestine immigration (Aliyah Bet) ship to have its crew interned at Acre. There, Litwin took pictures of the crew including Henry Mandel. It was at this notorious fortified prison that the British jailed and executed Jewish resistance fighters. At Acre, Litwin surreptitiously took photographs of the Irgun members, who were freed in the famous breakout of May 1947. This episode was dramatically depicted in the movie *Exodus*. At Acre, Litwin was given a special hand carved medal by the Irgun.

Wallace Litwin was born in Brooklyn and lived in New York for most of his life. He served with distinction in the US Merchant Marine in World War II, traveling the dangerous North Atlantic sea route to Murmansk in the Soviet Union. After the war in 1946, he went to photography school in New York. His first major job as a photojournalist was on the SS *Ben Hecht* in 1947. Litwin established his career with the artistic dramatic photos he took on the ship. From 1947 into the early 1980s, Litwin was one of America's

---

13   Mandel interview by Shuster, 2000.

most accomplished photographers. His images adorned the pages of America's most prestigious magazines and the walls of the rich and famous. He was the first professional photographer to be featured in advertisements by the Canon camera company. He produced over 170 major photographic essays for noted magazines, such as *Look, Collier's,* and *Esquire*. As one of the leading photojournalists for *Town & Country*, he documented numerous American and European art, business, and society notables, including Albert Einstein, Jackie Kennedy, I. M. Pei, and Dr. Michael DeBakey. While working as a photojournalist onboard the aircraft carrier the USS *Franklin D. Roosevelt* CVA-42 in 1952, Litwin took the first color photographs of a UFO (the photographs have never been released to the public).

By the end of the 1950s, Litwin was part of the New York celebrity social scene. In 1962, he married author and playwright Muriel Resnik, who penned the play *Any Wednesday*, which ran on Broadway for almost 1000 performances, and was made into a Hollywood feature film starring Jane Fonda. He co-authored *Son of Any Wednesday: The Making of a Broadway Hit*. In 1973, Wallace and Muriel divorced. He eventually moved to North Carolina, where he fell into relative obscurity passing away in 2006. Amazingly, Litwin kept the majority of his vintage prints and negatives. It is highly unusual that a noted twentieth century photographer's main body of vintage prints and negatives remain intact. In 2007, Stanley B. Burns, MD acquired Litwin's life's work. Wallace Litwin's significance and place in photographic history rightfully stems from the series of photographs related to his voyage on the *Ben Hecht*.[14]

***

HM: This is an award [images at page 236] that was given to me by a member of the Irgun when I was a prisoner in Acco, in the town of Acco, that is, the old crusaders' castle. On the back of this award is the inscription "To a brave sailor from his comrades, members of the 'Irgun Zevai Leumi.' Acre Prison," and then my name, Henry Mandel.

David Kaplan later recorded that in Acre Central Prison, the Irgun prisoners included Chaim Luster (Eitan Livni's alias), Yehuda Levi, Katz, and

---

14   Dr. Stanley Burns, conveyed via email from Elizabeth Burns to the editor, October 9, 2020.

Peleg Tamar. "Levi and his friends carved olive wood medals for each of the crew. . . . As far as I know, none of the crew were officially and formally inducted into the Irgun. I understand that this was a formal ceremony and took place with Irgun commanders in Eretz."[15]

***

HM: But I have one of the [photographs] . . . while we were in lock-up in Akko. And Akko is where today Israel has a mental institution. But at that time they had prisoners . . . It was a former castle, surrounded by a moat, and they had a building outside the moat, and we were kept in that building. Because they did not mix...we were what were called remanded prisoners, we were not yet convicted. And inside they were convicted. They did not mix the remanded and the convicted prisoners. However, however, for Friday night and Saturday services, they had a Rabbi come in. The town of Akko was a hundred per cent Arab, except for one Jew, the Rabbi. The Rabbi was the only Jew who lived there, who took care of the needs of the Jews in the prison.[16]

The prison is now a museum.

HM [*as recorded in a* Jewish Week *profile*]: A rabbi was allowed into the prison once a week for services, and all of us said we wanted to attend. It was a way to get in contact with the other Jewish prisoners . . . We were searched each time we went in, but I had these paratrooper boots and I put three batteries in each one . . . I hobbled to services, but no one searched my shoes. [And he gave the batteries over to the Irgun prisoners.] I joined the Irgun because I felt all the Jews had to stick together. No Jew is an Island, and what happens to one, affects everyone. [Referring to the May 4, 1947 assault and breakout from Acre Prison,] I can't say for sure, but I have a feeling my batteries were a part of that operation.[17]

In Acre, David Kaplan received the Cohen blessing during the Torah service, and a visiting rabbi received the Levi blessing.[18] Kaplan later thought

---

15   Kaplan letter to the Israeli Defense Ministry.
16   Mandel interview by Goldschmidt Magid, 2006.
17   Mandel *Jewish Week* interview, 1998.
18   Editor's discussion with Abbe Kaplan, June 17, 2020.

this might have been Rabbi Aryeh Levin, known as the "Father of the Prisoners," but Rabbi Levin was not a Levi.[19]

> HM: So Friday night and Saturday they had services. And we wanted to attend services and they allowed us to join the convicted prisoners. So just for the services . . . We had to go over a bridge over the moat to go into the regular prison. And we were searched before we went, when we were going there to make sure we were not bringing anything in. And, when we were there, one of the . . . and we did more talking and discussing things than praying. You can imagine, there were a lot of things of interest to us and to them and so on. And one of the things they asked is "Do we have any batteries?" Among other things, among my other duties, I also was an electrician on the ship. And I had taken with me a box of batteries, I think twenty-four batteries, that hadn't been used. And I figured that I would throw it into my bag, my duffel bag. And I had it. They had never took it or looked through the thing. So I said I have batteries. So they asked to bring them in. I had paratrooper boots. And I put them on the bottom of my boots and I came in. I walked in and I brought them those batteries, which I never asked them what they needed it for. But I found out later. Because after we were sent back, while we were still at sea, on the *Marine Carp*, coming back to New York, they had a jailbreak.[20]

Actually, while the *Marine Carp* was at sea, Dov Gruner and three other members of the Jewish resistance, whom the Irgun was desperately attempting to free when the *Ben Hecht* crew were in Acre, were executed by the British in Acre Prison on April 16, 1947.[21] The Acre jailbreak took place later on May 4, 1947. The crew's release from Acre Prison had been secured by attorney Joseph Kaiserman whose contention, in the words of one of the crew men, "was that the British had jumped the gun by boarding the ship in international waters."[22]

> HM: And they blew out the wall at Akko Prison. Akko, which in English they call it Acre. A-C-R-E. But in Hebrew it is Akko. And they blew out the wall and I understand that they used these batteries as the source of the power to blow up . . . where they got the explosives, I don't know, but they needed

---

19 "Grave of Rav Aryeh and Wife," https://en.wikipedia.org/wiki/Aryeh_Levin#/media/File:Grave_of_rav_Aryeh_and_wife.JPG.

20 Mandel interview by Goldschmidt Magid, 2006.

21 *"The Gallows."*

22 Nicolai, "I ran Britain's Palestine Blockade," 26.

power to blow, to set it off, and these batteries, as a matter of fact, someone told me that a movie was made about it, and showed how they got batteries from an American prisoner. I never saw the movie and so on but that is what I was told. But they had that blow out. And many of the prisoners escaped. Not only the Jewish prisoners but Arab prisoners escaped. And they had some problems. Because in the escaping some of the cars they were having broke down and so on. But I only got that information second-hand because I was at sea at the time. But it was an interesting thing. I hobbled in a few times because I could not take twenty-four batteries at once.

AGM: Hmm . . .

HM: I think I took four and four in my two shoes in three trips.[23]

***

FS: Did you have any relationship with the Irgun in Palestine? Did you contact them?

HM: We had a relationship in the prison there. Because we were kept outside of the actual prison. Because we were what they called remanded prisoners. And the main prison had convicted prisoners. So they did not have us mixing. But for services, a Rabbi would come in. Acre is a completely Arab town. And the only Jew living in that town was a rabbi who was the chaplain for the Jews in the prison. And he would come in on Friday night and Saturday. And he would conduct services. Now we insisted that we wanted to go to services, so they let us go into the main prison to be with the Jewish prisoners there for Friday night and Saturday. And while we were there, and they would search us every time we went in there to make sure we did not bring in any contraband, while we were there, I was asked by one of the prisoners if I had any batteries. And I had a dozen batteries. I said yes, I have batteries, he said can you bring them in. So, the next time that he came in, I put these batteries in my shoes, I had what they call paratrooper boots. They were the high shoes and I put them in my shoes and I hobbled in. And when they searched us, they searched us very . . . not very deeply, just . . . I forget, I am trying to get the word.

FS: Thoroughly?

---

23   Mandel interview by Goldschmidt Magid, 2006.

HM: They did not search us thoroughly at all.. Very superficially, they searched us. And I brought in the batteries. I did not ask them what they were using the batteries for. However, I found out later because about two weeks later after we were released, there was this breakout where they . . . the Jews in Acre Prison blew out the wall. They somehow had gotten in dynamite and they needed a power to set off the charge and they used these batteries. As a matter of fact, just about two years ago I met somebody they said they saw a movie made about this which showed that. [*HM smiles.*] I had never seen that movie, I still haven't but, it is an interesting....But that was our contact with the prisoners in Acre, Acco in Hebrew. But most of the Jewish prisoners there were either members of the Irgun or the Stern Group.

FS: Just for clarification, for the record, could you explain what the Stern Group is?

HM: The Irgun had a breakaway group that was more radical then . . . and it was led by a man named Abraham Stern. So he was, so they called that the Stern Group. They were much more radical then the Irgun. And the British called them the Stern Gang to make it sound worse than it was because of course they did not like it. And, but, it was a group led by Abraham Stern, a small offshoot of the Irgun. And in many instances the two groups cooperated.

FS: To achieve?

HM: To achieve the elimination of the British. As a matter of fact, about forty years after the liberation of Palestine the papers, the secret papers from the British were opened out because of the passage of time, they were no longer critical, and these papers showed that the action of the Irgun had a large effect on the thinking of Britain in getting out of Palestine.[24]

British historian Nicholas Bethel observed that

[i]n the three years of post-war conflict 338 British subjects were violently killed by Jewish groups. Compared to the number of Jew [*sic*] and Arabs killed in the five months of civil war that followed the United Nations decision, and estimated total of 5014, this is a low figure, a miniscule figure if compared with the number of Jews murdered in Nazi Germany. But since each of the 338 were killed in a personal way, either singly with bullets or in

---

24   Mandel interview by Shuster, 2000.

a small group with a bomb, their deaths made as much impact on British public opinion, perhaps more impact, than the heavy British casualties of the Second World War, which were endured with fortitude and resolution. The 338, it seemed, had died quite unnecessarily. Political pressure to bring the killings to a halt was therefore all the stronger.[25]

FS: Let me just clarify. The time that you were arrested, you were serving as an American as a Merchant Marine?

HM: Yes.

FS: Was there any outcry from the American government?

HM: Yes, there was. There was an outcry. The British claimed that we were within their territorial limits. But that wasn't the point. Our government did make certain representations to England, specifically I don't know [HM smiles], what they did specifically, but England when they saw that there were headlines in all the papers, the Times had headlines about it and so on, and when England saw that there was no way that they could win the propaganda war, because of the fact that we were claiming that the restriction of immigration was the illegality, not the getting immigrants going to Palestine, and this was not aiding and abetting illegal immigration. At that time, they felt discretion was the better part of valor . . . "Let them go . . . Let's get them out of our hair." And we were somewhat disappointed because we felt that our point, while it was made to a certain extent, it would have been more made if we had had a public trial. And because we were Americans, England could not have gotten away with a secret trial, it would have had to have a public trial.

FS: Being held prisoners with you, were there any Gentiles as well?

HM: Yes. We had two of our engineers who were Gentiles. Our bosun was a Gentile. Our chef [Walter Cushenberry] was a Black . . . Our radio operator was a Gentile. Two of our deck hands were Gentiles [James Heggie and Robert Nicolai].

FS: Do you remember any of their names?

25   Nicholas Bethell, The Palestine Triangle: The Struggle for the Holy Land, 1935–48 (New York: G. P. Putnam's Sons, 1979), 358.

HM: Well, the bosun was Walter Greaves, the radio operator was John Styrak....

FS: Are you in touch with any of these people since?

HM: The only one which I am in touch with is the other radio operator, Dave Kaplan . . . I sailed as an oiler on the *Marine Carp*, that was a separate story when we were expelled from Palestine . . .

Kaplan likewise said "Hank Mandel was a friend of mine. See, we became—those of us who knew about it became members of the American Veterans of Israel. American Veterans, this was formed many, many years ago by people from Machal [*mitnadvey chutz l'aretz*, overseas volunteers],[26] from Aliyah Bet. Basically, there were two groups; Aliyah Bet and Machal."[27] Mandel was a member of both groups.

***

On March 31, 1947, Levitan cabled home that he was returning on the *Marine Carp*.[28] The *Marine Carp*, Levitan described later, "was an American transport, troop transport, and it was carrying soldiers and soldiers' wives that they had married in Europe. And other people. And they put us on the ship in this room."[29] The *Marine Carp*, which had 843 passengers, including displaced persons, upon arrival in New York, had left Piraeus, Greece, April 3, 1947.[30] "The day before we were to be released," an imprisoned crewmember remembered, the British authorities gave the Irgun and Lechi prisoners "permission to give us a farewell dinner. It consisted only of meat stew, but there was much speech-making, singing and toasting. Then our hosts did the traditional Jewish dance, the Hora," a night he said he would never forget.[31]

---

26 Nir Arielli, "Recognition, Immigration and Divergent Expectations: The Reception of Foreign Volunteers in Israel during and after the Wars of 1948 and 1967," *Journal of Modern European History / Zeitschrift für moderne europäische Geschichte / Revue d'histoire européenne contemporaine* 14, no. 3 (2016): 374–390.
27 Kaplan Oral History, part 1, MZ.
28 Levitan collection, folder 5, USHMM.
29 Levitan Oral History, USHMM.
30 Halkenhauser, "Ben Hecht Seamen Tell of Seizure."
31 Nicolai, "I Ran Britain's Palestine Blockade," 35.

After Israel's independence was declared later, the captain of the *Marine Carp* insisted on stopping in Beirut as scheduled, despite the pleas of the American Jews on board who were traveling to Israel to volunteer for the Israeli Army. The American Jews were arrested by the Lebanese authorities and imprisoned for weeks until American protests secured their release.[32]

> HM: That when we were on a ship, we got to . . . We boarded in Haifa as prisoners. And the first stop was Alexandria. And one of the crew members, an oiler, I think it was, an oiler, was an Egyptian, and he got off. So they were looking for an oiler. So I went up to the purser and I said "I am an oiler." I showed them my papers that I was a machinist, and electrician, which is higher than an oiler. So I became part of the crew. And I came back to New York and that was the *Marine Carp*. I came back to New York as a crew member of the *Marine Carp*.[33]

The Chief Electrician of the Marine Carp, Charles Feeney of Baltimore, died of pneumonia during the journey, which may have rendered the ship further shorthanded. Daniel Agronsky, the son of the editor of the *Palestine Post*, made the journey to New York on the same trip of the *Marine Carp*.[34] According to David Kaplan, David Gutmann, *Ben Hecht's* oiler, was a nephew of Agronsky.[35]

***

> AGM: In my reading I came across that the Americans that were on the ship which were expelled from Palestine, they came back to New York and there was a reception in their honor at City Hall in Manhattan. Were you involved in that?

> HM: Well, when they had a reception I wasn't at the reception. It was an interesting thing. As a matter of fact, when we arrived in New York there were newspapers there and taking pictures and so on. And I was on watch and I could not come up there. They had the pictures in the newspapers. I have a copy of the picture which was in *The Daily News* of the crew of the

32 Renato Barahona, *The Odyssey of the Ship with Three Names: Smuggling Arms into Israel and the Rescue of Jewish Refugees in the Balkans in 1948* (Reno, NV: Center for Basque Studies, University of Nevada, 2013), 93.
33 Mandel interview by Goldschmidt Magid, 2006.
34 "Hecht Sailors Back; British 'Fair,' Says One," *The Daily News*, April 17, 1947, 29.
35 Kaplan Oral History, part 1, MZ.

Ben Hecht without me because I was on watch at the time [see image at page 243].[36]

Mandel was apparently at the City Hall reception (see page 237, bottom image, third row, far right). The reception he was not able to attend because he was on watch occurred the day the *Marine Carp* arrived in New York, April 16, 1947. There was also a dinner in honor of the *Ben Hecht* and the *Ben Hecht* crew at the Hotel Astor on April 21, 1947. The seating chart from the event shows crewmembers Jeno Berkovitz, Louis Binder, Louis Brettschneider, Walter Cushenberry, Walter Greaves, David Irving Gutmann, James Heggie, Harry Herschkowitz, Robert Levitan, Marvin Liebman, Wallace Litwin, Norman Luce, and Henry Mandel. Louis Markowitz was on the lower dais, and Robert Nicolai, Shepard Rifkin, Henry N. Schatz, Erling Sorensen, Edward R. Styrak, and Jack Winkler were seated on the dais or lower dais. Mandel's parents, labeled as Mr. and Mrs. Abraham Mandel, were seated at table 18.[37]

---

36 Mandel interview by Goldschmidt Magid, 2006.
37 Seating Chart of "Tribute Dinner Honoring Ben Hecht and Crew of the 'Ben Hecht,'" Grand Ballroom, Hotel Astor, April 21, 1947, Newspaper Clippings file, Bob Levitan collection, USHMM.

Chapter 7

Bazooka Plant

Born in Austria, but left quite young, Of his native land he has never sung. He took a ship and crossed the sea, with mom and Dory he was just three. To the Bronx they went, the family grew, girls and boys, quite a few. He started school when he was quite young, at Salanter his education had begun. His dad was a shochet, then sold Jewish books, and I know his mother sure could cook. High School was Yitzchak Elchanan (now MTA). I bet there was less work, more play. College took him quite awhile, As president of City, he did it in style. You know a war came in between, he and his brothers joined the Army and Merchant Marine. He saw the world, he went all around, Spent very little time on solid ground. In forty-seven he got a call, and said goodbye to one and all. To Palestine he went and volunteered. His mom said goodbye but shed many a tear. Forty-eight was very exciting, I don't know if he saw that much fighting.

—Bethsheba Mandel, Poem in Honor of Henry Mandel's Ninetieth
Birthday Celebration

FS: Let's finish with what happened during the war and then we will get to that. [*Mandel nods.*] When did your service in the Merchant Marine end?

HM: Well, it is a difficult thing to say. Technically, the service as a veteran ended when the official war ended. Which I don't recall, September 1, September 15, 1945. But I was in the Merchant Marines till about June 1947.

[*Mandel's Coast Guard identification papers appear onscreen in the interview recording* (see image at page 238): Mandel is smiling, showing his teeth, with a receding hairline, wearing a bow tie and jacket. It states: "Henry Mandel, (Illegible) 2-580712 D1; Date of Birth 9-6-20, Place of Birth, Austria,

Citizenship, USA, Home Address 1035 Kelly St., Bronx 59, New York," and above "signature of Mariner," Henry Mandel's signature.]

HM: . . . United States Coast Guard for Henry Mandel. And it indicates the different licenses in which I held. This [image at page 239] is the reverse side of the ID card which shows that I was licensed as a fireman, oiler, machinist, and electrician.

[the card reads: "Date Naturalized: 6-22-28. Naturalization No. 2554889 (Thru [through] Father's Papers) Height: 5 8. Weight 160. Complexion: Fair. Color Hair: Brown. Color Eyes: Blue. Social Security No. 105-12-2659. Endorsed at New York, N.Y. 7-July '47 Fireman. Oiler. Machinist Electrician."]

HM: This is my original certification in the Coast Guard as a machinist . . .

[*A photograph of Henry Mandel's United States Coast Guard discharge papers appears on the screen,* see image at page 240]:

HM: This is my discharge papers from the United States Coast Guard, and it indicates that I served in the Armed Forces of the United States of America.[1]

***

FS: Tell me what you did?

HM: Well, after I got out from the Merchant Marines, I went back to the Navy Yard 'till 1948. From 1947 to 1948.[2]

The United States State Department announced that it would stop issuing licenses for arms shipments to Palestine and surrounding countries on December 5, 1947. The American embargo was in reality one-sided, because until May 1948, the British government continued to sell arms to the Arab states that had invaded Palestine if the arms had already been contracted for before hostilities commenced.[3] The UN Security Council

---

1   Mandel interview by Shuster, 2000.
2   Mandel interview by Shuster, 2000.
3   Shlomo Slonim, "The 1948 American Embargo on Arms to Palestine," *Political Science Quarterly* 94, no. 3 (1979): 498–499, 512–514; David J. Bercuson, *The Secret Army: The Incredible Story of the Foreign Volunteers Who Formed One of the Toughest Modern*

also imposed a blanket arms embargo from May 29, 1948 to August 11, 1949. However, as described by a leading historian, "the Haganah—an underground organization well-versed in the clandestine arts—fashioned secret arms procurement networks in Europe and the Americas in 1947 and early 1948."[4]

> HM: Then in '48, the State of Israel was declared, I volunteered. Actually, I received a request to help in building, in setting up a bazooka shell plant, and then this plant we took to Israel.
>
> FS: Request from whom?
>
> HM: A . . . I came home from work one day, and there was a card in my mailbox. To please call a Mota Teumim. There was a phone number. I called Mota, and even though it sounds like Chinese, it wasn't. Mota . . . His Jewish [Yiddish] name was Motel, and his English name was Mota [HM smiles] M–O–T–A, and he was an engineer. And he was working on a plant for, I really don't know, the Jewish Agency, or someone . . . This was a surreptitious work, secret work, and someone had recommended me, I don't know, I have no idea to this day who. That I was a machinist and a toolmaker, and then I spoke to him and I . . . we were setting up . . . I was working in the Navy Yard at the time during the day and I finished it at a quarter to five. And then at six o'clock, I went to where they were setting up these machines, getting the machines ready. And I worked there from six to ten helping out. And then, when we just about were getting ready, I resigned from the Navy Yard. And then . . .[5]

Mota Teumim was a thirty-six year-old engineering graduate student who ran the bazooka plant at 119 Greene Street in New York for the secret organization being directed by Haganah operatives out of Hotel 14 on Fourteenth Street.[6] Though the Eastern Development Company officially owned the plant, it was really a front for the Haganah in New York. The Eastern Development Company was managed by Sam Sloan and Moses Hayman of the Sonneborn group of American Jewish business people who

---

Armies in the World and Fought for the Establishment of a Jewish State (Toronto: Lester & Orpen Dennys, 1983), 25.

4   Benny Morris, *1948: The First Arab-Israeli War* (New Haven, CT / London: Yale University Press, 2008), 206.

5   Mandel interview by Shuster, 2000.

6   Leonard Slater, *The Pledge* (New York: Simon and Schuster, 1970), 195.

secretly supported the Haganah's efforts to secure arms in the United States.[7] Moses Hayman, an inventor and explosives expert, and Sam Sloan, set up the 5,000-square-feet space at 119 Greene Street. Workers in the secret shop received "a dollar and a half an hour if they were skilled, a dollar an hour if they were unskilled." Most of the workers were unskilled. A chronicler of the clandestine arming of Israel in the United States during this period notes that "[o]f necessity, because of the nature of the project, the workers were all trusted Zionists." The Eastern Development Company eventually shipped its assembly line and some of its workers to Israel.[8]

> FS: And what were these machines being used for that you were helping to set up?
>
> HM: They were to make bazooka shells. And then we went and took this machinery and set it up in Israel. And we started making bazooka shells. At the time the war ended in Israel in '49 we were making all the bazooka shells, our plant was making all the bazooka shells for the entire Israel Army.
>
> FS: What was the name of that plant?
>
> HM: Well, it was part of the Army, our base was in Koordani. And that was part of Chayl Madda, the scientific branch of the Army. I was a lieutenant there.[9]

Mandel helped reassemble the plant in the Israeli town of Koordani, on a former British Army base. The Koordani plant eventually supplied all the bazooka shells for the Israeli Army.

> FS: This was in the Israeli Army?
>
> HM: In the Israeli Army . . .
>
> FS: Let me go back. What were the circumstances, which you joined the Israeli Army?
>
> HM: I had been asked to join this group to prepare for this bazooka shell set up. And then . . . which I did, I worked with them for a while here in the United States and then we went to Israel where we set up. And when we

---

7   Doron Rosen, *In Quest of the American Treasure: The Israeli Underground (the Haganah) Activity in the United States in 1945–1949* (Jerusalem: Ministry of Defense, 2008), 191 (Hebrew).

8   Slater, *Pledge*, 194–195, 319.

9   Mandel interview by Shuster, 2000.

came to Israel they signed us into the Army. And there I set up the turret lathe section and the punch press section of the plant.[10]

***

An unusual confluence created an international political environment that allowed for the creation of the State of Israel. Crucially, the Soviet Union was supportive, apparently based on the Leninist idea of Soviet countries being organized along ethnic lines and the strategic goal of undermining the British Empire in the Middle East. American and world public opinion were also shocked by the Holocaust, which lent popular support to the Jewish cause.[11] A critical manifestation of that support were the estimated 4,000 foreign volunteers who joined the Israeli Army between May 15 and July 9, 1948. The second truce between Israel and the Arab armies began on July 19, 1948.[12] Veterans of World War II volunteered for Israel, including specialists such as: "sailors, doctors, tank men, logistics, and communications experts, air-and ground crews. . . . [T]he air superiority provided by the experienced foreign air personnel proved to be a crucial advantage Israel had over her Arab opponents."[13] The Americans among them volunteered despite United States Criminal Code, Section 10, which forbade "Enlisting or entering into service of any foreign prince, state, colony, district, or people as a soldier, or as a marine, or seaman on board of any ship of war, letter of marque, or privateer." United States passports at the time stated they were "not valid for travel to or in any foreign state for the purpose of enlisting or serving in the armed forces of such a state."[14]

Prior to volunteering to serve Israel, Mandel had served two years as a machinist and electrician in the Merchant Marine in the Atlantic and Mediterranean. Mandel was living in New York City when he joined the

---

10 Mandel interview by Shuster, 2000.
11 Larry Collins and Dominique Lapierre, *O Jerusalem!* (New York: Simon and Schuster, 1988 [1972]), 48; Erich Hula, "The Nationalities Policy of the Soviet Union: Theory and Practice," *Social Research* 11, no. 2 (1944): 168–201; John Kent, "Britain and the Egyptian Problem," in *Demise of the British Empire in the Middle East: Britain's Responses to Nationalist Movements, 1943–55*, ed. Michael Cohen and Martin Kolinsky (Portland, OR / London: Frank Cass, 1998), 144.
12 A. Joseph Heckelman, *American Volunteers and Israel's War of Independence* (New York: Ktav Publishing House, Inc., 1974), 30.
13 Morris, *1948: The First Arab-Israeli War*, 268.
14 *Bercuson, The Secret Army*, 57–58.

struggle for Israel.[15] Mandel now transitioned from non-violent resistance to freedom fighting. His occupation at that time was a machinist and tool and die maker. He was twenty-seven years old. He was recruited to join the Israeli Army, though he never knew who had provided his name as a likely candidate. Mandel did not know that the Haganah front organization Land and Labor for Palestine obtained the Chaplaincy records which provided contact information about every Jewish American World War II veteran,[16] including Merchant Marine records.[17] Volunteers often left from New York on the *Marine Carp*, the converted Victory ship Mandel had returned home on, which provided inexpensive berths for the trans-Atlantic journey to Le Havre, France.[18] Initially, the ship continued on to Israel, until on one journey, at a stop in Beirut, Jewish passengers of the SS *Marine Carp* were detained for suspicion of traveling to join the Zionist armies in Israel.[19] From then on volunteers who reached France traveled to Marseilles, where they took boats crammed with displaced persons to Palestine.[20]

Mandel traveled from New York to Le Havre, France on the *Niew Amsterdam*, and then by train to a Displaced Person camp outside of Marseilles, and then in a boat crowded with former displaced persons, to Haifa.[21] Mandel traveled and served in the Israeli Army under his own name. Arriving in Israel in September of 1948, he was inducted into the Israeli Army at the Tel Litvinsky camp. He served in the Israeli Army from September 1948 until September 1949 at the rank of lieutenant in the Chayl Madda (Chemed, weapons development), stationed in Haifa. "We set up a bazooka shell plant in Koourdani, between Haifa and Acre. I was responsible for the punch press and turret lathe Depts."[22]

Mandel's Israeli Army identification number was 67674, indicating he was the 67,674th person to join the Israeli Army. He did not serve in combat in the Israeli Army, nor was he wounded. Stationed at the Technion in Haifa, he worked there developing a flamethrower until his release from

---

15   Mandel Machal questionnaire, AJHS.
16   Slater, *The Pledge*, 195.
17   Wandres, *Ablest Navigator*, 36.
18   Slater, *The Pledge*, 216.
19   Barahona, *The Odyssey of the Ship with Three Names*, 93.
20   Slater, *The Pledge*, 217.
21   Mandel Machal questionnaire, AJHS.
22   Ibid.

service in September 1949. He did not receive special pay for his service; though his pay rate as a lieutenant was, as Mandel noted, "more than most."[23]

***

In Chemed, the American volunteers spoke exclusively in English. On one occasion Chaim (Henry) went with another American to help set up a new kibbutz overnight in a strategic area. On the way, Chaim asked for directions in Hebrew. His friend was shocked: "Chaim, you know Hebrew?"

Hanukkah was celebrated while Chaim was stationed in Haifa. He was disappointed to discover that were no latkes, the traditional fried potato pancakes of the holiday that his mother Chana always made. Despite food rationing, Chaim bought potatoes; his landlady make some latkes for him.

In Haifa, Chaim asked a Hasidic rabbi, who was a cousin of the Bostoner Rebbe, whether he should observe the second day of *Yom Tov* (major festivals that are celebrated for two days in the diaspora and only one day in Israel). The rabbi asked whether he intended to return to America. Chaim answered yes. "But wouldn't you stay if the *Moshioch* [the Messiah] came?" the rabbi asked. Chaim said that in that case he certainly would. "So you don't really intend to leave the Land of Israel," the rabbi concluded. That determination was relevant because only a person who intends to return to the diaspora is obligated to keep two days of *Yom Tov* while staying in the Land of Israel. But, the rabbi concluded, in case *Moshioch* did not come, he told Chaim to keep two days of *Yom Tov*. The final advice of the rabbi was the same as the dominant position: that a visitor from the diaspora to the Land of Israel, or vice versa, should adopt the stringencies of both locales during the second day of *Yom Tov*.[24]

***

FS: Tell me about your discharge. You had mentioned something about a uniform?

---

23 Mandel *Jewish Week* interview, 1998.
24 See Yechiel Yaakov Weinberg, *Siridei Eish*, vol. 2 (Jerusalem: Mossod Rav Kook, 2003), sec. 161, 379–380.

HM: [*HM shakes his head.*] Oh, that was in the Israeli Army, when I was being discharged. See, in the Merchant Marine, discharge is that you simply stop. I have a withdrawal certificate from the union which says that I withdrew, as a retirement card. And at any time I want, I could simply by paying union dues become an active member of the union again. But there is no specific discharge like they have in the service. But in Israel, when I was a lieutenant in the Army there, and they had a special camp where they inducted and discharged the English-speaking, what they called the Anglo-Saxons, people that were in Televinsky, and I was sent down to Televinsky on a Sunday for a discharge, they made all the arrangements for me and so on, they paid me money, paid whatever was due me, and so forth, and then they were about to give me my discharge papers. And then they reviewed the papers and they said, "You know, our laws say that a soldier being discharged is only allowed to retain one uniform. I said "Well, I don't have more than one." He said, "We know that, we see that you never received a uniform from the Israeli Army." I said "I didn't." So he says, "We must give you one before we can discharge you." I said, "Well, give me one." He said, "Sorry, but the storeroom is already closed. You will have to wait until tomorrow, because the storeroom closes at one and it is now 3 o'clock." So they had to rework my papers, give me an additional day's pay, and the next day they gave me a shirt, a short sleeves shirt, and a khaki, a pair of khaki shorts, which they gave me the day I was discharged. And they gave me an extra day's pay. Of course, as a lieutenant, I was getting paid seven pounds a month, which was then . . . [*HM smiles*]. So it did not cost them that much for the extra day.[25]

Mandel departed Israel in September of 1949. He eventually received the War of Independence service ribbon. Some of the Machal volunteers felt that Hebrew-speaking Israelis were favored over them by the Israeli government.[26] The new state of Israel was plagued by semi-corrupt patronage and influence peddling, referred to as *protektzia* or "Vitamin P."[27] Mandel had been offered the opportunity to join a new shipping firm because of his technical knowledge. One partner was going to provide funding. However, another of the three partners was selected due to his political influence with the ruling Labor party. Furthermore, Mandel feared that he would have

25   Mandel interview by Shuster, 2000.
26   Wandres, *The Ablest Navigator*, 74.
27   James G. McDonald, *My Mission in Israel, 1948–1951* (London: Victor Gollancz, 1951), 143.

had to work on the Sabbath. Disappointed, Mandel decided to decline the offer and return to New York. The shipping firm later became part of Israel's leading shipping line, Zim.

Upon returning to the United States, the American Jewish community, concerned about charges of dual loyalty, failed to herald the bravery of American volunteers in the Israeli War of Independence until several decades later.[28] As of 1995, Mandel had not received the Fighters for the Defense of Freedom cluster to his Israeli Defense Forces service ribbon,[29] but on August 13, 1998 the Israeli Defense Ministry awarded him the Etzel medal and the Fighters of the State decoration.

28 Amy Weiss, "1948's Forgotten Soldiers?: The Shifting Reception of American Volunteers in Israel's War of Independence," *Israel Studies* 25, no. 1 (2020): 149–173.
29 Mandel Machal questionnaire, AJHS.

Part Two

Letters and Contextual Commentary

What ship is this that will take us all home? O glory hallelujah! 'Tis the old ship Zion . . . Come tell me of your ship and what is her name? Oh, tell me, happy sailor . . .
—"Old Ship of Zion" or "Happy Sailor," African American slave spiritual

Chapter 8

The Bergson Group

R. Simlai expounded: Six hundred and thirteen mitzvoth were given to Moses . . .
Isaiah came and reduced them to two: "Do what is just and observe what is right."
—Talmud Bavli *Makkot* 24a, quoting Isaiah 56:1[1]

The Bergson Group's leader, Peter Bergson, had been born as Hillel Kook in Lithuania in 1915. At the age of ten, his family immigrated to Palestine. Hillel studied in the Jerusalem yeshiva of his uncle, the Chief Rabbi of Palestine, Avraham Yitzhak Kook. His closest friend was David Raziel, who ultimately became an early head of the Irgun Tzva'i Le'umi. Kook joined the Irgun as a teenager. In 1937, he went to Europe to help organize the illegal immigration of Jews into Palestine as an emissary of the Irgun. He came to the United States in June of 1940, where Revisionist Zionist leader Ze'ev Jabotinsky was seeking support for the establishment of a Jewish army to combat the Nazis.[2] The Irgun was inspired by Jabotinsky but increasingly acted independently of him.[3] After Jabotinsky's death in 1940, the Irgun delegation in the United States and the American branch of the Revisionist movement distanced themselves from one another.[4] As the highest ranking Irgun member in the

---

1   Yaakov Elman, *The Living Nach: Later Prophets* (New York / Jerusalem: Moznaim Publishing Company, 1995), 137 (Hebrew).

2   David S. Wyman and Rafael Medoff, *A Race against Death: Peter Bergson, America and the Holocaust* (New York: The New Press, 2002), 14; Shai Horev, *Dawning Ships: The Story of the Clandestine Immigrant Ships from "Vilus" to "Ayalon Valley Battle"* (Haifa: Pardes, 2004), 26 (Hebrew).

3   Rafael Medoff, *Militant Zionism in America: The Rise and Impact of the Jabotinsky Movement in the United States, 1926–1948* (Tuscaloosa and London: The University of Alabama Press, 2002), 49.

4   Judith Tydor Baumel, *The "Bergson Boys" and the Origins of Contemporary Zionist Militancy*, trans. Dena Ordan, Foreword Moshe Arens (Syracuse, NY: Syracuse University Press, 2005), 13; Medoff, *Militant*, 65.

United States, Kook became the leader of the Irgun delegation, which informally became known as the "Bergson Boys" or the "Bergson Group."[5]

Both the American League for a Free Palestine (AFLP) and the Hebrew Committee for National Liberation (HCNL) were established by the Bergson Group. The non-profit corporation legal structure of the AFLP was set up in December 1943.[6] Kook and his colleagues in May 1944 founded the HCNL to fight for creation of a Jewish state in Palestine on the model of a revolutionary shadow government in exile for the Jews of Palestine and for the stateless Jews of Europe.[7] In their nomenclature they were "Hebrews," a term that was a forerunner for the modern label "Israeli," as opposed to the ethnic and religious moniker of "Jew."[8] Kook came to consider the activists of his group as the political leadership of a Jewish national self-liberation movement; he thought the Irgun leaders in Palestine who had undertaken an underground rebellion against British rule were merely military commanders whose authority he did not accept.[9]

The Revisionist movement was very active in organizing illegal immigration to Palestine from Central Europe through the Balkans before World War II from 1937 and during the war's early years.[10] Throughout the 1930s, the official Zionist movement urged that only the elite immigrate to Palestine, those who were capable of economically developing the country and of building a new type of pioneer Jew.[11] In July of 1931, Dr. Chaim Weizmann said in a World Zionist Congress address that Palestine was too small to receive more than a minority of world Jewry.[12] In August of 1937, Weizmann was the preeminent world leader of Zionism. In a speech at the World Zionist Congress he reported telling the British Peel Commission— which eventually recommended a partition of Palestine—"that the hopes

---

5   See Medoff, *Militant*, 70.
6   Harold Leventhal, of Ginsburg, Leventhal, and Brown, memorandum to Ambassador Abba Eban "Re: The Ben Hecht Case: Where do We Stand, and What should be Done," June 6, 1952, labeled "Confidential," 5, file 1816/6, Attorney General, the Ship "Ben Hecht," vol. 1, Israel State Archives (ISA), Jerusalem.
7   Wyman and Medoff, *Race against Death*, 167.
8   Louis Rapoport, *Shake Heaven and Earth: Peter Bergson and the Struggle to Rescue the Jews of Europe* (Jerusalem / New York: Gefen, 1999), 165, 173, 255 n.17.
9   Ben-Ami, *Years of Wrath*, 436.
10 Ben Hecht, *Perfidy* (New York: Julian Messner, Inc., 1961), 9; Aviva Halamish, *A Dual Race against Time: Zionist Immigration Policy in the 1930s* (Jerusalem: Yad Izhak Ben Zvi, 2006), 365, 369 (Hebrew).
11 Hecht, *Perfidy*, 18.
12 Halamish, *Dual Race against Time*, 10.

of Europe's six million Jews were centered on emigration. I was asked, 'Can you bring six million Jews to Palestine?' I replied, 'No'. . . . The old ones will pass. They will bear their fate or they will not. They were dust, economic and moral dust in a cruel world. . . . Only a branch will survive."[13] Weizmann consistently opposed illegal immigration in to Palestine[14] at a time in which Poland was aligning its foreign policy with Germany, unaware that it would soon be a victim of the Nazis too.[15] In 1949, Weizmann told the first American ambassador to Israel that the first generation of refugees "may be a liability, but the second will build Israel."[16] Weizmann's rival and successor in leadership, David Ben Gurion, also generally opposed illegal immigration until 1939, when he came to the conclusion that illegal immigration could be a non-violent weapon in the struggle to establish a Jewish state.[17]

After initially concentrating on advocating for the formation of a Jewish army to fight alongside the Allies against Germany as a separate unit,[18] on November 25, 1942, Kook was galvanized by an article that appeared on page 10 of the *New York Times*, announcing that two million Jews had already been killed in Europe, to try to stop the slaughter.[19] Less than six months earlier, on June 30, 1942, after State Department officials attempted to block the disclosure of the ongoing extermination of the Jews to quell pressure to admit Jewish refugees into Palestine and the United States,[20] the *New York Times* had reported that one million Jews had been killed.[21] Decades later, Kook reflected,

> I am still totally perplexed as how it was possible *not* to react—the way the Jewish leaders didn't react. And I believed then and I believe now that these were people who belonged to something else. They didn't have any real

---

13 Weizmann quoted in Hecht, *Perfidy*, 19–20.

14 Halamish, *Dual Race against Time*, 372.

15 William L. Shirer, *The Collapse of the Third Republic: An Inquiry into the Fall of France in 1940* (New York: Simon and Schuster, 1969), 415–416.

16 McDonald, *Mission in Israel*, 193.

17 Halamish, *Dual Race against Time*, 372–374.

18 Rafael Medoff, *The Jews Should Keep Quiet: Franklin D. Roosevelt, Rabbi Stephen S. Wise, and the Holocaust* (Philadelphia: Jewish Publication Society / University of Nebraska Press, 2019), 147.

19 Wyman and Medoff, *Race against Death*, 29.

20 See Medoff, *Keep Quiet*, chapter 3.

21 Samuel Hynes, Anne Matthews, Nancy Caldwell Sorel, and Roger J. Spiller, eds. *Reporting World War II: American Journalism 1938-1946* (New York: The Library of America, 2001 [1995]), 164.

identity; because I don't think that they would not have reacted in this way if the pogrom was in New Jersey. I think they would have reacted. But because it was *there*, they didn't react.[22]

Starting in late 1942, the Bergson Group's untiring efforts to publicize the plight of the Jews under Nazi dominion and the United States' inaction in response to the Holocaust, including biting advertisements written by playwright and screenwriter Ben Hecht, and a march on Washington by hundreds of European-trained Orthodox Rabbis, contributed to the formation of the War Refugee Board in January of 1944.[23]

Prior to the creation the War Refugee Board, US government policy essentially forbade American Jewish organizations from disbursing funds within Nazi occupied Europe to attempt to rescue Jews.[24] The ostensible concern was that the funds would aid the German war effort. American policy was in line with the British opposition, in practice, regarding saving Jews in great numbers from the Holocaust who would find sanctuary in Palestine. The following British official document in 1943 was representative of British policy throughout the war: "We have received the views of the Foreign Office on the proposal of the US Treasury to license the remittance to Switzerland of 25,000 dollars as a preliminary installment, to be expended on the rescue of Jews from France and Roumania. The Foreign Office is concerned with the difficulties of disposing of a considerable number of Jews, should they be rescued."[25] Members of the Irgun believed then, and all the more so when government files were made public later, that "[a]n entire nation, six million men, women and children, sank into an abyss, in a planned campaign of annihilation which lasted five whole years, because the Germans decided to destroy it, and the British—and others—decided not to rescue it," as Irgun commander Menachem Begin wrote later.[26]

Jewish powerlessness, which was so blatant during the Holocaust, meant that the pleas of the Jews could be safely ignored by the British and the gates of Palestine could be locked to the Jews of Nazi-occupied

22   Wyman and Medoff, *Race against Death*, 133.
23   Medoff, *Keep Quiet*, 148–149.
24   Howard M. Sachar, *Diaspora, An Inquiry into the Contemporary Jewish World* (New York: Harper & Row, 1985), 4.
25   Menachem Begin, *The Revolt*, rev. ed., trans. Samuel Katz, ed. Ivan M. Greenberg (London: W.H. Allen, 1979), preface to the revised edition, XVII.
26   Ibid., XVII.

Europe.[27] "Was the Jew so worthless that all nations felt free to bedevil and murder him? The answer," Ben Hecht and the Bergson Group felt, "was yes—or silence. The German slaughter of Jews had in a way given the Jews a bad name: the name of defenseless, expendable creatures to be shoveled out of existence as human garbage."[28] The British Empire had fought Hitler alone for a long harrowing time, and had withstood terror bombing of its people seeking only, as Winston Churchill explained to an American emissary of President Roosevelt when trying to persuade the United States to fight Germany, "the right of man to be free; we see seek his right to worship his God, to lead his life in his own way, secure from prosecution. As the humble laborer returns from his work when the day is done, and sees the smoke curling upwards from his home in the serene summer sky, we wish him to know no rat-a-tat-tat of the secret police upon his door will disturb his rest."[29] Regarding Great Britain's record during the Holocaust and its aftermath, Ben Hecht would later describe her as the most "honorable" of enemies, and the "gallant defender of civilization, 1939–1945; nevertheless, an enemy of the Jews. This is what makes a Jewish historian seem hard to please. He has to scowl when all other historians look happy."[30]

The "popular support spearheaded by the Bergson Group" helped Secretary of the Treasury Morgenthau convince President Roosevelt to establish an American government agency, the War Refugee Board,[31] though it came too late for the vast majority of European Jews.[32] The War Refugee Board demonstrated that America attempted to alleviate the Holocaust, albeit belatedly and only in ways that did not burden the war effort. The War Refugee Board did succeed in saving the lives of thousands of Romanian and Hungarian Jews.[33] Under the auspices of the War Refugee Board, the World Jewish Congress and the American Jewish Joint

---

27 Sachar, *Diaspora*, 145.
28 Hecht, *Perfidy*, 22
29 Erik Larson, *The Splendid and the Vile: A Saga of Churchill, Family, and Defiance during the Blitz* (New York: Crown, 2020), 351.
30 Hecht, *Perfidy*, 26, 15.
31 Rebecca Erbelding, *Rescue Board: The Untold Story of America's Efforts to Save the Jews of Europe* (New York: Doubleday, 2018), 275.
32 Saul Zadka, *Blood in Zion: How the Jewish Guerrillas Drove the British out of Palestine* (London / Washington: Brassey's, 1995), 127.
33 Ben Hecht, *Guide For The Bedeviled* (Jerusalem: Mila Press, 1996), 212; idem, *A Child of the Century, with an introduction by Sydney Zion* (New York: Primus [Donald I. Fine] Plume, 1985 [New York: Simon & Schuster, 1954]), 576–581; Rakeffet-Rothkoff, *Silver Era*, 221–222.

Distribution Committee were permitted to sustain many Jews who otherwise would have perished, though it is impossible to quantify the exact numbers saved.[34]

In contrast to the HCNL, the AFLP, though in reality run by the same individuals, was intended to be an organization of American citizens, Jew and Gentile alike. The widespread sympathy of many Americans, regardless of background, reflected the roughly contemporaneous observation of a scholar that "America is either a cosmopolitan nation—a great cross-section of general humanity, distinguished from other nations not by any peculiarity of blood or color but only by geography and tradition and spirit—or it is nothing at all."[35] The Bergson Group had many high-profile non-Jewish supporters, including celebrities like Frank Sinatra, who participated in the "We Will Never Die" pageant that in 1943 brought attention to the Holocaust and highlighted the need to stop the slaughter. The AFLP's Chairman was former (and future) Senator Guy Gillette of Iowa.[36] Gillette's initial interest may have been inspired by his wife Rose, who was Jewish, but he was also a longstanding opponent of British imperialism.[37]

The AFLP drew inspiration from the Irish National Movement, especially its tactics of organizing opposition to British rule in Northern Ireland among the American public and in Congress.[38] The British Foreign Office hired a law firm to investigate the ALFP's legal status, but the firm, Coudert Brothers, concluded that the ALFP was acting legally under American law.[39] Bergson sought to attempt to appeal to the American public at large, as he later explained: "Our whole feeling was, from the very beginning, . . . that we are a national liberation movement, and we thought we will appeal to the American people, and we deserve their support. Why should Americans help

34 Erbelding, *Rescue Board*, 275, 277.

35 George F. Kennan, *Realities of American Foreign Policy* (New York: W. W. Norton and Company, Inc., 1966 [1954]), 109.

36 Paul H. Silverstone, *"Our Only Refuge, Open the Gates!": Clandestine Immigration to Palestine 1938–1948* (New York: P. Silverstone, 1999), 23.

37 McClure, Stewart E. "Stewart E. McClure: Chief Clerk, Senate Committee on Labor, Education, and Public Welfare (1949–1973)," Oral History Interviews, Senate Historical Office, Washington, D.C., on the staff of Guy Gillette, Interview #1, Wednesday, December 8, 1982, 16–17, https://www.senate.gov/artandhistory/history/resources/pdf/McClure1.pdf.

38 Baumel, *Bergson Boys*, 266–267.

39 Fritz Liebreich, *Britain's Naval and Political Reaction to the Illegal Immigration of Jews to Palestine, 1945–1948* (London / New York: Routledge, 2005), 103.

Ireland and not us? We were a good cause."[40] *Ben Hecht* crew-member Henry
Mandel reflected fifty years after its voyage that "[i]f I were Irish I would be
proud to be Irish. If I were Italian I would be proud to be Italian. But I am not,
I am Jewish," he said with a smile. "And I am proud to be a Jew."[41]

Maurice Rosenblatt, a vice-chairman of the AFLP, hired Stewart E.
McClure, who worked on writing publicity materials, fundraising letters,
and speeches for the AFLP.[42] Bergson Group advertisements promised that
there should be separation of church and state in the incipient Hebrew
nation in Palestine: "Join our efforts to bring about the early recognition of
the Hebrew Republic of Palestine, so that progress might prevail for all—
Christian, Muslim or Jew."[43] Another advertisement stated that all the survivors of the concentration camps wanted was to "be allowed to go home.
Home to Palestine. . . . To do what in Palestine? To throw out the Arabs
who live there?," the ALFP advertisement asked rhetorically. The answer
was "NO"; their true aim was "[t]o build, side, by side with them, a modern progressive democracy in what was once the cradle of democracy, and
which they, and they alone, can restore to that role."[44]

Yitshaq Ben-Ami was a native of Palestine, who during World War
II helped organize various Bergson Group alter ego entities, including the
American Friends for a Jewish Palestine, the Committee for a Jewish Army,
and the Emergency Committee to Save the Jewish People of Europe. After a
stint in combat with the American Army in Europe, he served as the executive director of the AFLP between 1946 and 1948.[45] Ben-Ami, who was a
core Bergson Group member responsible for the outfitting of the *Ben Hecht*
before it set sail from the United States, explained in his memoirs that

> [o]ur idea was to force the British to arrest United States citizens, then
> challenge their actions in the courts in Palestine, and if that failed, in the
> United States courts and Congress as well. The ship was manned by a

---

40   Wyman and Medoff, *Race against Death*, 113.
41   Mandel interview by Shuster, 2000.
42   McClure Oral History, 9–10.
43   "It's O.K. to Steal . . . when you're the British Government," ALFP Advertisement, *PM*,
     December 10, 1946, 19, available at New York Public Library (NYPL), SASB M1—
     Periodicals and Microforms Rm 119 *ZY (*PM* daily), November/December 1946.
44   "Foes of Democracy are Forgiven . . . Will Its Friends Be Amnestied?," ALFP
     Advertisement, *PM*, December 27, 1946, back page, available at NYPL.
45   "Yitshaq Ben-Ami, 71; Zionist Active in U.S.," *New York Times*, January 3, 1985, sec. B,
     8, https://www.nytimes.com/1985/01/03/nyregion/yitshaq-ben-ami-71-zionist-active-
     in-us.html.

volunteer crew of American sailors, several of whom were not Jewish, who were not necessarily associated with any particular ideology but who were animated by a desire to help survivors of the Holocaust. The voyage was intended to simultaneously serve as an attempt to gain entry of several hundred Jews into Palestine, provoke a trial in which the legality of Britain's barring of Jewish immigration to Palestine would be challenged, and to publicize the plight of Jewish "Displaced Persons" (DPs for short), who sought to immigrate to Palestine.[46]

By the end of 1945, 100,000 Jews, who refused repatriation to their pre-war homes in Eastern Europe, lived in camps in occupied Germany.[47] The majority of the European Jews that survived the Holocaust were defined in 1946 as displaced persons, part of "Europe's futureless, floating population."[48] During a pogrom incited by a blood libel, forty-six Jews were killed in the Polish town of Kielce on July 4, 1946, where many Jews had congregated on their way to their hometowns. Hundreds of thousands of Jews thereupon fled Poland. In 1946 and 1947, an additional 150,000 Jews who had survived the war in the Soviet Union arrived at the DP camps after fleeing an upsurge of antisemitism in Poland. Because World War II was over, these Jews were not recognized as refugees by the Western powers.[49] It was these forlorn people that the Jewish illegal immigration movement sought to save from a stateless, hopeless future. In August 1946 the British announced that future illegal immigration would be directed to detention camps in Cyprus.[50]

Former Senator Guy M. Gillette said in a statement that entered into the Congressional Record on August 1, 1946, that "It is 1946 in America; it is 1776 in Palestine. Americans who won their own freedom from despotism cannot believe that once more the only course open to the British Government is the course which means inevitable strife. We cannot believe that there is no alternative offered to the British Government but the course laid down by Adolf Hitler." Dr. David Wdowinski, at a rally for the Hebrew Committee of National Liberation at Carnegie Hall, on November 16, 1946, said "If you would help us, tell the world the truth,—that we are patriots

---

46 Ben-Ami, *Years of Wrath*, 403, 450.
47 Sachar, *Diaspora*, 5.
48 *The Black Book: The Nazi Crimes against the Jewish People* (New York: Jewish Black Book Committee, 1946), 5.
49 Sachar, *Diaspora*, 326, 5–6.
50 Wandres, *The Ablest Navigator*, 30.

fighting to liberate our soil and our people. And wish us the same success that your forefathers had in the same struggle against the same oppressor in 1776. It is 1776 in Palestine today."[51]

Novelist, playwright, and screenwriter Ben Hecht was the first writer in the general American press to attack Allied governments and Jewish leaders alike for failing to help the Jewish victims of the Nazis, leading to his recruitment by the group that became AFLP/HCNL.[52] Ben Hecht liked to imagine that he was a descendant of a Jewish mariner who had been a follower of the medieval seafaring renegade Roger de Flor, "a man without country who brought Christian and Moslem empires alike to their knees."[53] When the Irgun delegation in the United States asked Hecht in 1941 to support their cause, he later wrote that "a little to my surprise, I agreed. And the old stateless, flagless ghost of a Jew in me rejoiced."[54] Writing in 1985, Sydney Zion said "Today the world is definitively in on Roosevelt and the Jews (see, for example, David S. Wyman's massively documented work, *The Abandonment of the Jews*) but it took . . . forty years after Ben went after FDR. Hecht did not wait to write a book, he attacked in full-page ads while the massacre was going on. If there is a synonym for courage, spell it Ben Hecht."[55] Though his personal disposition played a part, much of his work as a propagandist for the Jewish cause was motivated by his love for his family: "It was they who were under attack by the German murderers and the sly British . . . Although I never lived 'as a Jew' or even among Jews, my family remained like a homeland in my heart." Hecht also credited his second wife, Rose Caylor, who came from a family with rabbinic lineage, for his emergence "as a propagandist for the Jews of Europe and Palestine."[56] Yitzhaq Ben-Ami, the Bergson Group member who would take the lead in organizing the outfitting of the *Ben Hecht* in the United States, felt as Ben Hecht rediscovered "his Jewish roots" that "for all his bitter frustration at the Jewish establishment he found a certain peace and a sense of identity he had never known."[57]

---

51 Isaac Zarr, *Rescue and Liberation: America's Part in the Birth of Israel* (New York: Bloch Publishing Company, 1954), 197, 215–217.

52 Ben-Ami, *Years of Wrath*, 283; Mark Cohen, *Not Bad for Delancey Street: The Rise of Billy Rose* (Waltham, MA: Brandeis University Press, 2018), 152.

53 Hecht, *Child*, 78

54 Ibid., 521.

55 Sydney Zion's introduction to Hecht, *Child*.

56 Hecht, *Child*, 109, 350, 355.

57 Ben-Ami, *Years of Wrath*, 285.

Some historians have concluded that "[t]he Holocaust did not occur because the United States stayed silent; rather, the Holocaust happened because the Nazis wanted to kill Jews and had more access, control, and will over them than the Allied nations had to protect them."[58] Hecht was not sure if a unified fierce public protest by the leadership of American Jewry and more resolute measures by the Allied governments could have stopped the Holocaust, but he had enough faith in humanity that he hoped that it would have. He was outraged that it had not been attempted.[59]

In 1946, Ben Hecht's Broadway play *A Flag is Born* brought attention to the Zionist cause when it played for ten weeks on Broadway and then on tour.[60] The play opened in the Alvin Theater in New York City on September 5, 1946 (now the Neil Simon Theater), before it went on the road with Sidney Lumet taking over the role of David.[61] The music of *A Flag is Born* was written by Kurt Weill and its star was Paul Muni, with a young Marlon Brando as David.[62] In the play, Tevya, played by Muni, who had starred in Hecht's groundbreaking 1932 gangster movie *Scarface*,[63] reproves the English government: "For a little oil you are willing to put out the lights of English honor? Why? Because you don't want to do wrong by the Arabs? Since when does England care about doing wrong to the people whose land it steals?" In response to the argument that the British law prohibited immigration of Jews into Palestine, Tevya asks "If somebody makes a law against humanity—who is the law breaker?"[64] David asks "Where were you, Jews? Where were you when six million Jews were being burned to death in the ovens?"[65] and reprimands the audience, directly: "You Jews of America! You Jews of England! . . . Where was your cry of rage that could have filled the world and stopped the fires? Nowhere! Because you were ashamed to cry out as Jews."[66]

---

58 Rebecca Erbelding, *Rescue Board: the Untold Story of America's Efforts to Save the Jews of Europe* (New York: Doubleday, 2018), 278.

59 Hecht, *Perfidy*, 193.

60 Medoff, *Militant*, 154–159.

61 Rafael Medoff, "A Zionist Play that Changed History," *Jerusalem Post*, September 4, 2006, https://www.jpost.com/Features/A-Zionist-play-that-changed-history; Medoff, *Militant*, 154–159.

62 Silverstone, *Our Only Refuge*, 23.

63 Gorbach, *Notorious*, 53.

64 Ben Hecht, *A Flag is Born* (New York: American League For a Free Palestine, Inc., 1946), 39, 35.

65 Medoff, *Militant*, 156.

66 Hecht, *A Flag is Born*, 20.

Because Ben Hecht insisted that his play would not be performed in a segregated theater, a Washington, D.C. performance was canceled, and a substitute performance of *A Flag is Born* was the first play performed in Baltimore before a mixed-race audience. All of the profits from the play went to the AFLP.[67] Ben Hecht claimed in his memoirs to have netted the Irgun nearly a million dollars with *A Flag is Born*,[68] though that cannot be verified because of a lack of documentation.[69] *A Flag is Born* generated funds for the purchase and refitting of the *Abril*; part of the profits went to the Irgun in Palestine,[70] and close to a quarter of a million dollars was wired to Europe to fund Bergson Group operations there,[71] with the aim of gaining the French government's support for Jewish independence.[72]

The *Abril*, a 753-ton, 200-feet-long private yacht,[73] was built by the Krupp company in Keil, Germany, in 1930, and initially was named *Argosy*. It was subsequently renamed *Vita*, and then was bought by a Cuban and renamed *Abril*. The ship had carried Republican Loyalist gold bullion to Mexico shortly before the victory of Franco in March, 1939.[74] A Spanish Jew had captained her during that trip; he later became the captain of the Israeli tanker *Haifa*.[75] The *Abril* became the USS *Cythera* (PY-31), which served as a radar picket that searched for German U-boats on the Atlantic coast with a crew of sixty men. The US Navy sold the PY-31 as surplus to the Tyre Shipping Company for $36,100.[76] The vessel was made available to the AFLP for only $38,000.[77]

---

67 Medoff, *Militant*, 159–160, 154–159.
68 Hecht, *Child*, 614.
69 Medoff, *Militant*, 263 n.4.
70 Ben-Ami, *Years of Wrath*, 403.
71 Adina Hoffman, *Ben Hecht: Fighting Words, Moving Pictures* (New Haven, CT: Yale University Press, 2019), 173.
72 Gorbach, *Notorious*, 239.
73 Rifkin, *What Ship*, 3.
74 Wandres, *The Ablest Navigator*, 120; Anonymous [David Kaplan?], "A M/V BEN HECHT Story," Website of the American Veterans of Israeli conflicts, found in Illegal Immigration collection, The *Ben Hecht (Avril)* file, reference code: K6-5/21, Jabotinsky Institute (MZ) (MZ *Ben Hecht [Avril]* Newspaper Clippings file).
75 David Kaplan Oral History, part 1, MZ.
76 Stewart, *Palestine Patrol*, 97; Aharoni, *Leaning Masts*, 22; "Mystery Ship Seen as Exiles' Haven: Ship Built in 1931 Believed Carrying Refugees to Palestine" (January 1947), found in Newspaper Clippings File, Levitan collection, USHMM; Silverstone, *Our Only Refuge*, 36; "600 Refugees Ship Towed into Haifa," *Palestine Post Bureau*, Sunday, March 9, 1947, front page, Palestine Post Bureau, dateline Haifa, Saturday, March 8, 1947; Lazar, *Immigration Ship "Ben Hecht*," 5.
77 Ben-Ami, *Years of Wrath*, 404; Stone, "Refugees Driven on Cyprus-Bound Ships like Cattle."

In October 1946, the *Abril*, Ben-Ami later recalled, "was rusty and spotted with peeling paint, just about ready for the scrap pile."[78] The ship was in poor condition due to rough usage in the war, and it required months of repairs in a dock in Brooklyn to become seaworthy. Julian Licht, an engineer, assured Ben-Ami that by removing all partitions and bulkheads the ship could carry over 500 people, and that the retrofitting would only cost $100,000 if the AFLP undertook the work itself. Licht had recently received confirmation that his parents were killed in the Kovno ghetto. He, Dr. Irving Shendell, other engineers, and crew members, including Mandel, worked twenty-hour days on a dock on Brooklyn's Gowanus Canal overhauling the *Abril*.[79] Ultimately, expenditures for reconditioning of the ship in New York were $100,000.[80] Despite Licht's fiscal conscientiousness, radio operator David Kaplan insisted that state-of-the-art radio equipment be installed.[81] Ultimately, despite all these economies, the AFLP eventually spent $300,000 for the *Abril*'s entire journey.[82]

Ben-Ami later described the Tyre Shipping Company as a cover for the AFLP.[83] In a confidential memorandum written by an attorney retained by the Israeli government to represent it in litigation over the ownership of the *Abril/Ben Hecht* in the early 1950s, the Tyre Shipping Company was described as "set up as a creature" of the AFLP to hold "nominal title" for the ship. Tyre's original directors were Morris Brenner and Julian Licht, and Alexander Wilf served as its President. The AFLP succeeded in selling only $8,500 worth of subscriptions to Tyre stock. Tyre used the funds to purchase the yacht. In an agreement executed in October of 1946, Tyre agreed to restore the ship or its value to the AFLP, and the AFLP agreed to advance costs to Tyre for its corporate purposes, which presumably was to fund the ship, alterations, and supplies for the retrofitting of the ship. The AFLP advanced $171,93.39 to Tyre for its corporate purposes; Tyre repaid $35,518.49, leaving a net debt to the AFLP of $125,455.[84]

The Irgun in Palestine thought that Bergson did not adequately financially support its struggle against the British Palestine Mandatory

78 Ben-Ami, *Years of Wrath*, 404.
79 Rifkin, *What Ship*, 3; Ben-Ami, *Years of Wrath*, 404–405.
80 Zarr, *Rescue*, 217.
81 Kaplan Oral History, part 1, MZ.
82 Lazar, *Immigration Ship "Ben Hecht,"* 5.
83 Ben-Ami, *Years of Wrath*, 405.
84 Leventhal memorandum, 2 and 5, ISA.

government; they felt that resources expended on the *Ben Hecht* would have been better spent on arms. The Irgun leaders in Palestine argued that the Haganah was paying enough attention to the refugees and illegal immigration efforts and that the purchase of the *Ben Hecht* was a waste of funds once the Irgun began an armed revolt in Palestine in 1944. Senior Irgun leadership, including Menachem Begin, the commander of the Irgun in Palestine, and other senior Irgun leaders there, felt that the funds raised by the AFLP should be devoted exclusively to fund the Irgun's desperate armed rebellion against British rule in Palestine, and not be diverted towards actions intended to garner publicity for the cause.[85]

The colorful history of the ship as a yacht, smuggler, and naval vessel was written up by someone with the AFLP, probably for the benefit of the press. Crew member Shepard Rifkin apparently did not think Ben Hecht should have allowed the eponymous illegal immigrant ship, with its hallowed and supposedly secret mission, to be named after him. However, the ship's organizers argued that donations would increase with news that the funds aided illegal immigration.[86] Publicity and putting public pressure against Britain's Palestine policy was a primary goal of the AFLP, and a famous name attached to the ship helped achieve that goal. In any event, the preparation of the ship to bring refugees to Palestine was hardly secret, because, as Ben-Ami acknowledged in his memoirs, "[f]or funds we were forced to bring several important potential donors to visit the pier even though this was a breach in security."[87]

In practice, Bergson did not accept Begin's authority, nor his strategic judgment that the armed struggle against Britain was primary rather than the Bergson Group's publicity campaign. Bergson had similarly refused to accept the authority of the establishment leaders of American Jewry in their less aggressive approach for advocacy for the victims of the Holocaust.[88] Ben-Ami, conflicted over the expense of the *Ben Hecht*'s voyage, ultimately felt that the Bergson Group had to demonstrate to the Haganah "if they did not act, we surely would, backing up with action our public campaign for free immigration. And also, we were gaining experience in moving people across the continent and running the present blockades for future armed

---

85   Zadka, *Blood in Zion*, 122; Baumel, *Bergson Boys*, 235.
86   Rifkin, *What Ship*, 20, 98, 162.
87   Ben-Ami, *Years of Wrath*, 405.
88   Zadka, *Blood in Zion*, 124–127.

landing."[89] It was anticipated by the AFLP that the ship would attempt to beach itself to allow the immigrants to wade onto the Palestine coast.[90]

While the *Abril* was being retrofitted in Brooklyn, crew member David Kaplan reports that "[r]umor had it that the British C.I.D. [Criminal Investigation Division, part of the British intelligence apparatus] knew about" the *Abril*'s purpose[91] and that it was thought among crew members that there had been at least one British effort to sabotage the ship in New York; a mattress factory opposite to her berth mysteriously caught fire in the early hours of the morning.[92] The official British Naval history of the Palestine blockade reports that "there was little secrecy concerning the purchasing and the repair of the *Abril*,"[93] which lends credence to that supposition. At that time, British intelligence eavesdropped on American Jews involved in arms purchases for the Jews in Palestine and provided that information to the FBI.[94] The ship was under active FBI surveillance because of the ALFP's suspected connections with communist sympathizers,[95] even though the group stressed its opposition to Communism.[96] There was concern that if the ship's departure was delayed, the FBI would stop it from sailing. The FBI searched the ship for arms in December of 1946, but only found hundreds of life belts.[97]

On December 26, 1946, the *Ben Hecht* sailed for France from Staten Island, registered, as reported in a press account in January 1947, as a Honduran ship with a crew of twenty-eight men and equipped with 1000 army mess kits and 1500 lifejackets.[98]

---

89   Ben-Ami, *Years of Wrath*, 405.
90   Rifkin, *What Ship*, 4, 22.
91   Kaplan, "This Is the Way It Was."
92   "A M/V BEN HECHT Story."
93   Stewart, *Palestine Patrol*, 97.
94   Wandres, *The Ablest Navigator*, 35.
95   Ben-Ami, *Years of Wrath*, 405.
96   Baumel, *Begson Boys*, 267.
97   Ben-Ami, *Years of Wrath*, 405–406.
98   "Mystery Ship Seen as Exiles' Haven," Newspaper Clippings file, Levitan collection, USHMM.

Chapter 9

The Mission and the Crew

You have to only listen to a professor to know there are too many books in the world—
and too many professors. There are too few mariners and too many geographers.

—Ben Hecht[1]

During World War I, the British Empire was fighting for its life in its battle
with Imperial Germany. Chaim Weizmann and Nahum Sokolow convinced
the British government, led by Prime Minister David Lloyd George, that
the loyalty of the Jewish people could be won in this struggle by supporting Zionism. British foreign secretary Arthur James Balfour issued a declaration supporting "establishment in Palestine of a national home for the
Jewish people," with the proviso "that nothing shall be done which may
prejudice the civil and religious rights of existing non-Jewish communi-
ties in Palestine" on November 16, 1917.[2] At the San Remo conference in
1920, the Balfour Declaration, which until then had only been the national
commitment of Great Britain, was confirmed in an international agreement
that dictated the future of former Ottoman territories.[3] Under the League of
Nations Covenant, Mandatory powers, such as Great Britain in Palestine,
were to act as a type of fiduciary in the fulfillment of their responsibilities
for the benefit of those peoples who were to be subject to the authority of the
Mandate, and not to pursue their own goals.[4] Article 6 of the Mandate doc-

---

1   Hecht, *Guide*, 123.
2   Bethell, *Palestine Triangle*, 16–17.
3   David A. Andelman, *A Shattered Peace: Versailles 1919 and the Price We Pay Today*
    (Hoboken, NJ: John Wiley & Sons, 2008), 106.
4   Evan J. Criddle, "Fiduciary Principles in International Law," in *Oxford Handbook on*
    Fiduciary Law, ed. Evan J. Criddle, Paul B. Miller, and Robert H. Sitkoff (New York:
    Oxford University Press, 2019), 347–348.

ument issued July 22, 1922, the authority by which Britain ruled Palestine under the auspices of the League of Nations, guaranteed that "Administration of Palestine, while ensuring that the rights and position of other sections of the population are not prejudiced, shall facilitate Jewish immigration under suitable conditions. . . ." On May 22, 1939, the House of Commons adopted a White Paper limiting Jewish entry to Palestine to no more than an additional 75,000 immigrants. The Permanent Mandates Commission of the League of Nations declared the White Paper in conflict with Britain's Mandate. Nonetheless, on November 20, 1940, with World War II raging and European Jewry desperately seeking to escape the conquering Germans, the British Government declared that no illegal immigrants who attempted to enter Palestine would be allowed into the country. The crew of illegal immigrant ships would be subject to eight-year prison terms.[5]

After World War II, Great Britain's military leaders felt that the maintenance of British military bases in Palestine were critically important to bolstering their nation's power.[6] Those bases had been built as part of an effort to secure a route from Great Britain to the British Empire in India.[7] In 1945, Earl Harrison, in a report to President Truman, wrote that the DPs wanted to leave the camps and that "Palestine is definitely and preeminently their first choice."[8] Convinced, President Truman asked the British government for the end of the White Paper's immigration limitations that stopped Jews from entering Palestine, "which represents for so many of them the only hope of survival," and called for the immediate entry of 100,000 Jewish refugees into Palestine. The British Foreign Office, led by Ernest Bevin, however, felt that Jews should remain in Europe, that the Palestinian Arab cause was just, and that alienating the Arabs would undermine British influence in the Near East, which was seen as crucial for sustaining the British Empire.[9]

Bevin argued that "I want the suppression of racial warfare, and therefore, if the Jews, with all their sufferings, want to get too much at the head of the queue you have the danger of another anti-Semitic reaction through it all." On another occasion, he said "[r]egarding the agitation in the United States, and particularly in New York, for 100,000 to be put into Palestine,

---

5   Bethell, *Palestine Triangle*, 20, 64, 69, 211, 92.
6   David Reynolds, *Britannia Overruled: British Policy and World Power in the Twentieth Century* (New York: Pearson Education, 1991), 156.
7   Abba Eban, *Personal Witness: Israel through My Eyes* (New York: G. P. Putnam's Sons, 1992).
8   Idem, *An Autobiography* (New York: Random House, 1977), 59.
9   Bethel, *Palestine Triangle*, 210–211, 202–203.

I hope it will not be misunderstood in America if I say, with the purest of motives, that that was because they do not want too many of them in New York."[10] If Bevin's remarks were examples of typical British irony, the joke was lost on Jews. Bevin ostensibly had been referring to the Democratic Party's successful effort to return to power in the 1945 election of William O'Dwyer as Mayor of New York City after twelve years of the mayoralty of the liberal Republican Florio LaGuardia and its failed efforts to retain control of Congress in the 1946 midterm elections.[11] But, in the evaluation of the moderate Jewish diplomat Abba Eban, "[i]t was evident from [Bevin's] hooligan tone that the Jewish people had come face to face with one of its cruelest adversaries."[12] A contemporary account observed that "[t]he feeling of the average Englishman was aptly summed up by Foreign Minister Bevin" and "[t]he English man-in-the-street has now perfected a stereotype of the 'New York Jew.' He is a man like Ben Hecht."[13] But Jews around the world, and much of the American public, felt that the Nazi Holocaust, and America's and Britain's indifference despite the horrors having been made public in 1942, made a Jewish state in Palestine necessary.[14]

***

Mandel explained in an interview that unlike illegal immigrant ships organized by the Haganah, the sailors on the *Ben Hecht* had not attempted to avoid arrest by melting in with the passengers. The Haganah arranged for Aliyah Bet crews to join the passengers upon capture without identifying themselves so as to avoid important information being exposed to the British during interrogations.[15] In contrast, the *Ben Hecht* crew instead sought to attract attention to the cause of Jewish refugees seeking to enter Palestine in a public trial:

> We were American sailors. The ship had . . . was flying the Honduran flag.
> But we were American; the crew was American. And the British locked us

---

10   Zaar, *Rescue,* 159, 186.

11   Mason B. Williams, *City of Ambition: FDR, LaGuardia, and the Making of Modern New York* (New York: W. W. Norton, 2013), 386–389, 391.

12   Eban, *Autobiography,* 60.

13   Paul S. Green, "Average Briton Believes 'New York Jews Are behind the Scenes in Palestine,'" *The Sentinel,* July 3, 1947, 7.

14   Bethell, *Palestine Triangle,* 204.

15   David Shari, *The Cyprus Exile 1945–1949* (Jerusalem: Zionist Library, 1961/1962), 81–82 (Hebrew), quoted in Lazar, *Immigrant Ship "Ben Hecht,"* 16.

up. They charged us with the technical crime of aiding and abetting illegal immigration. And we were prepared to fight, saying that the immigration was not illegal because that was part of the Mandate; and if the Mandate was not illegal then we were not aiding or abetting anything illegal. So, we had committed no crime.[16]

Levitan noted that in "some ships, the crew mingled with the passengers, put on old clothes and mingled with the passengers and went to Cyprus. But on our ship we didn't do that. We declared ourselves as the crew of the ship and we said what you are doing is wrong. We should have been able to take our people in."[17]

As noted before, the legal argument articulated by the *Ben Hecht* crew men was rooted in the award of the Mandate for Palestine to Great Britain on April 25, 1920 by the victors of World War I, which was ratified by the League of Nations as a matter of international law in 1922, and which became legally effective with the signing of the peace treaty with Turkey at the Lausanne conference in 1923. As adopted by the League of Nations, Great Britain as the Mandatory power was responsible for putting into effect the Balfour declaration of 1917 that called for the creation of a Jewish "national home" in Palestine.[18] The Bergson Group reasoned that whatever the Balfour declaration meant by the term "national home" it could not mean that Jews were to be barred from immigrating to Palestine.[19] As real as the claims and British promises of statehood to the Palestinian Arabs were, the central goal of the international legal authorization of British rule in Palestine was to provide a refuge for homeless Jews. As an anonymous letter writer argued in the Palestine Post in 1947, British Army officers were in Palestine

together with [their] comrades in arms and administration, to carry out the League of Nations Mandate, by which, and by which alone, Great Britain is internationally permitted to be in Palestine. Whether or not the mandate is "legal" in the English Officer's view is not the point. But if it is legal, he is here in Palestine to assist in carrying it out—and that means helping to establish the Jewish National Home here, not as a piece of humanitarian philanthropy as he magnanimously thinks, but as an international duty. If it is not legal. . . .

---

16   Mandel interview by Shuster, 2000.
17   Levitan Oral History, USHMM.
18   Barbara W. Tuchman, *Bible and Sword* (New York: New York University Press, 1968 [1956]), 339, 344–345.
19   Merlin, *Millions of Jews to Rescue*, 21.

The English Officer has no conceivable right to be here at all. This is a fact too often forgotten by English Officers, as well as English Civilians.[20]

For the *Abril / Ben Hecht*'s navigator and eventual acting captain, Hyman Robert (Bob) Levitan, and for many crewmembers, "[t]he principle of the people behind this operation was that the British were morally and legally wrong for stopping us" and that if the ship were to be captured the incident would be publicized as to the British "policy of keeping Jews out of Palestine."[21] The ship was primarily staffed by a volunteer crew of American citizens who understood World War II as a war for freedom and against forms of oppression, including the British Empire.[22] It is notable that the Nazi death camps were organized so that their commanders never had to personally kill anyone, and that subordinates could tell themselves that they were just following orders.[23] At the end of the war, in the words of novelist James Jones, the American soldiers who liberated German concentration camps encountered fearful consequences of a "state's legally adopted policy of political and social violence."[24] Upon the liberation of the concentration camps in 1945, world public opinion recognized the Holocaust as the ultimate horrifying symbol of immorality and mass murder.[25] Still, the victors of the war allowed the survivors of the Holocaust to be left to rot in limbo in the displaced persons camps.[26] Volunteering on an "illegal" Jewish immigrant ship was the personal, exceptional response of crew members to the Holocaust. They responded by helping others in the same way they would have wanted to be helped.

Years later, when asked for a brief explanation of his motivation to volunteer, Mandel wrote "I was a Zionist, and I also felt that it was my duty to help my fellow Jews."[27] Levitan, when asked about what motivated the

---

20 "English Civilian," Readers' Letters, "Legality: British and Jewish," *The Palestine Post*, Monday, August 11, 1947, 4.

21 Robert Hyman Levitan notes for synagogue presentation, 7, file 5, Bob Levitan collection, USHMM.

22 Jones, *WWII*, 212.

23 Gitta Sereny, *Into That Darkness: An Examination of Conscience* (London: Andre Deustch, 1974).

24 Jones, *WWII*, 210.

25 Paul Johnson, *The Quest for God: A Personal Pilgrimage* (New York: HarperCollins, 1996), 67.

26 Elie Wiesel and Richard D. Heffner, *Conversations with Elie Wiesel*, ed. Thomas J. Vinciguerra (New York: Schocken Books, 2003), 5–6.

27 Mandel Machal questionnaire, AJHS.

crew, reflected that "I can only talk about the twenty men that were on my ship, and if you had twenty men you have twenty different reasons" for why they had volunteered on the *Ben Hecht*. Levitan explained that as a teenager learning of the oppression of the Jews in Europe, he saw "here was Great Britain and France and the United States and they couldn't do anything, so what could I do? . . . I was an impotent little Jewish kid in Brooklyn; couldn't do anything about it. So when he approached me with this situation, so I automatically quit my ship and jumped in and volunteered. . . . I didn't even hesitate a second. I just said yes and jumped right in." Levitan later recalled wanting to help "the Jews that came out of the concentration camps. . . . They had no place to go, they had no place to live. I spoke to one man and told him 'the war was over, you know. You lived in Germany before, why don't you just go back there now?' And he says he can't. He says 'the earth there in Europe burns his feet.' And he just wanted to get out of there."[28] A similar story was told by the ship's purser, Marvin Liebman. In October of 1946, Liebman's mother received a letter from the sole survivor of her Polish hometown. "The letter described vividly," Liebman recounted, "how my aunts and uncles, in addition to hundreds of other Jews in that vicinity, were made to dig in their own graves and then were buried alive in them." He shared with the readers of the *PM* newspaper one line of that letter in particular that Liebman said he would not forget: "The earth of Europe burns our feet."[29] Perhaps that vivid image of the very earth of Europe singeing the feet of the survivors reflected a widespread psychological need to leave the blood-stained continent where the Holocaust took place among Jewish displaced persons in the aftermath of World War II. "There was this expression that I heard about during World War II," Levitan remembered when asked whether he was willing to die for the cause, "I was not thinking of dying; I was just thinking of doing my job."[30]

***

The initial AFLP appointee to run the *Abril* project was Gershon Hakim, who had aided the Irgun as a teenage runner in the mid-1930s in Palestine and had served in the United States Army, though Hakim was ultimately

---

28 Levitan Oral History, USHMM.
29 Marvin Liebman, "'Ben Hecht' Purser Poses as Refugee, Tells of Life on Cyprus," *PM*, April 20, 1947, found in file 24/5–6 [*chof*] no. 22, Aliyah Bet, MZ (Hebrew).
30 Levitan Oral History, USHMM.

reassigned to another task before the ship sailed.[31] The most significant personnel decision was choosing a Captain for the ship. Hillel Kook initially attempted to recruit Elliot Roosevelt, a son of President Roosevelt, to serve as the Captain, under the theory that the British would not suspect him of steering an illegal immigrant ship and when the former yacht arrived in Palestine it would receive tremendous publicity, but his mother, Eleanor Roosevelt, would not permit him to undertake the adventure.[32] Robert Clay, who had been initially assigned to be Chief Mate, became the Captain, which the AFLP eventually felt was a mistake. The AFLP's rivals in the Haganah turned down at least one potential ship captain, Adolph Oko Jr., the son of Hebrew Union College librarian Adolph Oko and a friend and co-writer with legal scholar Nathan Isaacs, because it was felt that his reasons for volunteering were too emotional.[33] In Captain Clay, the AFLP apparently decided to choose an emotionally uninvolved captain. Shepard Rifkin's *roman-à-clef* (autobiographical novel), which appears to be a generally reliable account of major events in the *Ben Hecht*'s voyage, describes concern that the Captain character would founder the ship, with several hundred refugees aboard. Upon the ship's arrival in France, that Captain character, like Clay in real life, was dismissed on the recommendation of the crew.[34] Levitan initially signed on as second mate, and was promoted to be first mate and navigator under Captain Clay during the first leg of its journey across the Atlantic, but he eventually served as the de-facto acting captain.

Levitan was born and raised in Brooklyn, New York, and was a graduate of New York Maritime College. He served in the Merchant Marine during and after World War II as a mate and navigator in both the Pacific and Atlantic theaters. When a friend who had been a classmate at the New York Maritime College told him that a ship that was going to bring displaced persons to Palestine was looking for sailors, he quit the ship he had been sailing on in Norfolk, Virginia and went to New York.[35] Levitan himself

---

31 Ben-Ami, *Years of Wrath*, 406.
32 Dr. Rafael Medoff, "Why Elliot Roosevelt Shouldn't Have Listened to His Mother" (May 2003), http://new.wymaninstitute.org/2003/05/why-elliot-roosevelt-shouldnt-have-listened-to-his-mother/.
33 Barahona, *Odyssey*, 46–47.
34 Rifkin, *What Ship*, 118, 142.
35 Levitan Oral History, USHMM; Ben-Ami, *Years of Wrath*, 405; "A M/V BEN HECHT Story," MZ *Ben Hecht* (*Avril*) Newspaper Clippings file.

described his somewhat ambiguous and shifting role on the *Ben Hecht* in the following manner:

> I started out as second mate. I had an American second mate license and I was an experienced navigator. But when we left New York the man who was supposed to be chief mate never showed up. So boom, I am promoted, I am chief mate. We sailed across the Atlantic into the Azores region and we went to south France and the man who was the captain of the ship was very inadequate.

As explained in more detail hereinafter, the first Captain, Robert Clay, recklessly directed a course into the path of Atlantic storms that almost sank the ship.

> The crew said they would not sail with him anymore. So the organization took him off the ship and said "You run things and we will get another captain." We were there like four weeks and they never came down with another captain. When the people from the displaced persons camps came down and boarded the ship, they said when you take it across . . . what can I say . . . I was never more . . . really more than a navigator but I was the captain of the ship.[36]

Levitan became the most senior officer, Louis Markowitz became second mate, Walter Greaves became third mate, and James Heggie became bosun for the ship's voyage from France to Palestine.[37]

Mandel explained his role in a letter to the Israeli Defense Ministry in 1998:

> I was to assist in raising a crew, as well as to get the ships ready to go to sea. I would go to the Seamen's Union Hall and try to enlist volunteers. I got a number of volunteers, but not all of them sailed when the ship left. The crewmen that I enlisted that sailed were Lou Brettschneider, an engineer, who I last heard was working in Germany, and Dr. David Kaplan, a radio operator, who presently lives in [Suffern, NY,] USA. There were also some Betarim who came aboard at the last minute. One was Louis Binder who is now deceased. Another is Eli Freundlich who mixed with the passengers and was interned in Cyprus. Eli now lives in New Jersey, but I do not know the address.[38]

---

36   Levitan Oral History, USHMM.
37   Kaplan, "This Is the Way It Was."
38   Mandel letter to the Israeli Defense Ministry.

The tombstone of Eli Freundlich (May 10, 1925–July 15, 2016), who would also go on to serve in the Israeli Army, bears the Hebrew inscription "Volunteered with the help of God with Heroism."[39] Louis Binder (August 31, 1929–June 14, 1979) was the youngest crew member of the *Ben Hecht* and was nicknamed "Baby" on the ship. Binder was active in Revisionist Zionistic youth groups, and at age fifteen he had run off to join the Army Air Corps. During the summer of 1945 he had served seventy-four days before being found by his parents and the FBI. The seventeen-year-old Binder had told his parents he was going to work on a farm, when in fact he had joined the *Ben Hecht*. It was the second time that he had left Boys' High School in Bedford–Stuyvesant, Brooklyn for adventure. He died relatively early at age forty-nine.[40] David L. Gutmann (1925–2013) was born September 17, 1925 in New York City. His mother died shortly thereafter; his father was a steelworker with an interest in psychoanalysis. Gutmann's father had been trained as an engineer in Palestine after his family moved there in 1905, but after immigrating to the United States he was not able to find work as an engineer and he died at age fifty-two. Gutmann joined the Merchant Marine at age seventeen during World War II, and he had been an oiler for three years when he volunteered for the *Ben Hecht*. Prominent Israeli painter Nachum Gutmann was his uncle.[41]

David Kaplan told an interviewer:

In 1946, I had been in the Merchant Marine as a radio operator, Naval Reserve and Coast Guard. And I had sailed during the Second World War in this capacity as Radio Officer. By 1946, the war was over. And I was, at that time, I had been on a troop ship bringing back the American soldiers from Europe. And on the same ship was a man by the name of Henry Mandel, who was the electrician, the ship's electrician. And we became friendly. And he advised me that there were ships needed to take people from the DP

---

39   Eli Freundlich (1925–2016) Find A Grave Memorial no. 192035197, Mount Sinai Cemetery, Lakewood, Ocean County, NJ, USA, maintained by "wharfrat" (contributor 48079906).

40   Halkenhauser, "Ben Hecht Seamen Tell of Seizure"; Hochstein and Greenfield, *Secret Fleet*, 175; "Louis Binder," US Department of Veterans' Affairs BIRLS Death file, 1850–2010, Ancestry.com, original data: Beneficiary Identification Records Locator (BIRLS) Death File, Washington, D.C.: US Department of Veterans' Affairs.

41   Stephanie Gutmann, *The Other War: Israelis, Palestinians, and the Struggle for Media Supremacy* (San Francisco: Encounter Books, 2005), 10–11; Jon Rose, Margaret Huyck, and Jerome Grunes, "David L. Gutmann (1925–2013)," *American Psychologist* 69, no. 5 (July/August 2014): 549.

camps of Europe . . . And he advised me of a need for Jewish seamen, or seamen, to man these ships to bring the DPs from the camps of Europe to Eretz Israel [Hebrew for the Land of Israel]. And at that time, I agreed that whoever—we agreed that whoever heard of such a ship would contact the other. And subsequently, I was sailing on a tanker, the *Gulf Wing*, which was a World War I reparations tanker from Germany, going from Philadelphia down to Punta Cardon in Venezuela . . . Coming back from Venezuela, I received a radio message from Mr. Mandel—from Henry, we called him by . . . his nickname, Hank—from Hank, telling me that there was a ship available. So, I arranged to get off the *Gulf Wing*, to leave the ship in New York and Philadelphia. And I met with Hank. . . .

Hank took me down to introduce me to the American Free League for Free Palestine, the Bergson Group. And we were brought to their headquarters in New York, where I was interviewed by Lieutenant Commander Yehuda Finkelstein, I believe his name was. And advised of what they wanted to do and told that we would live on the ship and help repair the ship, while it was here in New York and Brooklyn. And then that our pay would be two cartons of cigarettes a week. And whatever food they could manage to find to give us. And that's exactly what happened. Two cartons of cigarettes in Europe at that time had some value. It wasn't much, but it was something.[42]

Shepard Rifkin was born September 14, 1918 in New York, but he was raised and went to school in Omaha, Nebraska. After his father's business failed, his family returned to New York. His 1936 Evander Childs High School in the Bronx yearbook said of Rifkin "His pen is mighty, it's his sword, but for a genius, he is quite bored."[43] He attended City College. Rifkin was rejected by the Army for poor eyesight, but he joined the Merchant Marine as a steward and became a deckhand, sailing in submarine infested waters in the Atlantic Caribbean and Pacific.

Several key members of the crew were not Jewish. Third Mate and Bosun Walter "Heavy" Greaves was born in New Bedford, Massachusetts. Heavy was a big, tough, tattooed, fun-loving seasoned sailor with a soft heart.[44] He served in the Merchant Marine during World War II, during which he survived his ship being torpedoed and sunk three times. He saw

---

42 Kaplan Oral History, part 1, MZ.
43 "Shepard Rifkin," 1936 US School Yearbooks, 1900–1999, Ancestry.com, original data: Evander Childs High School, Bronx, New York.
44 See Rifkin, *What Ship*, 67.

one of the American League for a Free Palestine's advertisements requesting contributions, and he contacted the office and within a day was aboard
the *Abril* in New York.[45] He became the unofficial leader of the crew. The
knowledge that he would fairly dispense justice and would be there to give
the right orders in case of an emergency kept the ship's crew together.[46]
Also representative of the seven *Ben Hecht* crewmembers who were not
Jewish,[47] was James (Jimmy) Heggie, who eventually served as boatswain,
an Irishman born in Glasgow, Scotland, who was a professional seaman.
Heggie, who was not married, received a stipend of one-third of the standard seaman's pay for his family during his time on the *Ben Hecht*. He joined
the ship after reading of the "inhuman treatment" suffered by "those poor
people," the displaced persons, and for the sake of the "adventure."[48] Other
crew members later recalled that Heggie "hated the British," had volunteered for the opportunity to oppose the British,[49] and had threatened to
leave "because we didn't carry a machine gun to fight the whole British
Navy."[50] Ed Styrak's parents were Polish immigrants who had antisemitic
attitudes. But Styrak explained that after he went to college and then serving in the Merchant Marine, he realized that antisemitism was senseless.[51]
Chicagoan Robert O'Donnell Nicolai, who in 1947 was twenty-five years
old, had served in the elite 101st Airborne Division during World War II.
Nicolai recalled that he signed on the *Ben Hecht* "because I didn't like seeing a minority kicked around. Religion had nothing to do with it."[52]

Walter Cushenberry was a professional maritime chef whose closest
relatives were his siblings and an aunt. He volunteered without pay on the
Ben Hecht. In an interview at the New York office of the AFLP after the
crew's return to New York, Cushenberry was described as tall and wearing
rimless glasses; he had a southern accent and his voice was so soft that it
was hard for an interviewer to hear him. Cushenberry had not known much
initially about the problem of Jewish displaced persons. He had been at the

---

45   Finegood, "Greaves."
46   See Rifkin, *What Ship*, 67.
47   Hoffman, *Fighting Words*, 174.
48   Halkenhauser, "Ben Hecht Seamen Tell of Seizure."
49   Levitan Oral History, USHMM.
50   Kaplan Oral History, part 1, MZ.
51   Harold Livingston, *No Trophy No Sword: An American Volunteer in the Israeli Air Force during the 1948 War of Independence* (Chicago, Berlin, Tokyo, and Moscow: Edition Q, 1994).
52   Nicolai, "I Ran Britain's Palestine Blockade," 24.

Seamen's Church Institute waiting for a job on a ship when a former skipper of his, apparently Captain Robert Clay, approached him. At the AFLP's office, Cushenberry became convinced that Palestine was the only place to establish homes for the displaced Jews of Europe. When he was asked why he felt he had to do something about it, he gently replied that his union, the National Maritime Union (NMU), "teaches that regardless of race or creed there should be no discrimination on ships . . . So frankly, I do think it's my business." Cushenberry related that after meeting and taking on the hundreds of passengers, talking to them, and seeing their conditions, "it would make you thank God for being there" and he reflected [t]here was quite a nice understanding between all of us on the crew." Cushenberry felt that "[w]e all seemed to work to the same point quite a bit, the same belief."[53]

The crew and their ages and homes at the time of the *Ben Hecht*'s voyage were:[54]

1. David L. Gutmann, age twenty-one, third oiler. He lived on Sedgwick Avenue in The Bronx.

2. Harry Hershkowitz, age thirty, able bodied seaman (an able seaman is certified to perform routine maritime duties).[55] He lived on Eleventh Street on Manhattan's Lower East Side.

3. Shepard Rifkin (1918–2011),[56] then age twenty-eight. He lived on West Eighth Street in Manhattan.

4. Henry Mandel, age twenty-six, first oiler. He lived on Kelly Street in The Bronx.

5. Louis Brettschneider, age twenty-four, third engineer He lived on Fifty-Second Street in Brooklyn. He graduated from New Utrecht High School in 1940.[57]

---

53 "How Ship's Cook Walter Cushenberry Won his Hand-Cut Olive-Wood Medal," *PM*, March 12, 1947, *PM* reel 53, 24 3/2–4/30/47, NYPL.

54 Unless otherwise noted, sourced from "The Bergson Group, Voyage of the Ben Hecht," http://new.wymaninstitute.org/2017/01/the-bergson-group-voyage-of-the-ben-hecht/.

55 Barahona, *Odyssey*, 171.

56 "Shepard Rifkin," US Social Security Death Index, 1935–2014, Ancestry.com, original data: Social Security Administration, Social Security Death Index, Master File.

57 Louis Brettschneider US School Yearbooks, 1900–1999, Ancestry.com, original data: New Utrecht High School, Brooklyn, New York.

6. Robert O'Donnell Nicolai, age twenty-four, able bodied. He lived in Midlothian, Illinois.

7. Edward R. Styrak, age twenty-three. He lived in Mount Clemens, Michigan.

8. David Kaplan, age twenty, first sparks and second radioman. He lived at 606 Bedford Avenue in Brooklyn. Kaplan was born on November 12, 1926.[58]

9. Jeno Berkovitz (December 29, 1918–April 17, 2013), then age twenty-eight, messman, of Wales Avenue in The Bronx. Served in the Merchant Marine during World War II, and later worked as a maître d' in restaurants, including the Four Seasons.[59]

10. Walter Rexie Cushenberry, thirty-three, steward, born in Mayfield, Kentucky, and living in Brooklyn at the time of the *Ben Hecht*'s voyage.[60]

11. Walter "Heavy" Greaves (June 3, 1917–July 29, 1969, Brooklyn), then twenty-nine, third mate, of South Street in Manhattan.[61]

12. James Heggie, thirty-three, bosun, able bodied, of 62 Clymer Street in Brooklyn.

13. Hyman Robert Levitan (May 3, 1922–1998), then twenty-four, (acting) captain, of 3510 Fourteenth Avenue in Brooklyn.

14. Albert L. Hirschkoff, twenty-six,[62] press, of Fifty-Seventh Street in Brooklyn.

---

58 S.S. *Marine Carp* Manifest, Sailing from Haifa, Palestine Roll T715, 1897–1957, Arriving Port of New York, NY, April 16, 1947, Passenger and Crew Lists (Including Castle Garden and Ellis Island, 1820–1957), Ancestry.com.

59 Obituary for Jeno Berkovitz, April 17, 2017, https://www.foresthillspalmcityflorida.com/obituary/berkovits-jeno.

60 "Cushenberry, Walter R. 'Rexie,'" http://www.wertheimer.info/family/GRAMPS/Haapalah/ppl/a/3/bce473e1a207e40303a.html.

61 "Walter Greaves," Jr. Rhode Island, Historical Cemetery Commission Index, 1647–2008, Ancestry.com, Original data: Find A Grave database and images (https://www.findagrave.com, accessed October 25, 2019), Walter Greaves, Jr. (1917–1968) Find A Grave Memorial no. 126202393, Moshassuck Cemetery, Central Flls, Providence County, Rhode Island, USA, maintained by "Lasting Memories" (contributor 47977729).

62 "Albert L. Hirschkoff," New York, Passenger and Crew Lists (including Castle Garden and Ellis Island), 1820–1957, Ancestry.com, original data: Passenger Lists of Vessels Arriving at New York, New York, 1820–1897, microfilm publication M237, 675 rolls, NAI 6256867, Records of the US Customs Service, Record Group 36, National Archives at Washington D.C.; Passenger and Crew Lists of Vessels Arriving at New York, New

15. Wallace Litwin, thirty-two, photographer (wiper), of Eighth Street in Manhattan. Born November 22, 1914.[63]

16. Norman Edward Luce, forty-four, cook, of South Street in Manhattan.

17. Louis Markowitz, fifty-three, second mate, of Washington Avenue in The Bronx. Markowitz was born in Lithuania[64] and was naturalized as a citizen in San Francisco;[65] he died while living in the Bronx in 1966.[66]

18. Harry Nathan Schatz, forty-eight, oiler, of Indianapolis. Born on December 18, 1898.

19. Jack Winkler (April 25, 1926–May 29, 2002), age twenty, ordinary seaman, of Milwaukee.[67]

20. Haakom Lilliby, age unknown, chief engineer, of Norway.

21. Erling Sorensen, age unknown, first engineer, of Brooklyn and Norway.

22. Louis Binder (August 31, 1929–1979), Brooklyn.[68]

23. Marvin Liebman, 272 Ninetieth St., Brooklyn. Liebman died at age seventy-three in 1997.[69]

York, 1897–1957, microfilm publication , 8892 rolls, NAI: 300346, microfilm roll 7425, 71, line 10.

63 S.S. *Marine Carp* Manifest.

64 "Louis M. Markowitz," New York, Passenger and Crew Lists (including Castle Garden and Ellis Island), 1820–1957, Ancestry.com, original data: Passenger Lists of Vessels Arriving at New York, New York, 1820–1897, microfilm publication M237, 675 rolls, NAI: 625867, Records of the Immigration and Naturalization Service, Record Group 36, National Archives at Washington, D.C.; Passenger and Crew Lists of Vessels Arriving at New York, New York, 1897–1957, microfilm publication T715, 8892 rolls, NAI: 300346, Records of the Immigration and Naturalization Service; National Archives at Washington, D.C.

65 S.S. *Marine Carp* Manifest.

66 "Louis M. Markowitz," Newspapers.com Obituary Index, 1800s–current, Ancestry. com, original data: *Daily News*, February 26, 1966, https://www.newspapers.com/imag e/463378797/?article=d36c6a63-1bfa-423e-9526-f329c136c457&focus=0.030904047,0 .64238244,0.21679369,0.7276238&xid=2378.

67 "Jack Winkler," US Department of Veterans' Affairs BIRLS Death file, 1850–2010, Ancestry.com, original data: Beneficiary Identification Records Locator Subsystem (BIRLS) Death File. Washington, D.C.: US Department of Veterans' Affairs.

68 "Louis Binder," New York Birth Index, 1910–1965, Ancestry.com, original data: New York City Department of Health, courtesy of www.vitalsearch-worldwide.com, Digital Images.

69 "Marvin Liebman, 73, Dies."

24. Eli Freundlich (May 10, 1925–July 15, 2016),[70] lived in Brooklyn at the time of the *Ben Hecht*'s voyage.[71]

***

Some members of the crew were confused by the superficial contradiction of an Orthodox Jew serving on the ship. In Rifkin's novel, the Orthodox character Heinkel, like Mandel, refrained from eating the kosher salami on board because he did not know if a rabbi had supervised the slaughtering of the meat.[72] When questioned by crewmates on this stringency and his faith, the character Heinkel responded that he could not prove that God exists, but if there was one, "I'll be in a much better position to meet Him than anyone else" among the crew. Heinkel is described as praying throughout the journey, bracing himself as the ship rolled, and even laughing at jokes, but continuing to sway in prayer. Rifkin also describes a character, perhaps inspired by himself, who envies Heinkel because his "orthodoxy led him to a calm fatalism" that "had solved the problem of avoiding tension." The Americanized orthodoxy practiced by Mandel was novel to the crew. A character presses Heinkel "[h]ow can you not be completely Orthodox? That's like not being completely pregnant. The Bible says you must not shave. It doesn't say you can shave in certain conditions. It says no work on the Sabbath. It doesn't say you can work on the Sabbath if you're on a ship that's running Jews to Palestine."[73] Actually, the *Rema* permits work that would normally violate the Sabbath once a sea journey has already commenced. The *Magen Avroham* commentary argues that the Shulchan Arukh supports the same position, as he permits travelling in a desert in a caravan on the Sabbath during a time of danger in order to preserve life.[74]

---

70   Eli Freundlich Find A Grave Memorial no. 192035197.

71   "Eli Freundlich," US World War II Army Enlistment Records, 1938–1946, Ancestry. com, original data: National Archives and Records Administration, Electronic Army Serial Number Merged File, 1938–1946 [Archival Database] ARC: 1263923, World War II Army Enlistment Records, Records of the National Archives and Records Administration, Record Group 64, National Archives at College Park, College Park, MD; Hochstein and Greenfield, *The Jews' Secret Fleet*, 176.

72   Rifkin, *What Ship*, 50; David Gutmann, Machal and Aliyah Bet Records, undated, 1930–2010, I-501, AJHS, Center for Jewish History, New York.

73   Rifkin, *What Ship*, 95, 101, 127–128, 95.

74   *Rema* and *Magen Avroham Orach Chaim* sec. 248, subsec. 1, *Sif Kattan* (4).

Mandel very often told his family that the greatest rabbis found leniencies that served the needs of their congregants. Later in life, he often praised Rabbi Moshe Feinstein, who found leniencies to free the marital chains of widows of Holocaust victims, to prevent them from become *agunot* and to resume their lives free to remarry under Jewish law after the war. Above all, Mandel's efforts on behalf of the refugees reflected his understanding of his religious and moral obligations. There is no more important requirement of Jewish religious law, no greater *mitzvah*, than the redemption of captives. Captivity is worse than death, violence, and hunger because all of these are encompassed in it.[75] Every moment of delay when it is possible to accelerate redemption is as if blood were shed.[76] Nonetheless, the Mishnah ruled that captives are not to be redeemed at too high a price because of *tikkun olom*, a regulation to protect society. Nor are captives to be rescued, either for the sake of society or for the remaining captives left behind.[77] The Talmud asks whether the rationale of the decree was to avoid providing the enemy an incentive for taking more hostages or to avoid overburdening the Jewish community financially, but leaves the question unresolved.[78] Similarly, the classical responses of Jewish law to oppression struggled with the moral dilemmas posed by threatened reprisals if prisoners were not handed over to oppressors, permitting the sacrifice of individuals specifically demanded by oppressors, but not permitting Jewish officials to select those who would die, though even passive collaboration was frowned upon.[79] By examining the 1947 voyage of the Jewish illegal immigrant ship *Ben Hecht*, this book explores a historical example of what the obligation to redeem captives, established in the Talmud and medieval codes,[80] can mean in modern times.

---

75 *Bet Yosef, Yoreh De'ah* sec. 252:2.

76 *Bet Yosef, Yoreh De'ah* sec. 252:3.

77 Mishnah *Gittin* 4:6.

78 Talmud Bavli *Gittin* 45a.

79 Elman, *The Living Nach*, 357 (citing Mishnah *Terumoth* 8:12, Genesis Rabba 94). See David Daube, *Appeasement or Resistance and Other Essays on New Testament Judaism* (Berkeley: University of California Press, 1987), 79; David Daube, *Collaboration with Tyranny in Rabbinic Law* (London: Oxford University Press, 1965), quoted in Lucy S. Dawidowicz, *The War against the Jews 1933–1945* (New York: Bantam Books, 1978), 384–385.

80 Talmud Bavli *Bava Batra* 8b; Maimonides, *Mishneh Torah*, Laws of Gifts to the Poor 8:10; *Shulchan Arukh, Yoreh De'ah* sec. 252.

Chapter 10

Atlantic Crossing to the Mediterranean Sea

O thou afflicted, tossed with tempest, and not comforted
—Isaiah 54:11

The *Ben Hecht* sailed from Port Richmond in Staten Island for a North Atlantic crossing in late December 1946.[1] One of the diesel engines malfunctioned the first day after the ship left New York and was not reliable for the rest of the journey, and the generators also malfunctioned, leading crew member Robert O'Donnell Nicolai to suspect that the *Ben Hecht* had been "jinxed from the start."[2] Another witness described the crossing across the Atlantic as "a difficult one, stormy almost constantly, a mostly inexperienced crew, little, if any opportunity for either noon sun or night time star sights."[3] Captain Clay's decision that the first port of call would be Ponta Delgada, Portugal involved a route that put the ship in the midst of dangerous winter mid-Atlantic storms. The waves were so high that the ship nearly capsized as it approached the Azores. Even experienced sailors became seasick. It fell to Levitan to navigate the ship through the dangerous crossing.[4] During the Atlantic voyage, as the vessel approached the Azores, the ship rolled so much in one storm that there was a fear water would enter the stack, the boilers would be destroyed, and the ship would be wrecked

---

1   "A M/V BEN HECHT Story."
2   Nicolai, "I Ran Britain's Palestine Blockade," 24.
3   "A M/V BEN HECHT Story."
4   Kaplan, "This Is the Way It Was"; "A M/V BEN HECHT Story."

and sunk.[5] Fourteen days after leaving New York, the ship did arrive in Ponta Delgada and stopped for fuel, food, and water.

Passing the British base at the Straits of Gibraltar, the entrance to the Mediterranean, where every ship was asked "What ship?" by British forces, was a major challenge[6] (Rifkin's novelization of the journey is entitled *What Ship? Where Bound?*).[7] After being battered by severe storms and rough seas in the crossing of the Atlantic Ocean due to Captain Clay's misjudged route, the *Abril* arrived on January 10, 1947,[8] six days behind schedule, in Port-de-Bouc, a small coaling port near Marseilles, France.[9] The *Ben Hecht* had "fruit juices, and 1,600 pounds of salami" when it arrived in Port-de-Bouc.[10] Due to his conduct during the Atlantic journey, crew members were concerned that the captain would founder the ship with several hundred refugees aboard.[11]

Abraham Stavsky, also known as Mr. Palest (as in Palestine), Abrasha, or Nebraska,[12] was awaiting the ship in Marseilles, where he had been organizing the transport of the Jewish displaced persons. Abraham Stavsky was born in Brisk (Brest Litovsk), in what is now Belarus, in 1906, and had immigrated to Palestine.[13] He had been accused of the assassination of Chaim Arlosoroff, a leading labor Zionist leader, on a Tel Aviv beach in June of 1933.[14] The British imprisoned an extreme right-wing ideologue, Abba Achimeir, for the assassination of Arlosoroff, as well as Stavsky and Zvi Rosenblatt.[15] Only Stavsky was convicted, but in 1934 the conviction was reversed on appeal.[16] Stavsky was most probably framed for the murder. Arlosoroff's wife identified Stavsky as the culprit, but though the murder took place on the Tel Aviv beach, several witnesses placed Stavsky in Jerusalem at the time of the shooting. Chief Rabbi Kook's advocacy for

---

5   Rifkin, *What Ship*, 103.

6   Barahona, *The Odyssey*, 95.

7   Rifkin, *What Ship*, 120.

8   Ben-Ami, *Years of Wrath*, 406; Silverstone, *Our Only Refuge*, 23; Rifkin, *What Ship*, 121.

9   Kaplan, "This Is the Way It Was."

10 Nicolai, "I Ran Britain's Palestine Blockade," 25.

11 Rifkin, *What Ship*, 108, 118.

12 Heckelman, *American Volunteers*, 41.

13 Horev, *Dawning Ships*, 25.

14 Wyman and Medoff, *Race against Death*, 251 n.10; Medoff, *Militant Zionism in America*, 69.

15 Merlin, *Millions of Jews to Rescue*, 17.

16 Medoff notes in Merlin, *Millions of Jews to Rescue*, 205–206; Heckelman, *American Volunteers*, 41.

Stavsky's innocence was so strong that some attributed it to divine inspiration, though it is possible that trusted confidential sources vouched for Stavsky.[17] The case against Stavsky eventually collapsed, but not before the Revisionist movement, with which Stavsky was associated, became associated with violence in the public mind. Stavsky organized illegal immigration by ship to Palestine for the Revisionist movement in the late 1930s and early 1940s,[18] and also worked with the War Refugee Board as part of his efforts.[19] Hecht described Stavsky as "a tall man with bulging shoulders, heavy hands, bushy brows and a smile. . . . His face was a shade brighter than most men's faces, as if his soul were nearer its surface." Hecht asked Stavsky directly, 'Did you kill Arlosoroff?' Stavsky replied just as directly: 'No. I have never killed a Jew.'"[20]

***

Several weeks were needed in Port-de-Bouc to repair storm damage to the *Abril*, replace Captain Clay with Levitan, and to ready the ship for its intended Displaced Person passengers by building shelves for the purposes of sleeping accommodations.[21] The Mossad Aliyah Bet in France knew the AFLP was outfitting the vessel and provided some assistance.[22] Despite the misgivings of the Irgun command in Palestine, the Irgun in France aided in the practical work of preparing the illegal immigrant ship. Irgun operative HaCohen-Brandes recalled that when the *Abril* arrived in France, Eliyahu Lankin, the newly appointed head of overseas Irgun operations who had recently arrived after escaping a British prison camp in Eritrea; Eri Jabotinsky, a leader in the Betar Revisionist youth movement who worked with the Bergson Group; and Abrasha Stavsky, who was the group's expert on Aliyah Bet, organized the preparation of the vessel for the immigrants.[23] Lankin sought to bridge differences and mediate the disagreements between

---

17   Shnayer Z. Leiman, "R. Abraham Isaac Ha-Kohen Kook: Letter on Ahavat Yisrael," *Tradition: A Journal of Orthodox Jewish Thought* 24, no. 1 (1988): 84–90.

18   Heckelman, *American Volunteers*, 69.

19   Wyman and Medoff, *A Race against Death*, 251 n.10.

20   Hecht, *Child*, 619, 621.

21   "A M/V BEN HECHT Story."

22   Ze'ev Hadari, *The Mossad L'Aliyah Bet Operational Logbook* (Beer Sheva, Israel: The Ben-Gurion University of the Negev Press, 1991), 24, 28 (Hebrew).

23   Yehoshua HaCohen-Brandes Oral History, October 15, 1992, testimony reference code: TS5-16, Jabotinsky Institute (MZ), 13 (Hebrew).

the Bergson Group and the Irgun leadership in Palestine commanded by Menachem Begin.[24]

Irgun member Yehoshua HaCohen-Brandes, who helped prepare the *Ben Hecht* in France for its journey to Palestine and bring about 500 displaced persons from Germany into France, recounted: Stavsky "decided this ship had room for 600 people. There was below three bedrooms, one or two restrooms, and an engine room. But there was a big deck. And he began to design." HaCohen-Brandes related that Stavsky

> designed to install planks extending out over the sea . . . to expand the deck. At the end of these planks he set up a small shack without a roof and without a bottom, like a telephone booth. He built like eight booths like these. These were the bathrooms. There was no need for a special installation because everything fell into the sea. According to the design, all the men needed to do was stay on the deck—"which ever way" [said in English in an interview otherwise in Hebrew], by standing, by sitting, by lying down. In the rooms below, it was necessary that only sick women or sick men descend, that would be the infirmary. And thus about 600 people were able to travel in that ship—if you call her a ship.

"When I heard '600 people,'" HaCohen-Brandes reminisced, "I thought, that is not serious. I did not know whether to call him an expert or something worse. But he was correct. He knew his trade. He had already transported six hundred people in ships that were smaller, in the framework" of the illegal immigration from Europe before and during World War II, organized by the Revisionist movement.[25]

Crew member David Kaplan later remembered that upon the *Ben Hecht*'s arrival in France, "we had taken a terrible beating in the trip over. The ship was really not in good shape. And neither were the men. And we got to Port-de-Bouc where we were divided into groups of three. One to stay, or help work on the ship with the French workmen, who were putting in the shelves for our people." Kaplan related that one group of *Ben Hecht* sailors "went to Monte Carlo. And I was put in charge of that group because I speak French. And a job like that, I never want again. Because this bunch of *meshuganim* [Yiddish for 'crazy persons'] . . . You had to have the patience of a Job. And they were crazy. They put us in a hotel, the Mirabeau. The Mirabeau Hotel

---

24   Zadka, *Blood in Zion*, 123; Baumel, *Bergson Boys*, 237.
25   HaCohen-Brandes Oral History, 13, MZ.

in Monte Carlo is for retired British colonials. Very sedate. Very quiet." But after the crew came by "they have that hotel turned upside down. Absolutely crazy." Kaplan remembered that "In Port-de-Bouc, we had a lot of trouble. Jimmy Heggie, one of the men, just drank a little bit to excess. He ended up with the delirium tremens. And we had to leave him there."[26]

Another group, including Henry Mandel and Harry Hershkowitz, went sightseeing in Paris. Hershkowitz, who had in the summer of 1946 published an avant-garde magazine with the shocking title of *Death Magazine*,[27] met Sartre while in Paris,[28] and returned to the ship as a "Jean-Paul Sartre maven."[29] Jean-Paul Sartre's *Réflexions sur la Question Juive* (*Reflections on the Jewish Question*), written in 1944, was a critical analysis of antisemitism, but it did not ascribe positive content to Judaism.[30] Sartre was the world's most influential philosopher in the late 1940s,[31] and the Bergson Group had obtained his support.[32] Sartre taught that "A man is what he wills himself to be" and that "It's what one does, and nothing else, that shows the stuff one is made of. . . . You are—your life, and nothing else."[33]

Stavsky and Hakim dismissed Captain Clay soon after the arrival of the *Ben Hecht* in France.[34] At a meeting at their invitation, Captain Clay "was surprised by being flash-photographed, then he was handed an envelope full of cash and told that if he valued his safety, he had better forget all he had learned or seen up to then. He was put on a plane back to the United States."[35] Though the crew was told that a new captain would be found, no replacement appeared. Bob Levitan, the ship's navigator, assumed the mantle.[36]

***

26 Kaplan Oral History, part 1, MZ.

27 Stuart D. Hobbs, *The End of the American Avant Garde* (New York: New York University Press, 1997).

28 Cf. Rifkin, *What Ship*, 127.

29 Kaplan Oral History, part 1, MZ.

30 Translated in Jean-Paul Sartre, *Anti-Semite and Jew*, trans. George J. Becker, preface Michael Walzer (New York: Schocken Books, 1995 [1948]).

31 Johnson, *Quest*, 22.

32 Gorbach, *Notorious*, 239.

33 Jean-Paul Sartre, *No Exit and Three Other Plays*, trans. S. Gilbert (New York: Vintage International, 1989), 43.

34 Ben-Ami, *Years of Wrath*, 454; Kaplan Oral History, part 1, MZ.

35 Ben-Ami, *Years of Wrath*, 406.

36 Levitan letter to Finegood; Shaul Horev, *"I Will Gather Them From the Outermost Parts of the Earth": The Revisionism and the Civil Illegal Immigration to Palestine in Mandate Times* (Haifa, Israel: Duhifat Publishers, 2012) (Hebrew).

Contrary to the Haganah's practice, the *Abril*'s outfitting was not a well-kept secret.[37] Levitan later recounted[38] that although the Haganah had succeeded in bringing some illegal immigrants to Palestine, it was at a rate at which it "would have taken two lifetimes to get them over there. So the Irgun was interested in getting people over there but they were more interested in getting the world opinion changed so that the British would let the European refugees get into Palestine."[39] Back in the United States, the Haganah felt that the AFLP's energetic and entertaining publicity campaigns threatened to siphon off donations from their own clandestine operations.[40] On January 22, 1947, the British informed the French authorities of the arrival in France of the *Abril*, along with a Haganah ship, which were both suspected of being illegal immigration ships, and requested that the ships be seized.[41] Crew members complained to Stavsky about the publicity about a supposedly covert mission. Stavsky replied that "You know who the security leak is—it's you."[42]

In Rifkin's novelization, Heinkel, the Orthodox Jewish crew member character, tells fellow crew member "Eisenberg" (probably based on Lou Bretschneider) that "when I was in this kosher restaurant I saw a couple of American-looking guys come in. They sat down near me. I could see they come there all the time to eat . . . So they started to talk . . . and from the way they talked, and the way they talked about us . . ." Eisenberg interrupts Heinkel, but he continues: "Lemme finish. I mean our ship. So I bet you five bucks they're on a Haganah ship." Eisenberg insists that Heinkel show him the restaurant. Eisenberg then makes contact with the Haganah sailors in the restaurant, and a few crew members visit the Haganah's office, offering their services. In the novel, Eisenberg asks the Haganah man in Marseilles for guidance, who tells him that when the ship based on the *Abril* arrived in port, the price of bribery of officials doubled, and prices of supplies went much higher due to the publicity attached to the ship. "The biggest favor you can do for us," the Haganah operative says, "is to get that goddamn ship out of here as fast as possible."[43] Gutmann later recounted that the Haganah

---

37 Silverstone, *Our Only Refuge*, 23.
38 Levitan letter to Finegood.
39 Levitan Oral History, USHMM.
40 Slater, *Pledge*, 95–96.
41 Swarc, "French Connection," 159.
42 Jeffrey Weiss and Craig Weiss, *I Am My Brother's Keeper*, 33.
43 Rifkin, *What Ship*, 49, 146–147, 165.

representative told them "[t]he best thing you can do for us is to get [the] ship out of here and get yourselves arrested" (expletives deleted).[44]

Levitan emphasized to a researcher that "[t]he *Ben Hecht* was a small vessel that could only handle the 600 people aboard. There were six small rooms available crammed with 100 people each." With the arrival of the refugees "the entire crew of 20 slept in shifts in a room behind the bridge."[45] Rifkin's novel claims the ship had only taken on children if their parents were men and women of fighting age, and few old people.[46] However, his crewmate Kaplan said "[w]e had mostly women, older men, older women and very younger children, and a very small scattering of what you would call 'fighting material.' These were refugees, but they weren't fighting refugees . . . Some ships took only those who could *keyn machers* [Yiddish for those who could be productive]."[47] Crew member Robert O'Donnell Nicolai later recalled that "[w]e were rather surprised when we first saw these refugees; they were all well-dressed. Later we discovered that they had been given the pick of wearing apparel at their DP camps, for they were really the Chosen People from among all the Jews of Europe—they were getting out."[48] Some passengers had black leather coats, some had suitcases.[49] The passengers "were dressed in city clothes, suits, shirts, ties, dresses and each person carried like one bag, either a suitcase or a big sea bag or burlap bag," Levitan recalled. "They had their worldly possessions with them." Decades after the journey, Levitan told an interviewer that "even though the people on the ship look like you and I, they had been through some terrible, horrific times. And they were survivors of that which I don't even want to think about anymore."[50]

***

Betar activists Moshe Shiff (some sources list his name as Moshe Schwartz)[51] and Simcha Berlin were escorts (*melavim*) of the passengers and organized

---

44   Jeffrey Weiss and Craig Weiss, *I Am My Brother's Keeper*, 31, 33, 40.
45   Levitan letter to Finegood.
46   Rifkin, *What Ship*, 192.
47   Kaplan Oral History, part 1, MZ.
48   Nicolai, "I Ran Britain's Palestine Blockade," 25.
49   Rifkin, *What Ship*, 193.
50   Levitan Oral History, USHMM.
51   "Avril, Cytherea—Ben Hecht," http://palmach.org.il/en/history/database/?itemId=5100; Ron Bar-Yaakov, "A Flag is Born in Days of Conflict," https://www.ybz.org.il/_Uploads/dbsArticles/bar_yaacov.pdf (Hebrew).

the passengers onboard.[52] The escorts who commanded the passengers were not subordinate to the captains of illegal immigration ships.[53] The escorts assigned thirty young men to keep order among the passengers.[54] The *Ben Hecht* carried Wallace Litwin, a professional photographer whose work had appeared in *Life Magazine*, and who also served as a wiper, a member of the crew;[55] Jacques Méry, a correspondent of *Paris-Preuse*; and Albert Hirschkoff, who hailed from Brooklyn, New York, and who claimed after the vessel's capture to be a freelance journalist and accredited string writer planning to write a book on Palestine.[56] Jabotinsky described "an American observer" as being aboard the ship;[57] Hirschkoff was apparently one of two observers who acted at the direction of Abrasha Stavsky or Hillel Kook.[58] One of these observers had worked in the Office of Strategic Services, the precursor to the American Central Intelligence Agency, and another in the British security forces. Both of them hid from sight "the moment the ship arrived. They saw everything we did," HaCohen-Brandes remembered. A novelization of the *Ben Hecht* story describes a former US Army lieutenant who had been studying at the Sorbonne called Korngold, who had become involved with the Irgun through contacts in Paris.[59] Korngold was appointed by a character apparently based on Bergson Group member Yitshaq Ben-Ami (styled as Ben Ari) to be the go-between through whom "all orders for the passengers were to be filtered through" and that "he together with a police that he had formed among the passengers were to ensure good order and discipline."[60] In a memorandum describing his *Ben Hecht* related activity, Jabotinsky refers to a "L.H.," an American citizen who fits this description.[61] HaCohen-Brandes recalled that the veteran of British security services called himself "Hershko." HaCohen-Brandes recounted that "Stavsky and Kook said, 'he is a writer who knows security . . . he promises to write the story afterwards. Therefore he wants to join

52   Shari, *The Cyprus Exile*, 81–83, quoted in Lazar, *Immigrant Ship "Ben Hecht,"* 16.
53   Barahona, *Odyssey*, 114.
54   Lazar, *Immigrant Ship "Ben Hecht,"* 8.
55   Eri Jabotinsky, "Request on the 'Ben Hecht' Transport in France," March 10, 1947, MZ *Ben Hecht (Avril)* Newspaper Clippings file.
56   "3 Pressmen among 21 Detained," *The Palestine Post*, Tuesday, March 11, 1947, 3, Palestine Post Bureau, dateline Haifa, Monday, March 10, 1947.
57   Jabotinsky, "Request on the 'Ben Hecht' Transport in France."
58   HaCohen-Brandes Oral History, 13, MZ.
59   Rifkin, *What Ship*, 190; "Ben Hecht," http://paulsilverstone.com/ship/ben-hecht/.
60   Rifkin, *What Ship*, 190.
61   Jabotinsky, "Request on the 'Ben Hecht' Transport in France."

us and know everything."' HaCohen-Brandes apparently was referring to Hirschkoff. In fact, Hirschkoff was acting as an observer on the *Ben Hecht* on behalf of the Bergson Group. Both *Ben Hecht* crew member David Kaplan and Irgun activist Yehoshua HaCohen-Brandes wondered why they did not hear from Hirschkoff again after his release from British custody.[62] Harry Herschkowitz is mistakenly described as the leader of the passengers in two Israeli studies of Aliyah Bet, probably confusing him with Albert Hirschkoff.[63] An otherwise valuable Israeli study of Jewish illegal immigrant ships misidentifies a photograph of Henry Mandel as that of Harry Hershkowitz.[64]

***

Eri Jabotinsky challenged the moral basis of the Haganah's policy of encouraging unarmed Holocaust survivors to physically resist the British Naval boarding of illegal immigrant ships. He told a French journalist who accompanied the *Ben Hecht* before the immigrants' journey to Palestine that "many repatriation vessels have resisted for several hours her Majesty's wartime units. But, our organization considers that it should not force unarmed beings to fight the British fleet, which does not hesitate to use the most violent means of repression."[65] Though the Irgun acquiesced to the use of the *Ben Hecht* as a refugee ship and assisted in its mission, there was in fact an attempt to militarize it. Irgun operatives trained a group of young men affiliated with the Revisionist youth movement Betar to violently resist the British with small arms. Irgun member Yehoshua HaCohen-Brandes, who helped prepare the *Ben Hecht* in France for its journey to Palestine, recounted: "I trained a group in use of weapons. We knew that they would try to halt them on the journey. . . . This time the 'ship' was not a ship and not a boat but a yacht that was big enough, that it was the private yacht of Ben Hecht, the Hollywood writer."[66] Actually, the *Abril* was not Ben Hecht's

---

62 HaCohen-Brandes Oral History, 13, MZ; Kaplan Oral History, part 1, MZ.
63 Horev, *I Will Gather Them*, 158, 188; Aharoni, *Leaning Masts*, 22.
64 Horev, *I Will Gather Them*, 189.
65 Jacques Méry, *Let My People Go*, preface Albert Camus (Paris: Éditions du Seuil, 1947), 29–30 (French, editor's translation).
66 Lankin interview, MZ.

personal yacht. A picture of the ship appears in his autobiography *Child of the Century* with the simple legend "A yacht I never sailed on."[67]

Yehoshua HaCohen-Brandes remarked that as part of his task he chose eight men among the young Betar youth group members and in an empty wooded area near Marseilles "trained them in the use of submachine guns, pistols, and hand grenades." That order was contradicted by the instructions of Betar leadership. HaCohen-Brandes did not know at that time that Baruch Giladi, the president of Betar, who also went by the name Gideon Abramowitz, gave instructions to the men who received the training "the moment you meet the British, throw the weapons into the sea and do not cause bloodshed." In contrast, HaCohen-Brandes gave the Betar youth group members the contradictory instructions: "Do not allow the British to come close to the ship. They will not be able to fire at you because there will be too many people sitting on the deck. The ship needs to continue with speed to reach the coast. Beach yourself in the coast . . . In that manner, perhaps a portion of you will succeed in slipping into the Land."[68]

***

Thus, with the cooperation of the Mossad for Aliyah Bet, a branch of the Haganah, six hundred Jewish refugees were transported to the *Ben Hecht*.[69] According to Ben-Ami, the Jewish displaced persons who were to become the *ma'apilim* passengers of the *Ben Hecht* "were gathered from the American zone in Germany, France, and Italy, and their travel papers were prepared with visas to Bolivia."[70] The majority of the *Ben Hecht*'s passengers began their journey from displaced persons camps in the American occupied zone in Germany.[71] Dr. Shmuel Ariel, who at that time was the representative of the Irgun in Europe, and Claire Vaydat, the director of the Assistance aux réfugiés et déportés associated with the Fédération des sociétés juives de France, who had been active in the French underground resistance, helped arrange the passage of the displaced persons to the *Ben Hecht*. On February 18, 1947, Vaydat obtained three collective visas issued by the Bolivian consulate in Paris dated February 1, 1947, which were

---

67 "Committee Faces," in Hecht, *Child*.
68 HaCohen-Brandes Oral History, 13–14, MZ.
69 Horev, *Dawning Ships*, 25.
70 Ben-Ami, *Years of Wrath*, 406.
71 Jabotinsky, "Request on the 'Ben Hecht' Transport in France."

delivered to the French Consul in Munich for 658 immigrants.[72] Claire Vaydat has been described as the Irgun's "French connection."[73] One historian has speculated that the Federation subsequently broke ties with Vaydat due to her cooperation with the Irgun.[74]

On February 21, 1947, with the permission of the American Army and the French liaison in Frankfurt, 658 immigrants traveled from Munich to Kahl and then onto Karlsruhe.[75] Continuing on, the train was delayed at Rastatt, and then again in Kehl, a German city directly opposite the French city of Strasbourg, in part because the passengers did not have Displaced Person identification cards and the only documentation they had was a collective visa for the entire group. Ariel and Vaydat accompanied the transport over the French border at Strasbourg and smoothed over the difficulties after a delay of a few hours. False reports of the capture of the *Ben Hecht* were published on February 23, 1947, and the supposed news reached Palestine, though it could not be confirmed. During the night of February 23, 1947, and in the early morning of February 24, 1947, 535 immigrants crossed the border in France at Kehl on a train with twenty cattle trucks with stoves in each truck, and arrived in Strasbourg at 10 p.m. They traveled by train to Grenoble, arriving on February 24, where the transport was greeted by the President of the Fédération des sociétés juives de France, Alain Scheidman. Scheidman had vouched for them to travel by train to Grenoble.[76] The immigrants were sent to eight hotels in the area, where they stayed for six days.[77] Ten people left and did not travel on the *Ben Hecht*, and four others were left behind for medical attention. Forty-five immigrants joined the group at Grenoble, and forty others went directly

---

72   Swarc, "French Connection," 159; Lazar, *Immigrant Ship "Ben Hecht,"* 7.

73   Roger Friedland and Richard Hecht, *To Rule Jerusalem* (Santa Barbara, CA: University of California Press, 2000), 534 n.30.

74   Swac, "French Connection," 222.

75   Horev, *I Will Gather Them*, 189; Jabotinsky, "Request on the 'Ben Hecht' Transport in France"; John L. Campbell, 1st Lt. Repatriation Movements Officer (Frankfurt), To: Headquarters, Third US Army, APO 403, US Army (Attn: Screening and Repatriation Section, Displaced Persons Branch, G-5 Division), February 18, 1947, signed by C. L. Butler, Major CLC Commanding, 1st. Ind., Displaced Person Branch, G-5 Division, HQ., US Forces, European Theater, APO 757, February 19, 1947, file: Etzel Diaspora Headquarters, Paris, Illegal Immigrants ship "Ben Hecht" (Abril), reference code: K18-4/5, Jabotinsky Institute (MZ).

76   Lazar, *Immigrant Ship Ben Hecht,"* 7.

77   Jabotinsky, "Request on the 'Ben Hecht' Transport in France."

to Port-de-Bouc.[78] Ten members of the Mossad L'Aliyah Bet, the Haganah's organization for clandestine immigration, were allowed to travel with the transport from Germany as a matter of courtesy.[79] The French Ministry of Foreign Affairs accepted the visas as valid on February 26, 1947.[80] On February 28, the immigrants left Grenoble in the middle of the night, traveled to Marseilles[81] by railroad cars[82] and arrived in Port-de-Bouc at 6:30 a.m.[83]

---

78   Reubin Aharoni, *Leaning Masts: Ships of Jewish Illegal Immigration and Arms after World War II*, ed. Efi Meltzer (Ef'al: Merkaz, 1997), 22 (Hebrew).
79   Jabotinsky, "Request on the 'Ben Hecht' Transport in France, 10/3/47."
80   Swarc, "French Connection," 159.
81   Jabotinsky, "Request on the 'Ben Hecht' Transport in France."
82   Kaplan Oral History, part 1, MZ.
83   Lazar, *Immigrant Ship "Ben Hecht,"* 8.

Chapter 11

The Palestine Run

Their ropes are slack, They cannot steady the sockets of their masts, They cannot spread a sail.

—Isaiah 32:23

Some Jewish displaced persons, who had not been brought by the Revisionists or another Jewish organization, happened to be in the area of Port-de Bouc and were added on as passengers.[1] Most of the passengers were associated with the Revisionists, but there was also an Orthodox group associated with Agudath Yisrael.[2] Some of the Polish refugees had served in the Soviet Army,[3] and among the passengers there was a group of Jews from Tunisia who were members of Betar and planned to form a Kibbutz.[4] The passengers boarded the *Abril* on Friday, February 28, 1947.[5]

The identity and travel authorization papers issued by the Hebrew Committee for National Liberation distributed to the passengers had a practical purpose, along with its ideological and legal claim of the right to enter Palestine. Holders of papers with a white background were permitted to sleep on their bunks only during the day; holders of papers with a blue background could sleep at night in the bunks emptied of their previous inhabitants. Invalids, children, pregnant women, and the sick were given yellow documents that would permit them to rest all day. Upon boarding, holders of the yellow papers were sent below deck to the belly of the vessel

---

1   Rifkin, *What Ship*, 187–188.
2   Horev, *I Will Gather Them*, 189.
3   Nicolai, "I Ran Britain's Palestine Blockade," 34.
4   Méry, *Let My People Go*, 71.
5   Ben-Ami, *Years of Wrath*, 406.

where there was a room with approximately seventy beds, while holders of white and blue papers filled up all the decks from front to back. The travel documents issued by the Hebrew Committee arrived a few minutes before the ship left the dock, but they were distributed to the passengers before they boarded.

The *Ben Hecht* cast away anchors at 4 p.m. Friday, February 28, 1947, before Sabbath began.[6] *Ben Hecht* purser Liebman recalled that "some of the refugees refused to board on the Sabbath. After many entreaties, they did, with the promise that we would not move until Saturday night," but "[w]hen the engines revved up during the day, no one asked to debark."[7] But since the ship left the dock before the Sabbath started, there was no violation of Jewish law. Based on the Talmud,[8] the Shulchan Arukh, the authoritative law code, states it is permissible to board a boat on the eve of the Sabbath if the journey is necessary for a *mitzvah* (a good deed). Immigration to the land of Israel is the archetypical *mitzvah* and justifies travel that otherwise would be forbidden on the Sabbath,[9] as confirmed by the verse, "I will gather them from the uttermost parts of the earth."[10] So while the behavior of the Jewish law observant passengers seemed inconsistent to Liebman, in fact their position was justified under traditional Jewish law.

As the *Ben Hecht* prepared to leave Port-de-Bouc, the French harbor pilots went on strike. Left with little choice, Levitan attempted to leave the harbor without the aid of a pilot. The *Abril* sailed from Port-de-Bouc, France on Saturday, March 1, 1947 at 16 hours (4 p.m.).[11] The French police exit register reported that the ship's stated destination was Bolivia, and that it was carrying 620 Jewish immigrants and twenty-seven crew members.[12] In

---

6   Lazar, *Immigrant Ship "Ben Hecht,"* 8, 10.

7   Liebman, *Coming Out Conservative*, 60.

8   Talmud Bavli *Sabbath* 19a.

9   *Shulchan Arukh Orach Chaim* sec. 248, subsec. 1 and 4.

10 Jeremiah 31:8. See also Tosfot, s.v. "*halakha k'rabanan Gamaliel b'sifinah*" (*Erubin* 43a); Talmud Bavli *Shabbat* 19a; Alyssa M. Gray, "Reading Tosafot as (Law and) Literature," *Jewish Law Association Studies* 27 (2017): 308, 310, 316–317; *Bet Yosef Orach Chaim* sec. 248; *Shulchan Arukh Orach Chaim* sec. 248, subsec. 3; *Mishnah Beurah* 248:21.

11 "In Memory—Hyman Robert Levitan," November 2001, American Veterans of Israel website, found in Illegal Immigration collection, The *Ben Hecht* (*Avril*)—Newspaper Items and Publications (including 1949–1953, 1985, 2001, 2007), reference code: K6-5/21, Jabotinsky Institute (MZ).

12 Méry, *Let My People Go*, 38; Ben-Ami, *Years of Wrath*, 406; HaCohen-Brandes Oral History, MZ.

fact, the *Ben Hecht* carried, along with the approximately 600 refugee passengers,[13] twenty-odd crewmen, and three journalists (one of whom was also a secret operative)[14] for a total count of 626 people aboard the overcrowded former yacht,[15] though some accounts, apparently inaccurately, credit the ship with having carried 800[16] or 900 passengers.[17] Mandel later described that some of the refugees "were in a very pitiful state. They had not recovered from the concentration camps and the work camps which they had been in during the war. And they were a few [Jewish] Russians who had been in the Russian Army."[18]

Crewmember Marvin Liebman later wrote: "With the passengers standing on deck, the Panamanian [Honduran] flag was brought down, the Star of David was hoisted, and everyone spontaneously started to sing" the Zionist anthem *Hatikvah* (*The Hope*).[19] One of the Betar commanders declared the new name of the vessel: the *Ben Hecht*.[20] "Passengers were still cheering the departure," according to Jabotinsky, when the ship ran aground on a sandbank 200 meters from the dock as she attempted to leave the harbor, though fortunately the ship was not damaged by the soft mud it had gotten stuck upon.[21] "Everybody raced to the side to see what had happened, and the vessel began to keel over," crew member Robert O'Donnell Nicolai, who was a former US Army paratrooper, later related. "But a few of us used our heads and chased half the people over to the other side. The ship righted itself just in time."[22] Tug boats were needed to free the ship and to allow it to continue on its journey.[23]

Once the ship left port, it headed north-east, hugging the coast. The first night of the journey passengers sat upon equipment on deck and sang "how good, how pleasant, it is for brothers to sit together." That first night and day of the journey was the Sabbath and the seas were calm. Groups of passengers prayed in the morning silent prayers full of gratitude.

---

13 Naor, *Haapala*, 114; Rifkin, *What Ship*, 124; Kaplan Oral History, part 1, MZ.
14 HaCohen-Brandes Oral History, 13, MZ.
15 Zadka, *Blood in Zion*, 122.
16 Naor, *Haapala*, 65.
17 Stone, "Refugees Driven on Cyprus-Bound Ships like Cattle," 1.
18 Mandel Interview by Shuster, 2000.
19 Liebman, *Coming Out Conservative*, 60.
20 Hoffman, *Fighting Words*, 174.
21 Rifkin, *What Ship*, 197–198.
22 Nicolai, "I Ran Britain's Palestine Blockade," 25.
23 Eri Jabotinsky, "Request on the 'Ben Hecht' Transport in France."

Passengers mingled, searching for friends and trading stories. March 3, 1947, corresponding to 11 Adar according to the Jewish calendar, was Tel Hai day, observed by Revisionists in memory of the heroic death of Joseph Trumpeldor, which was marked by singing and group activities. The Fast of Esther, held on 13 Adar, fell on March 5, 1947, the fourth day of sailing. In the afternoon, rough waves crashed over part of the deck and rendered most of the passengers seasick. On the fifth day of the journey, the holiday of Purim, March 6, 1947, the waves calmed, but many were still too sick to eat the Purim festive meal. Those who felt well enough socialized on deck.[24]

Other dangers soon assailed the vessel. The journey from France to Palestine took longer than planned.[25] "The trip across the Mediterranean was made without benefit of mine charts," and the passengers had to be warned not to congregate on the same side of the boat "for fear of capsizing."[26] The conditions for the passengers were difficult. "Refugees' bunks were just bare shelves. They had to supply their own bedding, never could take their clothes off, had no washing facilities, and . . . slept packed like sardines." Indeed, "[r]efugees covered every inch of space. Sleeping quarters were any place they could find that was long enough to lie down on. Bunks accommodated most of them, but the rest had to cuddle in where they could. They even slept on the flying bridge over the wheelhouse," an open area reserved for observations by the Captain and officers of the ship.[27]

Crew member and photo-journalist Wallace Litwin, of the North American Newspaper Alliance, recounted that there was a group of Russian partisans, including a former bomber pilot, aboard.[28] One of the two physicians onboard who set up a makeshift infirmary (there were five pregnant women passengers)[29] was a former Lieutenant in the Red Army.[30] Among the passengers there was a Russian officer who had deserted due to antisemitic fellow officers. In Rifkin's novel, one of the Russian veterans explained he had gotten "sick of the other officers calling him a kike."[31] David Booker, then a thirty-two-year-old sculptor, before the war had been a student of the Polish sculptor Bakrokev, and during the war he served in

---

24   Lazar, *Immigrant Ship "Ben Hecht,"* 10.
25   Ben-Ami, *Years of Wrath,* 403.
26   "A M/V BEN HECHT Story."
27   Nicolai, "I Ran Britain's Palestine Blockade," 33, 25–26.
28   Zaar, *Rescue,* 220.
29   Kaplan Oral History, part 1, MZ.
30   Méry, *Let My People Go,* 23.
31   Rifkin, *What Ship,* 223–224.

the Red Army and fought at Stalingrad. He had deserted and traveled to Paris to return to sculpture, and there he joined a group of immigrants on the *Ben Hecht* who had not been associated with Revisionist Zionists.[32]

When asked about the mood of the ship, Levitan thought "a lot of the people were faithless. You know what could happen to them. What could happen to them worse? It already happened to them."[33] One of the passengers had survived in hiding by eating a dog that had consumed human corpses.[34] A French Jew who had been active in the Resistance experienced lasting mental effects of trauma after he and his sister were sadistically tortured by depraved German soldiers; their fate was worse than the Talmud's description of the son and daughter of Rabbi Yishmaël, who became captives to the Romans upon the destruction of the Second Temple and at least passed away before being exploited.[35] A Jewish Frenchwoman whose husband had been killed in the Resistance decided to leave for Palestine. Upon emerging from hiding, she encountered antisemitism among her fellow townspeople.[36] Crewmember David Kaplan heard second-hand that a Nazi had smuggled himself aboard, but was recognized by a former victim, and was thrown overboard by the passengers.[37]

But all was not dour during the voyage to Palestine. A wedding took place aboard the ship.[38] A seventeen-year-old French citizen, Henrietta Goldenberg, had the most romantic story: she had survived the war in hiding in a convent in relative luxury and was engaged to a Palestinian Jew, Bart Stroe of Tel Aviv, whom she had met while he served in the British Army's Royal Engineers as a mine sapper.[39] One of the Gentile crew members recounted that "[a]t first the refugees were inclined to be suspicious of us non-Jews; they couldn't understand why we had volunteered for the trip. But after they got the idea, which was they were hot-angry at the way the Jews of Europe had been treated, they thawed. From then on we were buddies."[40]

---

32   "The Pesach Seder in Cyprus Camp," *Al HaMishmar*, Monday, April 14, 1947, 4 (Hebrew).
33   Levitan Oral History, USHMM.
34   Méry, *Let My People Go*, 44.
35   Talmud Bavli *Gittin* 58a; Méry, *Let My People Go*, 61.
36   Méry, *Laissez passer*, 85.
37   Editor's discussion with Abbe Kaplan, June 17, 2020.
38   Méry, *Let My People Go*, 104–110.
39   Nicolai, "I Ran Britain's Palestine Blockade," 29; Méry, *Let My People Go*, 50–51.
40   Nicolai, "I Ran Britain's Palestine Blockade," 28.

Eri Jabotinsky spent the night after the *Ben Hecht* sailed in Marseilles, and was awakened early in the morning by a radio message from the ship that one of its engines was wrecked and requesting instructions. He consulted with his associates and ordered the return of the ship to port.[41] The ship's forward piston oil-pump rod of the port (left) engine had broken and pierced a hole in a crankcase an hour after sunrise the morning after the ship left Port-de-Bouc.[42] Crew member Shepard Rifkin's novel suggests that the breakdown was due to sabotage by French repair workers who had been bribed by British intelligence.[43] Another crew member stated in an interview that French workmen who were retrofitting the ship at port must have, "while they were doing some overhauling of the engines, sawed through, cut through with a hacksaw, one of the piston connecting rods on the twin diesels."[44] The British had certainly been collecting information on the ship,[45] including the ship's erstwhile captain Clay, who was known to the British "to be a tough customer."[46] The ship was in the middle channel on either side of which was "a vast mine field that had not yet been cleared," and the starboard (right) engine had failed several times during the Atlantic crossing. If it failed again at the same time as the port engine, they might drift into a mine. This would have been disastrous, as the small ship was not divided into water-tight compartments, and there appears to have been only two lifeboats and four rafts aboard, hardly enough for the over six hundred passengers and crew.[47] The route between the mine fields had been chosen to avoid suspicion, but, as Nicolai later recounted, "[a] mine that would only partially damage a larger vessel would blow the tiny *Ben Hecht* to hell."[48] Even before the ill fortune suffered by the engines, Kaplan later explained "this ship, with both diesels, never made ten knots. Got to eleven. It didn't make nine miles an hour" even though "we were advertised as a sleek, black gunrunner."

Levitan, now functioning as captain, had to consider the possibility that a returning voyage on a single engine would be just as hazardous as

---

41   Jabotinsky, "Request on the 'Ben Hecht' Transport in France."
42   Rifkin, *What Ship*, 202; Kaplan, "This Is the Way It Was," 3.
43   Rifkin, *What Ship*, 202.
44   Kaplan Oral History, part 1, MZ.
45   Méry, *Laissez passer*, 44.
46   Stewart, *Palestine Patrol*, 97.
47   Rifkin, *What Ship*, 201.
48   Nicolai, "I Ran Britain's Palestine Blockade," 26.

continuing on their original journey in that condition.[49] The chief engineer, Haakom Lilliby, and Erling Sorensen, the first assistant engineer, were diesel engine experts who were being compensated for their service.[50] The engineers made their own specialized tools to conduct the repairs.[51] Later in the day, the ship informed Jabotinsky that they would repair the motor in twenty-four hours and that the ship could persist in the voyage, and Jabotinsky told them to proceed.[52] Radioman Kaplan recorded in a memoir that "Louis Brettschneider, our second assistant and Hank Mandel, under terrible conditions, removed the damaged piston and patched the hole in the crankcase."[53] Working forty uninterrupted hours, the engine crew repurposed deck plates and hammered them into a patch which would not leak oil.[54] Kaplan describes that "Lou Brettschneider and the two Norwegian" engineers "did a job that must go down in the annals of history in marine engineering of making the repair underway, at sea, with a load like that. And making a patch job. And getting it working again. On a ship that had very little facilities, such as we did. We weren't prepared for that kind of repair."[55] Decades later, Brettschneider, who spent his later career as a civil engineer for the US Army in Germany, examined the ship—then a ferry between Naples and Capri—and discovered that the same patch was still in place. "They hadn't needed to do anything more than what these guys did at sea under terrible conditions," Kaplan mused. "So, we had some pretty good seaman mechanics."[56]

The ship experienced bad weather, which caused the water supply to be contaminated, and the passengers suffered from seasickness.[57] "We sailed," Levitan remembered, "across the Mediterranean and then . . . our course that I laid out took us from France up to the north side of the Mediterranean to the area of Turkey, and then we turned around and headed to the sea lane, going from Turkey to the Suez Canal. We tried to blend in with the traffic and when we got opposite" Palestine "we turned ninety degrees and

49   See Rifkin, *What Ship*, 202.
50   Kaplan, "This Is the Way It Was," 3.
51   Rifkin, *What Ship*, 202.
52   Jabotinsky, "Request on the 'Ben Hecht' Transport in France."
53   Kaplan, "This Is the Way It Was," 3.
54   Rifkin, *What Ship*, 202.
55   Kaplan, "This Is the Way It Was," 3.
56   Kaplan Oral History, part 1, MZ.
57   Silverstone, *Our Only Refuge*, 23.

. . . headed into Palestine."[58] The *Ben Hecht* arrived in Palestinian waters just south of Tel Aviv eight days after leaving port in France, on March 8.[59] One plan, according to the account in Rifkin's novel, was for the ship to run aground unto the Palestine shore.[60] However, Levitan did not intend to beach the *Ben Hecht* to land her passengers. It had been planned that the *Ben Hecht* would come close to shore off of the coast of Netanya and small boats would transfer the immigrants to land.[61] Netanya had been a landing place of Revisionist-organized illegal immigration ships before World War II.[62] Herb Silverman, a member of an audience who listened to Levitan speak about the *Ben Hecht* in 1987, claimed that he was waiting on the Palestine shore to help transport the refugees from the ship to land, but he too was captured.[63]

The emergency repairs rendered the engine operable with only five cylinders at a reduced speed, delaying the arrival of the ship near Palestinian waters by a day longer than the seven that had been allocated to the trip by the planners in Paris.[64] *Ben Hecht* crew members believed that the Irgun was not aware of that delay because of a failure to make contact with the Irgun radio operator in Palestine assigned to the *Ben Hecht*, much to the chagrin of David Kaplan, one of the vessel's radio operators.[65] The delay, caused by the possibly sabotaged engine and the lack of radio contact with the Irgun in Palestine, had serious operational consequences, as a series of Irgun attacks on British police stations and the cutting of electric power in Tel Aviv were not successfully coordinated with the ship's approach to the coast. The ship was not yet near Tel Aviv at the prearranged time, and the attacks failed to provide the expected distraction that might have allowed the *Ben Hecht* to attempt to land its passengers.

The plan which the crew was aware of was that the Irgun would attempt to coordinate a series of attacks on British installations to coincide with the anticipated arrival of the *Ben Hecht* off Tel Aviv on Friday evening with

58 Levitan Oral History, USHMM.
59 Jabotinsky, "Request on the 'Ben Hecht' Transport in France"; Levitan Oral History, USHMM.
60 Rifkin, *What Ship*, 235, 228.
61 Méry, *Let My People Go*, 133; Horev, *I Will Gather Them*, 189.
62 Shari, *The Cyprus Exile*, 81–83, quoted in Lazar, *Immigrant Ship "Ben Hecht."*
63 Hilary Saperstein, "Captain Faced Capture to Rescue Refugees," *Jewish Journal*, Thursday, April 23, 1987, Newspaper Clippings file, Bob Levitan collection, USHMM.
64 Kaplan, "This Is the Way It Was," 3; Méry, *Let My People Go*, 78.
65 Kaplan Oral History, part 1, MZ.

the intention of diverting attention and increasing the odds the *Ben Hecht* could break through the blockade.[66] The crew had been unsuccessful in communicating with the Irgun in Palestine. They did not know that the Irgun decided to strike the next night, Saturday. However, Jacques Méry reports that the Betar chaperones told the passengers that the Irgun would attack Saturday night.[67] Because Méry published the account shortly after the voyage, he may have been writing with the knowledge of subsequent events. It is also possible, however, that the Betar leaders on board knew more of the Irgun's plans because they perhaps had means of communicating with the Irgun that the American crew members were not told about.

On March 5, 1947, Leo Cohen, a Jewish Agency official, met with British Under-Secretary in Chief Secretariat Vivian Fox-Strangways, and told him they were aware of the imminent arrival of an illegal immigration ship organized by Peter Bergson. The British government felt that the passengers were terrorists, and would have a bad influence on the other illegal immigrants already imprisoned on Cyprus if they were interned there. Fox-Strangways asked for "advice" on how to deal with them. After consulting with Golda Myerson, who later became Israeli Prime Minister Golda Meir, Leo Cohen telephoned the following response the next day, on March 6: "The Jewish Agency is always prepared to discuss all aspects of Jewish immigration, but can't be expected to advise on a case of particularly difficulty outside of the context of immigration, as this is presented before us." Under-Secretary Fox-Strangeways took the implicit refusal with good grace, and replied that he understood that from the perspective of the Jewish Agency that the British government's approach in the matter could seem "unfair" and he did not wish to appear to the Jewish Agency that the request for advice was a trap.[68] In hindsight, the British government may have hoped to secure the Jewish Agency's cooperation with the expulsion of the *Ben Hecht* passengers back to Europe, the policy that they eventually imposed upon the illegal immigrants of the *Exodus 1947*.

The Saturday morning of March 8, 1947, an elderly rabbi and about twenty immigrants gathered, along with two sailors, probably Henry Mandel and Wallace Litwin. French journalist Méry described the scene in detail:

---

66   Mandel Interview by Goldschmidt Magid, 2006.
67   Méry, *Let My People Go*, 154.
68   Shari, *The Cyprus Exile*, quoted in Lazar, *Immigrant Ship "Ben Hecht,"* 16–17.

Never have prayers been more passionate than theirs. Never could the divine blessing be implied with so much ardor! Standing at the head of the *Ben-Hecht,* standing out against the blue sky, the faithful sway back and forth, kissing their Bibles [probably actually prayer books] bitterly, striking their breasts savagely. They sing without worrying about the neighbor. Then there are murmurs, and voices that get exasperated . . . Wallace's [Méry did not use the real names of crewmen in his book] face disappears under the folds of the tallit. And they glorify the LORD, and proclaim his power, and abjure his heresy, and draw with all his soul unto mercy. And when the Rabbi turns to the spardeck, arms crossed, white beard spread on the chest, I think I see Moses leading his people. "O Lord," preaches the old man, "grant the vows of our community. Our bodies suffered, our souls were tried. The wickedness of your enemies has been unlimited. Our fathers, our brothers, our sisters, our children, have perished by the millions. You know it. But you wanted Israel to stand among the nations. And it is a divine miracle that keeps Israel! Look at us, you, the Eternal. Viewing our little flock with no other monument than its faith, with no other force than its hope! Despite the executioners, the cremation ovens, we are there, raising the flag on which is written the ineffable name! O, lead us to freedom, to the land of Moses, this Promised Land. We want the wolf to no longer eat the lamb and the iron of the spear to be beaten into plowshares to salute Messianic times.[69]

---

69   Méry, *Let My People Go,* 129.

Chapter 12

Piracy on the High Seas

Spread over us the protection of thy peace; direct us aright through thine own good counsel; save us for thy Name's sake; be thou a shield about us; remove from us every enemy, pestilence, sword, famine, and sorrow; remove also the adversary from before us and from behind us. O shelter us beneath the shadow of thy wings.

—From the evening prayer service[1]

Freddy Liebreich, a one-time Jewish illegal immigrant who also subsequently served in the Royal Navy, identified documents[2] demonstrating that after a meeting of the British Cabinet on December 19, 1946, it had been decided "not to proceed with the Admiralty proposal that certain categories of illegal immigrant ships be arrested on the high seas and diverted to Cyprus."[3] The Admiralty was reluctant publicly "to open the door to developments in international maritime law which may work to our disadvantage,"[4] as the British government had "recently taken a very high line about international law at sea in the Corfu mining case" and the traditional 3-mile coastal territorial limit that favored a sea power like Britain. The Admiralty's proposal, rejected by the Lord Chancellor in December 1946, had "dealt with the arrest on the high seas of ships that had no status and no

1   Joseph J. Hertz, *The Authorized Daily Prayer Book Revised Edition* (New York: Bloch Publishing Company, 5715/1955), 313.

2   Liebreich, *Britain's Naval and Political Reaction*, 126–127, 143.

3   British Public Records Office ADM 116/5648, 1297582, C.M. (46) 107th Conclusions; Minute to Prime Minister, April 30, 1947.

4   C. J. Jeffries, Colonial Office, memorandum to J. G. Lange, Esq., CB, labeled "Secret," April 5, 1947, British Public Records Office ADM 116/5648, 1297582, Cabinet 350.

protector, and so could not claim the benefits of international law."[5] These secret British policy documents demonstrate that the British government believed that simply arresting a ship in international waters—which the British defined as three miles from the coast line, because such a restrictive limit gave the freest hand to the Royal Navy—was illegal, and was a step they hesitated to take publicly.

The practical tactics of the blockade forces, which did not have to be officially acknowledged, was quite a different matter. In practice, the Royal Navy did intercept Jewish illegal immigrant ships beyond the three-mile limit, including the *Ben Hecht*. In 1946, the Royal Navy, an officer later recalled, "normally had one destroyer on the three mile limit and another one about five miles further out at sea to try and divert" illegal immigrant ships.[6] Jewish illegal immigration ships were usually spotted by British patrol aircraft, which guided destroyers to the Jewish ships, which shadowed them until they were boarded, theoretically inside the three mile international territorial waters limit recognized under international law by the British government at the time.[7] British Admiralty memoranda from late 1946 demonstrate that the British Navy felt it needed to board ships outside the strictly limited territorial waters as it argued that faster and heavier ships were now being used by the illegal immigrants.[8] The British position at the time was that the three-mile limit from the shore was the extent of territorial waters, though it was already at that time being challenged by legal academics as outdated.[9] The ranking officer of the British Fleet in the Mediterranean felt that a ship that could travel twelve knots needed to be boarded twelve miles from the coast in order to assure that it would be intercepted.

Fritz Liebreich, who wrote an authoritative book on the subject, discovered and discussed Admiralty and Colonial Office memoranda, which shows that British officials thought an illegal Jewish immigrant "ship's master would be unlikely to know whether he has been stopped, just outside or just inside territorial waters," a view that had been put "privately to the

---

5   J. G. Lange, memo to Sir C. J. Jeffries, K.C.M.G, O.B.E, labeled "Top Secret," April 15, 1947, British Public Records Office ADM 116/5648, 1297582.

6   Alan Tyler interview by Mike Stone, September 20, 2017, https://reminiscences. uk/2017/09/20/alan-tyler/.

7   R. Dare Wilson, *Cordon and Search: With the 6th Airborne Division in Palestine 1945–48* (Nashville, TN: The Battery Press, 1984), 109, facing page 110.

8   Liebreich, *Britain's Naval and Political Reaction*, 323 n.49.

9   Ibid., 327 n.133.

Commander-in-Chief Mediterranean by the Vice Chief of Naval Staff and had become the basis for the Royal Navy's subsequent campaign against the illegal immigrants." Liebreich concluded that internal British government debates on arrests of the illegal immigrant ships on the high seas "were largely disregarded and proved without much practical influence on the issue."[10] However, as a great international law scholar later wrote when discussing another blockade, "at the level of the use of force in the classic sense . . . legal norm and moral precept are two expressions of the same deep human imperative."[11] The boarding of the Jewish illegal immigrant vessels by the Royal Navy was often opposed, and the often violent resistance resulted in casualties on both sides. The illegal immigrant ships needed to be towed to Haifa because the crews usually sabotaged the engines and threw away the radio equipment of the ships. The capture of the *Ben Hecht* fell into this general pattern. Only one ship, the Haganah-organized *Ulua* (the *Haim Arlosoroff*), succeeded in breaching the British Blockade during its height and managed to beach itself on the shore on February 28, 1947.[12] The Royal Navy's failed attempt to intercept the *Ulua* had taken place within the three-mile territorial limit. And there had been several sailors who were seriously injured during the attempt to board the illegal immigrant ship.[13] The British were apparently not willing to take that risk again.

The three British destroyers that ultimately boarded the *Ben Hecht/ Abril* off the coast of Palestine were still outside of the three-mile territorial limit recognized by the British at the time, and thus in international waters. The Royal Navy was intentionally violating their own professed interpretation of the international law of the sea. The Royal Navy's official account of the capture of the *Ben Hecht* consistently claims a later sequence of events than the timeline contemporaneously described by *Ben Hecht* crew members. This is significant because the British version of events implies that the *Ben Hecht* was much closer to the territorial waters of Palestine as defined by the British than was actually the case. The following description of the episode represents a reconstruction of events based on the weight of the available evidence:

---

10 Ibid., 125–127, 143.
11 Abram Chayes, *The Cuban Missile Crisis: International Crises and the Role of Law* (New York and London: Oxford University Press, 1974), 40:
12 Wilson, *Palestine Patrol*, 109.
13 Ibid., 243.

As the refugee boat approached within sixty miles of Haifa, two British Lancaster patrol bomber airplanes spotted the *Abril / Ben Hecht* at 10:40 a.m. on Saturday, March 8, 1947,[14] though one *Abril* sailor's account describes the sighting as having taken place at 10 a.m.[15] The second plane came within fifty feet of the ship, and photographed the *Abril / Ben Hecht*.[16] "As soon as the British airplanes flew, kept overhead, and then the British ships came," Levitan "knew we were captured. And that was the end of it. And I was disappointed. But I just did my job."[17]

The Royal Navy destroyer HMS *Chieftain* came in sight at 12:15 p.m.[18] Another destroyer, the HMS *Chevron*, arrived at 2:15 p.m. on the starboard (right) side of the *Abril/Ben Hecht*.[19] At that point the ship was 50 miles from the Palestinian coast.[20] The Royal Navy destroyers "converged on the Ben Hecht, warning her not to enter Palestinian waters, despite the request to land for food and water and supplies," a *Ben Hecht* crewmember later recalled.[21] A destroyer signaled "You are suspected of carrying illegal immigrants; it is my duty to inform you that once you enter Palestine territorial waters, I shall be forced to arrest you."[22] A British destroyer signaled the question "What ship? Where bound?," asking for the ship's name and destination, and the reply was that the name of the ship was the *Abril* and that the destination was Arica, Chile on the Pacific coast of South America.[23] That answer was hardly plausible, because at that point, Levitan was navigating the ship towards the direction of the Strait of Gibraltar, away from the Suez Canal, in an attempt to throw the British off the ship's trail.[24] "There was a long pause while they tried to understand why we were heading into the Mediterranean when Chile was in the other direction. At Bob Levitan's orders, I ignored the frantic signaling that followed," Kaplan described in a memoir of the journey.[25] "In the

---

14 Stewart, *Palestine Patrol*, 97; Rifkin, *What Ship*, 236; Nicolai, "I Ran Britain's Palestine, 26.
15 Liebman, "'Ben Hecht' Purser Poses as Refugee."
16 Rifkin, *What Ship*, 237.
17 Levitan Oral History, USHMM.
18 Rifkin, *What Ship*, 238.
19 Stewart, *Palestine Patrol*, 97; Rifkin, *What Ship*, 238.
20 Liebman, "'Ben Hecht' Purser Poses as Refugee."
21 "A M/V BEN HECHT Story."
22 Rifkin, *What Ship*, 239; Levitan notes for synagogue presentation, 6.
23 Rifkin, *What Ship*, 237; Kaplan, "This Is the Way It Was," 2; Levitan notes for synagogue presentation, 6.
24 Levitan notes for synagogue presentation, 6.
25 Kaplan, "This Is the Way It Was," 2.

meantime," the crew held "quick conferences with the Jewish leaders. The British might use tear gas; they might do anything."[26] Despite the British warning, the crew felt that at that point they had no choice and continued on their course.[27]

A rabbi who had been conducting a class for children about the biblical history of the Israelites throughout the voyage concluded the last session by noting that his holy book stated "that since the destruction of the Betar Fortress during the Bar Kochba revolt, Israelites have made no more attempts to regain their independence and Israel ceases to be a nation . . . this is no longer true today." A Betar escort explained the strategy to the passengers: "The English have no rights on this boat" because it was sailing in international waters, but "attempting to flee would be useless" due to the greater speed of the British ship. Some of the passengers disagreed with the decision not to physically resist the British boarding of the ship: "Can we accept to let ourselves be arrested as thieves? Have we so much patience, so much acceptance of sacrifice to quietly go to the English?" said one dissenter. "We will fight as the Jews fought the other boarded boats," said another passenger from Brussels, though eventually the Betar escorts' exhortations for non-violence were heeded.[28]

As Kaplan remembered,

> [T]hey communicated with us with a bullhorn, telling us that "You are approaching Palestinian territory water." We asked them, we said, "Look. We have no more water. We're running out of food. We need medical attention. Can we please go to . . . ?" "No, if you enter, we'll have to—if you enter Palestinian waters, we'll have to board you. And take your ship over." Now, we kept the dialogue going as long as we could. And we kept going, very slowly. But everybody was keeping pace with us.[29]

The *Abril / Ben Hecht* stopped sailing and the passengers were sent below.[30] The path of the *Ben Hecht* was blocked by the British destroyers at 4:30 p.m., approximately 10.3 nautical miles from the coast line of Palestine according

---

26   Nicolai, "I Ran Britain's Palestine Blockade," 26.
27   Levitan notes for synagogue presentation, 6.
28   Méry, *Let My People Go*, 147, 140, 154.
29   Kaplan Oral History, part 1, MZ.
30   Stewart, *Palestine Patrol*, 98.

to one *Ben Hecht* crewmember's account,[31] or 13 miles according to another (note that nautical miles are longer than conventional miles).[32]

The *Abril / Ben Hecht* then requested permission to enter Haifa, with the explanation that provisions and supplies were low, but the British again replied that the ship would be arrested if it entered the territorial waters of Palestine.[33] The *Abril / Ben Hecht* traveled north, parallel to the coast, until it reached a location straight away from Tel Aviv. However, the attempted ruse of concealing the *Ben Hecht*'s identity from the destroyers calling for the ship's surrender, with the intention of waiting in international waters until dark when it would attempt a fast approach to the coast, did not succeed.[34] According to one account, Levitan, the ship's navigator and the highest-ranking crew member, at that juncture also contemplated sailing away from Palestine, deeper into international waters, to evade British surveillance so that a second attempt to slip through the blockade could be attempted. However, the chief of the Betar escorts of the refugees insisted that the ship head straight to Tel Aviv in order to arrive in coordination with the Irgun's planned attack on British installations. The Betar escort argued that the Royal Navy destroyers would continue to follow the *Ben Hecht*; moreover, the ship did not have enough fresh water to continue the journey[35]—one of the two fresh water tanks had leaked overboard.[36] The decision was made to attempt the final run to the Palestine coast because food supplies were too low aboard the ship to further evade the British blockade, even though the British planes flying overhead and the Royal Navy destroyers shadowing the refugee boat made capture almost certain if the *Ben Hecht* made a final run to Palestine.[37] With only one day's food supply remaining for the passengers, Levitan felt he had no choice but to turn ninety degrees and start heading towards the Palestinian coast.[38] The refugees put on all the clothes they owned in the hope that the ship could manage to run aground and enable them to wade on to a beach and escape into Palestine.[39]

31   Kaplan, "This Is the Way It Was," 3.
32   Liebman, "'Ben Hecht' Purser Poses as Refugee."
33   Rifkin, *What Ship*, 240.
34   Horev, *I Will Gather Them*, 189–190.
35   Méry, *Let My People Go*, 147.
36   Kaplan, "This Is the Way It Was," 3.
37   Saperstein, "Captain Faced Capture."
38   Levitan notes for synagogue presentation.
39   Nicolai, "I Ran Britain's Palestine Blockade," 39; Rifkin, *What Ship*, 237.

When the British then asked for the nationality of the *Ben Hecht*, the ship's Honduran flag was lowered and Betar escorts hoisted the Zionist blue and white Star of David flag upon the illegal immigrant ship in its stead.[40] The Betar escorts led the passengers in singing the Zionist anthem, *Hatikvah*, and the Zionist Revisionist Party's hymn.[41]

A third destroyer, HMS *Chivalrous*, and the frigate HMS *St. Bride* came in sight at 5:30 p.m.[42] The *Chieftain* and *Chevron* positioned themselves on either side of the *Ben Hecht*, while the *Chivalrous* took a position 300 fathoms in front of the refugee boat.[43] The sizable flotilla of the three destroyers and the frigate presented an overwhelming display of British force. "You're not gonna argue with three destroyers," felt one crewmember. Kaplan related that Yossi Almog (who later commanded the *Abril /Ben-Hecht* when it became part of the Israeli Navy, and went on to lead the Clandestine Immigration and Naval Museum in Haifa), was later given a photograph taken by a Royal Air Force plane that showed the former yacht surrounded by the much larger naval vessels: "You see the little *Ben Hecht*, a tiny little ship in the middle. And these enormous destroyers all around it. There was . . . [a] French newspaper that had a picture that looked just like that. Here's a tiny little rowboat. And these enormous battleships in the Mediterranean. And with the caption 'They threaten the Mediterranean.'"[44] The cartoon, which reflected French public opinion, appeared during the *Exodus 1947* affair.[45]

The *Ben Hecht* was "now within sight of Tel Aviv, but it was hopeless to run for it. So we decided to surrender," a crew member later recounted. "It was night now; we prepared to blink acceptance."[46] The lead escort of the passengers encouraged them as they awaited the British attack: "From tonight in Tel Aviv, the Irgun will avenge us. Listen to us! The Irgun will be going to Tel Aviv tonight at a British barracks."[47] The British announced over loudspeakers "We know that you are illegal immigrants, and if you

40 "Abril Refugees Deported," *Palestine Post*, Monday, March 10, 1947; "'Abril' Immigrants to Cyprus," *Haboker*, Monday, March 10, 1947, front page (Hebrew).
41 Méry, *Let My People Go*, 144, 155; Kaplan, "This Is the Way It Was," 3.
42 Stewart, *Palestine Patrol*, 98; Rifkin, *What Ship*, 239.
43 Méry, *Let My People Go*, 148.
44 Kaplan Oral History, part 1, MZ; Stewart, *Palestine Patrol*, 97.
45 Bethel, *Palestine Triangle*, 341.
46 Nicolai, "I Ran Britain's Palestine Blockade," 26.
47 Méry, *Let My People Go*, 145.

dare to resist, we will not hesitate to use weapons."[48] *Ben Hecht* crew members knew what would be the bloody result of armed resistance, and gave an instruction that all weapons be thrown overboard. Rifkin's fictionalized account of the voyage of the *Ben Hecht* confirms that some members of the crew tried to persuade the Betar escorts that armed resistance would lead to great bloodshed: "the Limeys will get all excited and they'll start firing, and they got Stens. I don't want to get shot, even to put this heap on the beach, and lots of the people are going to get hurt." According to that account, shortly before the boarding by the British seizure of the ship, the Betar commander onboard ordered his men to throw their weapons into the sea.[49] Ultimately, it appears that Betar leader Baruch Giladi's (Gideon Abramowitz) standing instructions to the Betar escorts before the start of the journey—to not fire on the British—were followed, rather than the Irgun's plans for armed resistance. "They were not Irgun men. They were Betar men and they threw the weapons into the sea," Irgun operative HaCohen-Brandes later told an interviewer.[50]

Ultimately, eight separate attacks in Tel Aviv and along the coast of Palestine on British installations took place on that Saturday night, March 8, 1947, which could have served as diversionary attacks to distract attention from the *Ben Hecht's* landing of passengers, but the ship's crew was not informed of that plan. The casualties numbered four Jews and one British soldier killed, and approximately fifty Jews, British, and Arabs wounded:

> Among the assaults which occurred after electricity was cut in Tel Aviv were attacks on Citrus House (the British headquarters in Tel Aviv), a police station, and a Shell oil company tank which was blown apart. In response, Palestine High Commissioner Allan Cunningham called an emergency meeting of his executive civilian and military commanders. The five Jews and one Arab woman killed, along with eighteen Jews and Arabs wounded, were passersby uninvolved in the attacks who were shot in indiscriminate shooting by British troops.[51]

---

48 Lazar, *Immigrant Ship "Ben Hecht,"* 12.
49 Rifkin, *What Ship*, 208, 210, 244.
50 HaCohen-Brandes Oral History, 14, MZ.
51 Nicolai, "I Ran Britain's Palestine Blockade," 34; Wilson, *Cordon*, 262; "American Crew Members of Immigrant Ship under Arrest," *PM*, March 10, 1947, 1, 2, and 7, United Press, *PM* reel 53, 3/2–4/30/47, NYPL; Eliav Simon, "Five Killed in Attack on British Tel Aviv HA," *Sunday News*, March 9, 1947, Bob Levitan collection, USHMM; "Wild British Shooting Kills—Wounds Innocent Bystanders," Palcor, dateline March 10,

Before any surrender of the illegal immigrant ship could take place, the Royal Navy destroyer *Chieftain* went alongside the *Ben Hecht*. As nightfall approached and the Sabbath drew to a close, the British destroyers had nine-feet-high canvas covers fringing from their bows to conceal the boarding parties on deck, and shields on their fore (forward part of the ship) attached to the railings.[52] "The leading destroyer was unable to see our message [of surrender] because she had drifted behind our smokestack, which hid our signal light," recalled a *Ben Hecht* crew member. "When the commander threw his searchlight on our propeller, which was peaceably churning water, he figured we were going to try and make a get-away."[53]

The *Chieftain* rammed the refugee boat and succeeded in landing a boarding party of thirty-two officers and men and, in the euphemistic language of the Royal Navy history of its campaign against the illegal immigrants, "push[ed] the illegal vessel round to a westerly heading," and the ramming caused "slight structural damage."[54] The Royal Navy account states that the boarding took place at 7:15 p.m. after the refugee ship increased speed from ten, to thirteen, to fourteen knots and headed to Tel Aviv.[55] According to the *Ben Hecht*'s log, the British boarded the *Ben Hecht* about 10.2 miles off the coast. "Now, that's piracy on the high seas," Kaplan later described, because that was beyond the international three-mile coastal territorial limit recognized by Britain at the time.[56] One crew member, probably also Kaplan, later lamented that "[a]t 10.3 nautical miles from the shore, in international waters, the British boarded the ship, an act of piracy on the high seas, and no one to complain to."[57] Louis Binder thought the ship "was about 10 miles off Tel Aviv" when it was captured.[58]

Levitan later recalled:

> In fact, it was twilight, it was just getting dark. And you can hear the steel railings crunching and the side of the ship denting . . . These British ships which had huge canvas on each ship. When they got along side of us the

1947; "599 Visa-Less Jews Seized on 'Ben Hecht' Deported," *The B'nai B'rith Messenger*, Friday, March 14, 1947, 1, Palcor, dateline Haifa, March 10, 1947.

52 Rifkin, *What Ship*, 240; Levitan notes for synagogue presentation, 6.
53 Nicolai, "I Ran Britain's Palestine Blockade," 26.
54 Stewart, *Palestine Patrol*, 97.
55 Ibid., 98.
56 Kaplan Oral History, part 1, MZ.
57 A M/V BEN HECHT Story."
58 Halkenhauser, "Ben Hecht Seamen Tell of Seizure."

canvas dropped, and they had high pressure water hose sweeping our deck clearing our deck of people. There were no people on deck; I had them all below [deck]. But they swept our deck with these high-pressure water hoses. And then when they were right on top of us twenty British Royal Marines jumped from each of the British ships onto our ship.[59]

The boarders who jumped on deck of the *Ben Hecht* were armed with lead-tipped clubs, bayonets, pistols, gas masks, tear gas grenades, batons, javelins, and sub-machine guns.[60] The ship fell rapidly under the control of the sixty British Royal Marines. Levitan later recorded that "[d]uring this operation we were flooded by Cordon One lights which threw a high intensity light and light everything in a brilliant blue-white light while the shadows cast upon them were sharp and dark. It was weird. Day and night all at once!"[61] After the initial boarding party, according to the Royal Navy's official account, thirty more Royal Marines and sailors came from the *Chevron* and another twenty from the *Chivalrous*.[62]

***

Alan Tyler, a Jewish Royal Navy officer and World War II veteran who had begun his naval training at the tender age of thirteen, was born in London in 1924. His family were members of West London Synagogue, where he was confirmed and later married. Several months before the capture of the *Ben Hecht*, when Tyler joined the *Chevron* as a Lieutenant in the Summer of 1946, Tyler's commanding officer casually said after the King David Hotel bombing, "'I suppose you're prepared to come to Palestine to do the patrol,' I said of course, because we weren't very pleased with the IZL (Irgun) and the others."[63] Tyler regretted decades later "that the Government's arbitrary restriction on Jewish refugees entering Palestine provoked the violence which put our men's lives at risk but I do not regret my part in fighting that violence."[64]

---

59 Levitan Oral History, USHMM.
60 Horev, *I Will Gather Them*, 190; Nicolai, "I Ran Britain's Palestine Blockade," 26; Levitan notes for synagogue presentation, 6.
61 Levitan notes for synagogue presentation, 7.
62 Stewart, *Palestine Patrol*, 97.
63 Alan Tyler, "The View from a 'Brit,'" *AVI Newsletter*, Summer 1999, 13, AJHS Archive, reprinted from *Manna* (Winter 1997).
64 Tyler interview by Stone, 2017; Tyler, "The View from a 'Brit,'" 14.

Tyler later recounted the interception by the destroyer on which he was serving, HMS *Chevron*, of "a smart modern diesel yacht called *Abril*" flying the Honduran flag. Tyler addressed the ship in English and in German through a loudspeaker with a standard warning that the illegal immigrants "would not be allowed to land and should not resist as force would be met with force." He regretted the use of German, the "language of the hated Nazis," but Tyler thought it was necessary because "it meant that most of the immigrants knew the position and could not easily be misled by trouble makers."[65] A journalist aboard the *Ben Hecht* wrote that the British officer on loudspeaker offered to repeat his message in Yiddish, which led one passenger to whisper as the ship attempted to evade the destroyer that the British must have a recorded message in Yiddish "unless a Jew, a traitor, accompanies them on their ships."[66]

***

The Royal Marines "went right down to the engine room and took over. Another crew went right up to the bridge and took over."[67] When the boarding party took over the bridge, Jeno Berkovitz, who was at the helm, yelled "What the hell's going on here?'"[68] As Levitan later recounted, "by that time there were three British ships and sixty British Royal Marines on our ship and they had control of everything. The people, the bridge, the engine room."[69]

One of the women passengers was in the midst of childbirth and had been lying on the deck in a space specially reserved for her by a doctor. The doctor screamed at the British not to blast her with high pressure water hoses, but they did, forcing her to flee below deck in the midst of her labor crawling on her hands and knees. The captured passengers were crammed into small rooms with one hundred people and guarded by three armed British marines outside each room.[70] The passengers sat quietly while occasionally flashing looks of hatred at the guards. When a passenger asked why

---

65   Tyler, "The View from a 'Brit.'"
66   Méry, *Let My People Go*, 153.
67   Levitan Oral History, USHMM.
68   Nicolai, "I Ran Britain's Palestine Blockade," 26; Dr. Rafael Medoff, "Sailor's Role in the Birth of Israel," *The Jewish Star*, May 1, 2009 / 7 Iyar 5769, https://www.thejewishstar.com/stories/sailors-role-in-the-birth-of-israel,758?.
69   Levitan Oral History, USHMM.
70   Liebman, "'Ben Hecht' Purser Poses as Refugee"; Lazar, *Immigrant Ship "Ben Hecht*," 12.

they were imprisoned, he was clubbed on the head with a rubber truncheon. Enraged passengers began to rush the British, but Liebman recounted that a young passenger who had been a partisan in the forests of Poland and Russia calmed the crowd by shouting "Not yet! Our day will come to fight. Wait until we have our guns such as they. Our day will come and we will not forget."[71]

The crew members were ordered to report to the wheelhouse, where they were confined.[72] Kaplan "kept sending SOS messages telling the radio world of this attack until a marine pointed his rifle" at him in the radio shack.[73] Kaplan noted that the British Royal Marines who boarded the ship "were very good. They came on prepared for all kinds of trouble, but they were not abusive. They were not brutal."[74] In December 1946 the *Chevron* rescued nearly 800 refugees whose decrepit ship, the *Athina*, had sunk, leaving the passengers stranded without shelter or supplies on the Dodecanese island of Sirna. "We had a close view of these unfortunate people, genuine refugees apart from a few potentially hostile young men," Tyler later recalled, "and I believe this contributed to the fact that during all of our patrol time I never heard a hostile or anti-Semitic remark—even from a drunken sailor."[75]

Kaplan explained his frantic attempts to alert the world of the British boarding:

> The guy came into the radio shack. But meanwhile, I'm sending like crazy. And I was burning up my telegraph keys, telling the whole world, "Help! We are in international waters, piracy on the high seas!" And trying to reach that yoyo [the assigned Irgun radio operator in Palestine whom Kaplan never successfully contacted]. And I'm supposed to get a hold of that guy, who was never there. Mister nobody. Mister Goodbye Charlie. And I couldn't reach him. So, I transmit an international distress frequency, 500 kilohertz and the high frequency, 8280, to let the whole world know what was happening. And they boarded us. I was still sending, and the guy came in with the bayonet. He says "stop sending." So what am I gonna do? Argue with him? I stopped then. I never argue with a guy with a bayonet. Especially when he's bigger than I

---

71   Liebman, "'Ben Hecht' Purser Poses as Refugee"; Lazar, *Immigrant Ship "Ben Hecht,"* 14.
72   Nicolai, "I Ran Britain's Palestine Blockade," 26.
73   Kaplan, "This Is the Way It Was," 3–4.
74   Kaplan Oral History, part 1, MZ.
75   Tyler, "The View from a 'Brit.'"

am, and I can't run. I'm a very good runner. But I couldn't run anyplace. So, what happened is that they boarded us. We had children. We had infants. Mothers with infants. And it wasn't our job to fight the British. Our job was to get people to Israel. And so, we proceeded with them on board.[76]

While the professional photographer Wallace Litwin did photograph the boarding, his pictures were confiscated, while the photos taken by Nicolai remained undetected.[77] The armed naval boarding party was "prepared for combat," "but to their surprise did not encounter any resistance" upon boarding the deck of the immigrant ship. Once the British "were in control and no fighting occurred they settled down a bit," Levitan remembered. "The passengers were kept below and the entire crew was herded together" in a corner of the bridge under guard.[78] After approximately an hour, the ship was secured.[79] "Many of our passengers were in tears and worse, some threatening to jump overboard," a crew member recalled.[80] A journalist left the deck among the passengers because he could not "stand the tears that run on the bony faces of men."[81]

The British had believed that the *Abril / Ben Hecht* would fiercely resist capture because it was associated with the Irgun, which was engaged in an armed rebellion, and even the more moderate Haganah-organized ships had been engaging in fierce physical opposition to the boarding of their ships by the British.[82] The men and women passengers on some of the Haganah ships fought pitched battles against the British with every object at hand short of firearms, including hat pins, clubs, and silverware.[83] In light of this danger, Ben-Ami of the Bergson Group was relieved to hear in New York that the immigrants were safe after the interception by the British.[84] For the *Ben Hecht*'s mission was intended to be a non-violent act of civil disobedience.

Tyler claimed that the American crew "proved cooperative" and asserted that the Royal Marines "boarding party met with no resistance

---

76   Kaplan Oral History, part 1, MZ.
77   Nicolai, "I Ran Britain's Palestine Blockade," 26; Rifkin, *What Ship*, 70.
78   Levitan notes for synagogue presentation, 7.
79   Horev, *I Will Gather Them*, 190.
80   Kaplan, "This Is the Way It Was," 4.
81   Méry, *Let My People Go*, 159.
82   Stewart, *Palestine Patrol*, 97; Jeffrey Weiss and Craig Weiss, *I Am My Brother's Keeper*, 33.
83   Levitan Oral History, RGUSHMM.
84   Ben-Ami, *Years of Wrath*, 403.

and were actually offered tomato soup from her modern cook house. She was berthed peaceful in the harbor and her 600 passengers were transferred to Cyprus for internment."[85] He thought that the crew "were only too happy to get the ship turned over."[86] Tyler's account is echoed in the Royal Navy's official history of its campaign to blockade and intercept Jewish immigration to Palestine, which claimed that there "was no opposition" to the British boarders, and that "[c]ontrary to expectations the boarding parties were well looked after onboard by the American crew, being offered tomato soup and fudge from modern galleys."[87]

In contrast, Levitan later wrote, perhaps figuratively, "[w]hen we were captured by 3 British Destroyers and 60 British Royal Marines, the crew stood firm and stated 'England, you are the sinners, these Jews must go to Palestine.'"[88] The *Ben Hecht* crew dressed in American uniforms, making clear their identity, to prevent the holding and interrogation of the passengers.[89] Mandel explained the reason why the crew did not attempt to avoid arrest:

> On our ship, we felt that it was not sufficient to just try to get the refugees into Palestine. But we wanted to show more. We wanted to show that the British had no right to prevent Jews from coming into Palestine. We felt that they had a Mandate to create a Jewish homeland in Palestine from the League of Nations. That was their Mandate and they should have done that and not prevented Jews from coming in. So, in all of the other ships the crews melted in with the passengers and they came back to the United States. We did not. We stayed as a crew. And the British were rubbing their hands with glee. Ah, they finally got some people they could arrest for illegally aiding and abetting illegal immigration.[90] . . . British authorities wished to bring the sailors that manned the illegal immigrant ships to trial to discourage other sailors from helping the Jewish illegal immigrants.[91]

Henry Mandel wrote a previously unpublished letter dated August 30, 1999 to the editor of the newsletter of the American Veterans for Israel, which

---

85 Tyler, "The View from a 'Brit,'" 15.
86 Tyler interview by Stone, 2017.
87 Stewart, *Palestine Patrol*, 97.
88 Levitan letter to Finegood.
89 Horev, *I Will Gather Them*, 190.
90 Mandel interview by Shuster, 2000.
91 Naor, *Haapala*, 57.

had republished Tyler's account of the boarding of the *Ben Hecht*, to protest its suggestion that the crew of the *Ben Hecht* had docilely submitted to the British. He challenged a key detail of Tyler's account by asserting the ship had no tomato soup on board. Among the other revelations of this letter is that the *Ben Hecht* crewmen sabotaged the boat's steering mechanisms so that it could not be pressed into the service of Britain. The letter's theme was that the ship's crew did not resist, but neither did they cooperate.

Dear Sir:

I feel it is necessary to respond to "The View from a 'Brit'" published in your latest newsletter.

We must remember that the article was written by a British Sailor for a British audience, and his 'facts' are slanted towards that end, and justify the British role in their undeclared war against the Jewish people. My comments are aimed only to the part of the article concerning the "Abril" (MS *Ben Hecht*), as I was a crew member, and was present at the incident.

The "Ben Hecht" was a pre-World War I[92] yacht owned by Germans and seized by the U.S. government at the start of World War II and used by the U.S. as a mine tender in the Atlantic. It was declared surplus after W.W. II, and purchased at auction by "The American League for a Free Palestine," an American arm of the Irgun. It was a rusty hulk of a ship as it was roughly used all through the war without a major overhaul. It was purchased and towed from Baltimore to the Gowanus Canal in Brooklyn, and there it received a minor overhaul before setting sail out to France (Port de Bouc) to pick up our passengers. It could in no way be considered "modern," and had a top speed of 15 knots. We sailed short-handed from New York City. We had a number of crew members who claimed to have been in the Abraham Lincoln Brigade in Spain. As we were preparing to sail they all left the ship. We had only two radio operators, one of whom was David Kaplan with whom I had sailed previously and had invited to join the ship. Dave and Ed Styrak split the three shifts. In the deck department we had Walter "Heavy" Greaves who served both as third mate and bosun. In the engine department we had Lou Brettschneider who I also recruited and who served both as second assistant engineer and electrician. I myself served as third assistant engineer and oiler.

---

92   Other sources list the ship as having been built in 1930. See Stone, "Refugees Driven on Cyprus-Bound Ships like Cattle."

We had a breakdown in the Mediterranean and arrived near the Palestinian coastline Saturday morning rather than Friday evening as scheduled. The power station was taken over in Tel Aviv Friday evening and the city blacked out in the expectation that we would try to land there. Saturday, we were taken over by the British beyond the 20-mile limit in public waters, another illegal act. While we did not resist (another story in itself) we did not cooperate with the English. We disconnected the auxiliary motor to the rudder, and when the British took over the wheel it took two men to steer ("Those Jewboys must be bloody strong" was one comment by a wheelman.) We didn't have a "modern cookhouse" and we did not serve the British anything. They commandeered what they wanted, but they could not have had tomato soup, as there wasn't any aboard and our passengers and our own crew were never served tomato soup.

Mr. Tyler was trying to salve his own conscience, or trying to justify his own actions as a Jewish British sailor when he wrote his article.

After being released by the British, Lou Brettschneider, 'Heavy' Greaves and Dave Gutmann signed on to another Aliyah Bet ship. Eli Freundlich and I later served in the Israel Defense Services.

Best wishes and a Happy New Year

Henry (Chaim) Mandel[93]

***

After their adventure on the Ben Hecht, David Gutmann, Lou Brettschneider and Heavy Greaves again volunteered together on the Haganah ship *Paducah / Ge'ula*.[94] Eddie Styrak, who along with Dave Kaplan was one of the radio operators on the *Ben Hecht*, went on to volunteer for the Israeli Air Transport Command as a radio operator in the air.[95]

The official Royal Navy history of the Palestine blockade asserts that when the *Ben Hecht* was captured, the British were surprised to discover that Clay was no longer serving as captain, but that instead Levitan was in command. (The British misidentified Levitan as an ex-naval officer, as opposed to a Merchant Marine officer.)[96] The *Abril / Ben Hecht* was towed to Haifa, arriving, according to a crew member's account, at 7:30 p.m.,

---

93   Henry Mandel letter to *AVI Newsletter*, August 30, 1999 (in possession of the editor).
94   Patzert, *Running the Palestine Blockade*, 31–32, 47.
95   Livingston, *No Trophy*, 99–105.
96   Stewart, *Palestine Patrol*, 98.

March 9, 1947.[97] Note, that is hours earlier than the British chronology; the discrepancy may have been part of an attempt to obfuscate the fact that the ship was captured outside of Palestinian waters. Later, on July 18, 1947 the British would seize the *Exodus 1947* twenty miles off the coast of Palestine, well on the high seas.[98]

British Army Captain Linklater, Commanding Officer of the 317th Airborne Field Security Section, claimed in a post-arrest intelligence report dated March 9, 1947 that food was plentiful and sanitary arrangements adequate when the *Ben Hecht* was captured on March 8, 1947.[99] Despite the British perception, the food supplies on the *Ben Hecht* were in fact running low when it was captured. Walter Cushenberry was only responsible for feeding the crew, but as the *Ben Hecht* traveled through the Mediterranean Sea, the passengers' system of rations broke down and Cushenberry also assumed responsibility for feeding the passengers. He worked in the galley from 6 a.m. to midnight. When the supply of bread ran out on the fifth day of the voyage, he woke up even earlier to bake more bread.[100]

Cushenberry, in a newspaper interview given upon his return to New York after the crew's release from captivity, explained that when the *Ben Hecht* was captured outside of Palestine's territorial waters off the coast of Tel Aviv, and was being towed to Haifa, he distributed all of the supplies left in the ship's food stores to the passengers so they would not go hungry. Food was apparently distributed to the British who boarded the ships as well so they would not interfere. Members of the boarding party had entered the galley and ordered the ship's stewards to proceed with their work. Cushenberry took his "keys and opened everything I could and loaded the passengers with it. The most important things are the food. I didn't want the British to have it all. The passengers needed it. It was for them and they got it. I didn't tell the soldiers what I was doing, but they knew."[101] The British sailors and Marines misinterpreted this humanitarian act as indicating that there had been plentiful food aboard and lack of opposition to their commands. Shortly before the boarding of the ship, the crew sabotaged the vessel in several ways to render it useless for the British,

---

97   Liebman, "'Ben Hecht' Purser Poses as Refugee."
98   Bethel, *Palestine Triangle*, 326.
99   Swarc, "French Connection," 160–161.
100 "How Ship's Cook Walter Cushenberry"; Nicolai, "I Ran Britain's Palestine Blockade," 26; Rifkin, *What Ship*, 26.
101 "How Ship's Cook Walter Cushenberry."

including wiring the radio transmitter backwards and cutting off a line's fuel pump.[102]

***

The Sixth Airborne's procedure at Haifa for the reception of captured illegal immigrant ships was to seal off the port and the deployment of troops in the town itself, to avoid disturbances. Only press correspondents were able to witness the transshipment of the immigrants from the illegal immigrant ships to converted Liberty troop carrier ships, some of whom were sympathetic to the British, others to the Jews. Sometimes the immigrants protested and refused to go onto the prison ships that were to ship them to Cyprus, which the British felt was an attempt to influence the press. A British officer noted that among all of the passengers of the illegal immigration ships it was "apparent to one and all they valued their admission into the Holy Land more than anything else in the world." The prison ships then set sail to Famagusta in Cyprus. Ships were brought to Haifa first because of the concern that illegal immigrant ships would founder, at great loss of life. The captured ships were towed to a breakwater containing other seized illegal immigrant vessels.[103]

As the *Ben Hecht* was towed into Haifa harbor, Haifa's port was sealed off at 10 p.m. that Saturday night.[104] The *Ben Hecht* reached a cargo jetty in a new dock in the port at 2:30 a.m. early Sunday morning, March 9, 1947,[105] though one newspaper appears to have listed the time of arrival as 2:30 p.m. in error.[106] The vessel had no Hebrew name on its bow.[107] British forces "were placed in defensive positions" at port prior to the deportation order under the command of a British brigadier.[108] The captured *Ben Hecht* refugees included 385 men, 194 women, and 20 children, all carrying blue and white folders stamped "Identity Travel Certificates," issued by the Hebrew Committee for National Liberation in Paris, dated February 20, 1947, and

102 Kaplan Oral History, part 1, MZ.
103 Wilson, *Cordon*, 109–112.
104 "600 Refugees Ship Towed into Haifa."
105 "599 Abril Immigrants Sent to Island of Deportation."
106 "599 Visa-Less Jews Seized."
107 "Abril Refugees Deported"; "599 Abril Immigrants Sent to Island of Deportation."
108 "'Abril' Immigrants to Cyprus."

signed by Eri Jabotinsky, which were handed over to the border control official in the Port of Haifa.[109]

In contrast to the British sailors and Marines, the British Paratrooper "Red Devil" Division troops treated the Jewish immigrants roughly and beat them when forcing them into deportation ships in Haifa harbor.[110] *Ben Hecht* crew members recalled that Cushenberry, the ship's cook, had cried when the passengers were led off the ship. Cushenberry said "It was when the passengers began to tell how much they 'preciated what I'd done. Quite a few of them would cry after they were tellin' me that and naturally it got under my skin."[111] A history of the "Red Devil" Sixth Airborne's operations in Palestine noted that there was "no opposition encountered" during the *Abril / Ben Hecht* transshipment in Haifa. The British believed that all of the crew had been arrested.[112]

Captain Linklater, a British Army intelligence officer, was surprised by the lack of resistance aboard the *Ben Hecht* and the relatively uneventful transshipment of the passengers to the prison boats that brought them from Haifa harbor to Cyprus prison camps. He observed that confiscated photographs of neatly dressed immigrants during the voyage of the *Ben Hecht* contrasted with their dilapidated appearance upon their arrival as captives in Haifa.[113] Marvin Liebman, the *Ben Hecht*'s purser, unlike most of the crew, had decided to join the passengers and to conceal his identity. Liebman describes non-violent resistance of the passengers to being forced out of the ship, relating in his memoir that "word got around: 'Don't go easily. Give them trouble!' The women started shrieking, the men shouting curses, and I, who wanted nothing more than to walk off like a civilized human being, had to be carried off shouting feebly in Yiddish, 'Pigs, Pigs!'"[114] Two members of the British Red Devil Airborne division told Liebman, in his guise as an illegal immigrant, "Get moving, you Jew!" When Liebman sat, he was "clubbed over the head and shoulders and carried down the gangway and thrown into the dock." The passengers, whom Liebman had mingled with, were "forced to go through two lanes of British

---

109   "599 Visa-Less Jews Seized"; "'Abril' Immigrants to Cyprus."
110   Leon Edel and James Parlaton, "Ben Hecht Seamen Talk of Dov Gruner," *PM*, Thursday, April 17, 1947; Kaplan Oral History, part 1, MZ.
111   "How Ship's Cook Walter Cushenberry."
112   Wilson, *Cordon*, 247, 262.
113   Swarc, "French Connection," 160–161.
114   Liebman, *Coming Out Conservative*, 61.

soldiers" armed with clubs, and were then shoved into a long tent, ordered to strip, and sprayed with DDT.[115]

It took four hours from the arrival of the ship until all of the immigrants were transferred to two expulsion ships.[116] The *Abril* refugees were transported early in the morning to the *Empire Rest* and *Empire Shelter*, deportation vessels whose "reassuring names," one newspaper article sarcastically noted, belied their task. The deportation ships were originally American-built Liberty ships. The *Empire Rest* and *Empire Shelter*, conducting their first deportation runs to Cyprus, had "brand new wire cages, painted bright orange."[117]

A journalist reported that the refugees were swiftly transferred from the *Abril,* "once a private yacht, to deportation ships for quick shipment to Cyprus before a possible outbreak at Haifa. . . . Temporary canvas tents were erected on the dock, where the refugees were sprayed with DDT powder and searched for weapons before their transfer."[118] Before the entrance to the delousing tents that led directly from the dock to an awaiting prison ship, a six-foot officer of the British Sixth Airborne "Red Devil" division, known as the *Kalonniyot* (Poppies) among the Jews in Palestine after their red berets,[119] "kept shouting: 'One more! One up!,' taking one refugee at a time, giving the slow a shove, once hoisting a protesting refugee along by the seat of his pants."[120]

An *Abril / Ben Hecht* crew man remembered that

> in Haifa we were on one side of a dock that extended out onto the water and on the other side of the dock there was this British ship with cages over the hold. . . . . And the passengers on our ship went down the gangway across the dock up the gangway into the hold of this British ship. They had the cages over the hold. They never really even touched Palestinian land. The pier was sticking out into the water. They took all the passengers who were trying to get into Palestine and they loaded them into that ship and they took them to the island of Cyprus.[121]

---

115 Liebman, "'Ben Hecht' Purser Poses as Refugee."
116 "'Abril' Immigrants to Cyprus."
117 "Abril Refugees Deported."
118 Stone, "Refugees Driven on Cyprus-Bound Ships like Cattle."
119 Begin, *The Revolt*, 238.
120 Stone, "Refugees Driven on Cyprus-Bound Ships like Cattle."
121 Levitan Oral History, USHMM.

The deportation was conducted in accordance with established British tactics. However, a journalist noted an unprecedented aspect of the deportation: in response to the British Criminal Investigation Department police's request at the tent in which the immigrants were searched, whether they had a passport or visa, many men "handed over blue documents, with particulars and photographs. The one shown to the press party, dated Paris February 28, 1947, was printed in Hebrew, English and French, and carried the insignia of the Shield of David, with the Lion of Judah."[122]

***

Journalist I. F. Stone, at the start of the weekend on Friday night, March 7, 1947, had attended a wedding at a settlement named Ramat David where a Yemenite Jewish singer named Shoshana Damari performed. She would later become known as the "First Lady of Israeli song."[123]

> At the hotel [in Haifa on Saturday night] at one in the morning I found a message that an illegal ship was arriving and correspondents ordered to report to the Savoy Hotel for convoy to the carefully guarded, curfewed and darkened harbor. At the Savoy Hotel, four foreign correspondents, myself and three local reporters had tea and a chat with British officers - nice chaps, but bewildered, who conceive that their duty is to protect the Arabs from the influx of Jews. Then down to the docks, where huge flashlights were circling overhead. Soldiers, police, marines and Arab Legionnaires and detectives were all over the place, and road blocks on the dock itself.

From that vantage point he watched the deportation of the *Ben Hecht* passengers to Cyprus, which was hurried because the British feared disturbances from the Haifa Jewish community.[124]

The Palestine Post reported that

> [s]ome of the young people looked almost confident, the middle-aged wan and confused. One noticed a bandaged head here and there, heard an occasional half-suppressed cry from a frightened woman. There were a few brief scuffles between the soldiers and men who fought to hold on to their

---

122 "Abril Refugees Deported."

123 "Shoshana Damari," The Jewish Women's Archive, https://jwa.org/media/shoshana-damari.

124 I. F. Stone, "Panorama, 1947," *The Palestine Post*, Tuesday, March 11, 1947, 4.

belongings, which were being taken away for further inspection, but there was no violent resistance. The least suspicion that the ban on speaking to the refugees was being broken brought an immediate reprimand, making the pressmen wonder what the people had to tell that was being covered up by such strict incommunicado orders.

The press was not permitted to speak to the deportees, perhaps because the British desired to conceal that their ship had been boarded in international waters, but journalists were able to observe them. The gathered "journalists noticed that many documents other than the 'visas' were collected from the immigrants, and a small black box was carried away in great secrecy," documents that may have shown the ship's true position when it was arrested.[125] Stone reflected that

> the same people I had seen as happy farmers in the Emek, here the weary, the dirty, the sleepy-eyed, the long suffering, some shambling through, some walking with defiant erectness and slow gait, others anxious to avoid trouble; men, women and some small children. They moved along one by one, driven human cattle to who, these shouts, shoves and quick squirts with powder were but one more in a familiar series to be endured, though this time at the very brink of Eretz Israel.

Stone summed up his experience as a "weekend panorama, the humor and the tragedy, the rural peace and urban war, fulfillment on the land and frustration at the very shore, this my friends, is Palestine in 1947."[126] A British report broadcast on radio stated that the "men were transported without incident" to prison ships heading to Cyprus; and that the crew of the ship, twenty-three men, were all imprisoned.[127] The BBC soon clarified that the captured *Ben Hecht* had aboard 600 passengers possessing HCNL travelling documents with a crew of twenty, including eighteen Americans.[128] The *Empire Shelter* left port at daybreak and the *Empire Rest* an hour afterwards.[129] Two of the 194 woman on board were hospitalized: Irina Bundinia, a heavily pregnant seventeen-year-old who was expected to give birth shortly, and was rushed to a government hospital in Haifa;[130]

125 "Abril Refugees Deported."
126 Stone, "Panorama, 1947."
127 Horev, *I Will Gather Them*, 190.
128 Jabotinsky, "Request on the 'Ben Hecht' Transport in France."
129 "599 Abril Immigrants Sent to Island of Deportation."
130 "599 Visa-Less Jews Seized."

and M. Pyvyir, forty-five years old, who was brought to the Atlit prison camp.[131] Bundinia's husband was permitted to remain with his wife in a Haifa hospital, and thus was the only one of the 385 male refugees who was not immediately deported to Cyprus.[132]

"We were taken off," *Abril* crewmember David Kaplan later recalled, "and we were put into—not gently—into Haifa lockup."[133] A character that might be a stand-in for Rifkin in his fictionalized retelling of the *Ben Hecht*'s journey is injured by a paratrooper's club when he tries to defend a woman refugee who is shoved by British troops in Haifa as she is being deported to Cyprus.[134]

As mentioned previously, the British recorded 384 men, 195 women, and 20 children *Abril / Ben Hecht* passengers who were deported to Cyprus.[135] Most of the *Ben Hecht* immigrants were sent to Camp 66 in Cyprus, though Betar activists arranged for the North African passengers to be sent to Camp 55, where there was a larger group of North African immigrants. The appearance of the *Ben Hecht* passengers bolstered the number of immigrants affiliated with the Revisionists, increasing tension between them and the majority of immigrants who trusted the recognized authorities of the Yishuv.[136] Betar members organized military training in the Cyprus Camps, in which the *Ben Hecht* immigrants participated.[137]

Recalling the crew's treatment by the British soldiers, Levitan said

[t]hey did not pussy foot around. They gathered the crew together on the back of the bridge and when the passengers were all gone and on the ship to Cyprus, they took us down on the dock. And we walked to the end of the dock where they had a truck to take us to the prison . . . and halfway down the dock they had like a little hut. And you walk through one door and they hit us with DDT, for bugs or vermin or whatever and then we went out straight through out another door onto the truck. And went to a police station. And we sat and we were questioned for a couple of hours.[138]

---

131 "599 Abril Immigrants Sent to Island of Deportation."
132 "599 Visa-Less Jews Seized"; "Abril Refugees Deported."
133 Kaplan Oral History, part 1, MZ.
134 Rifkin, *What Ship*, 252.
135 "Abril Refugees Deported."
136 Lazar, *Immigrant Ship "Ben Hecht*," 17.
137 Ibid.; "Illegal Immigrant Ship 'Ben Hecht,'" http://www.palmach.org.il/history/database/?itemId=5100.
138 Levitan Oral History, USHMM.

The captured *Ben Hecht* crew spent two days in a Haifa jail, where the local Jewish population was surprised by their arrival because "there was no ship due in," but sent them fruit, cheese, bread, and sardines.[139] The local Jewish community probably did not expect the ship's arrival because the *Ben Hecht* was not organized with the Haganah-affiliated Mossad L'Aliyah Bet, and the security precautions that the British had taken to avoid demonstrations from the local Jewish community in Haifa were unnecessary. Louis Binder, the youngest *Ben Hecht* crewman, described his treatment by his British captors as "pretty good . . . [w]e were Americans and they didn't dare push us around. The food was fair and a lot of it brought in by the Jewish community. The British jabbed knives into it to make sure there were no weapons."[140] "We were kept there overnight" in cell 23 in Haifa prison, Kaplan recalled.[141]

The twenty crew members of the *Abril / Ben Hecht* appeared before Haifa Criminal Court Chief Magistrate Effendi Shadi Kahlil in Haifa lockup, who there in the prison remanded the *Ben Hecht* sailors on the charge of aiding and abetting 600 immigrants to enter in an illegal manner into the territorial waters of Palestine, instead of conducting the hearing at Haifa Magistrate Court, where the press was waiting. This unusual procedure was adopted because the British thought it was too dangerous for them to appear in court for security reasons. The men who were charged were Louis Binder, Louis Brettschneider, Jeno Berkovitz, Walter Cushenberry, Walter Greaves, David Gutmann, Albert Herschkoff, Harry Herschkowitz, David Kaplan, Haakom Lilliby, Wallace Litwin, Robert Levitan, Norman Luce, Henry Mandel, Robert Nicolai, Shepard Rifkin, Erling Sorenson, Edward R. Styrak, Henry Schatz, and Jack Winkler. Rifkin, who was ill, was not present, and had been taken to Government Hospital in Haifa.[142] Two policemen testified, recounting that the ship was arrested by three destroyers. The trial date of the twenty seamen was set by Chief Magistrate Kahlil for fourteen days hence.[143] The Judge issued an order of detainment for the remanded prisoners for three weeks. The information office of the Mandate

---

139 Nicolai, "I Ran Britain's Palestine Blockade," 35.

140 Halkenhauser, "Ben Hecht Seamen Tell of Seizure."

141 Kaplan Oral History, part 1, MZ.

142 "3 Pressmen Among 21 Detained"; "Abril Pressmen to Be Deported," *The Palestine Post*, Wednesday, March 12, 1947, 3, Palestine Post Bureau, dateline Haifa, Tuesday, March 11, 1947.

143 "British Hold 20 U.S. Seamen in Zion Refugee 'Smuggling,'" *New York Post*, Monday, March 10, 1947, AP, dateline Jerusalem, March 10, 1947.

government announced that all the crew were American citizens, except for the two Norwegian engineers, who had taken out the papers to apply for United States citizenship. Thirteen of the remanded prisoners were Jewish and seven were non-Jewish.[144] Other than Rifkin, who would join them later, the remanded crewmember prisoners were sent to Acre Prison on March 11, 1947 by truck.[145] Separately, two French citizens, apparently Jacques Méry of the *Paris Presse* newspaper and Henrietta Goldenberg, were also indicted, and continued to be detained in Haifa lockup along with photojournalist Wallace Litwin.[146]

In the New York newspaper *PM*, an article recounted that

> [n]ineteen U.S. crewmen of the ex-Navy ship *Ben Hecht*, intercepted off Palestine, are being held for trial on a charge of aiding and abetting illegal immigration. Orders to 'pursue' the prosecution regardless of the nationalities of the people involved were given by High Commissioner Gen[eral], Sir Alan Cunningham after receipt of secret information from the Palestine Criminal Investigation Department. . . . The crew members face heavy fines and prison sentences of up to eight years if found guilty. However, a high government source predicted that in the end the crew would be deported to their countries of origin.[147]

The statement that appears in one history—that the crew "were tried and convicted of aiding and abetting illegal immigration and were given 17-year prison sentences"—appears to be based on a misunderstanding.[148] A British Colonial Office official wrote to Sir Robert Howe of the Foreign Office, while arguing against prosecuting the *Abril / Ben Hecht* crew, "[i]t looks as if the *Abril* crew have either not been very clever, or else are deliberately seeking martyrdom, in order that the American League may use their arrest to raise a storm in the U.S. over detention by the British of U.S. nationals engaged in the humanitarian task of taking Jewish refugees 'home.'"[149]

---

144 Saperstein, "Captain Faced Capture."

145 "3 Pressmen among 21 Detained"; "Abril Pressmen to Be Deported"; Nicolai, "I Ran Britain's Palestine Blockade," 35.

146 "Abril Pressmen to Be Deported."

147 "British will Push Prosecution of Palestine Refugee Ship's U.S. Crew," *PM*, March 10, 1947, 1, 2, and 7, United Press, *PM* reel 53, 3/2–4/30/47, NYPL.

148 Hochstein and Greenfield, *The Jew's Secret Fleet*, 100.

149 Quoted in Ze'ev Venia Hadari, *Second Exodus: The Full Story of Jewish Illegal Immigration to Palestine, 1945–1948*, (London: Vallentine Mitchell, 1991), 205.

The deported immigrants were forced to stay in the holds of the prison ships for several hours before they were allowed on deck.[150] As mentioned earlier, early the next morning after the *Ben Hecht*'s capture, the immigrants were brought in the *Empire Shelter*, *Empire Rival*, and the *Empire Rest* prison ships to Cyprus. Liebman was shipped to Cyprus on the *Empire Rival*. He reported that the *Empire Rival* passengers were being forced to stand due to a lack of room, with no ventilation, and a stifling hot temperature, for two nights and a day. The *Empire Rival* arrived at Cyprus at 10 a.m. on March 11, 1947. The group of passengers Liebman had joined were sent to Special Camp 66. Adjoining was a prisoner of war camp with captive German SS soldiers, who had built Camp 66. "As we drove in on the trucks," Liebman remembered, "the Nazis laughed and shouted at us, taunting us."[151]

On Cyprus, Liebman witnessed a tragedy that unfolded after a soccer match between children from different parts of the detainment camp:

> The children were permitted to visit another camp for the game. As they returned to their own camp, they hoisted their winning soccer team to their shoulders. Suddenly British soldiers rushed in and tried to break up the parade, using weighted clubs unmercifully. When the kids resisted and people from the camp started to join them, they called in three tanks, which rode right through the crowd. One little boy had his foot crushed under the treads of a tank. . . . [Children were throwing rocks and sticks at the tanks and attacking soldiers with their hands at this point.] Then the order was given to fire . . . they meant to fire over the heads of the crowd, which was back behind the fence of the camp, but there were shots and a little blond kid with long curls standing next to me doubled up and fell. They picked her up, all covered in blood, and took her to the infirmary, but she died two days later.[152]

It was the British policy when dealing with unruly colonials that firing into the air could be considered a "bluff and an uninvolved person far away might be hit," so it was the practice to fire individual rounds "each one directed at one of the ringleaders."[153] Liebman's United States passport was

---

150 Liebman, *Coming Out Conservative*, 61.

151 Idem, "'Ben Hecht' Purser Poses as Refugee."

152 Liebman, "Brutality of British on Cyprus," *NY Post*, April 16, 1947, Bob Levitan collection, USHMM.

153 Bethel, *Palestine Triangle*, 219.

smuggled to him in Cyprus and he returned to New York on Saturday, April 12, 1947.[154]

Though news agency dispatches reported that 600 refugees were taken off the ship, in New York, the American League for a Free Palestine, which financed the vessel, said it had left Europe with 900 aboard.[155] This was an inaccurate claim, though it was made in good faith. Eri Jabotinsky claimed, in an internal Bergson Group memorandum describing the *Ben Hecht*'s outfitting in France in retrospect, that there "were on departure more than 600 passengers aboard" the *Ben Hecht*. "[T]he remainder either succeeded in landing or did not have traveling documents."[156] The AFLP insisted that the missing 300 "did not disappear into thin air or into the Mediterranean. Let the British try to find them."[157] Mordecai Chertoff, an American Jewish journalist who had recently arrived in Palestine, assured his family in a private letter dated March 23, 1947 that "NOBODY GOT AWAY in land-ing" and accused the Bergson Group of lying.[158] Most likely, Jabotinsky unintentionally provided the Bergson Group operatives in New York with an inflated number of refugees on the ship, and then they in good faith made the inaccurate claim that some of the refugees were able to infiltrate Palestine undetected.

With the arrival of the 600 clandestine immigrants of the *Abril* counted by the British, the Cyprus camps now exceeded a previously announced 10,000 detainee limit. There were 13,724 Jews in the camps, with 3,942 scheduled to leave Cyprus for Palestine as part of the allowed quota, thus leaving 9,782. The 600 *Abril / Ben Hecht* additional refugees resulted in a total of 10,382 refugees in the camps.[159] The stage was now set for the British government's fateful decision to send captured illegal immigrants back to the countries in Europe from which their ships had departed, instead of to the Cyprus camps. High Commissioner Cunningham informed his super-iors on March 9, 1947, that it was believed that an additional 25,000 Jews

---

154 Liebman, "Brutality of British on Cyprus."
155 Stone, "Refugees Driven on Cyprus-Bound Ships like Cattle."
156 Jabotinsky, "Request on the 'Ben Hecht' Transport in France."
157 Stone, "Refugees Driven on Cyprus-Bound Ships like Cattle."
158 Daniel S. Chertoff, *Palestine Posts: An Eyewitness Account of the Birth of Israel Based on the Letters of Mordecai S. Chertoff* (Jerusalem: The Toby Press, 2019), 58–60.
159 "Numbers of Illegal Immigrants Full in Cyprus," *Haboker*, Tuesday, March 11, 1947, front page (Hebrew); "Cyprus 'Full' with the Arrival of the 600 Clandestine Immigrants of the 'Abril,'" *Al Hamishmar*, Tuesday, March 11, 1947, front page (Hebrew).

were preparing to attempt to enter Palestine from Europe, which could not be prevented with the airplanes and destroyers available.

On July 18, 1947, the Mossad L'Aliyah Bet ship *Exodus 1947* (*President Warfield*) was boarded by the Royal Navy, and instead of being shipped to Cyprus, the passengers were sent to Europe. The British were determined to return the passengers to its port of origin, Port-de-Bouc, France. The Jewish deportees refused to disembark in France; cruelly, the British then forced them to land in Germany, to the disgust of world public opinion. The *Exodus* immigrants were eventually disembarked in Hamburg on September 9.[160] Haganah leaders thought "the *Exodus* was the most important event on the way of the Jewish people to an independent state."[161]

The American crew members of the *Ben Hecht* who were taken to the Acre Prison Fortress were imprisoned in a jail complex that allowed contact with permanent prisoners who were members of the Irgun Tzva'i Le'umi and Lechi underground militias. Several members of the imprisoned *Ben Hecht* crew became ill, including two who were hospitalized.[162] Levitan explained that

> there were twenty men in my crew, we were assigned to two cells. There were ten men in a cell. I had little rag mattresses that we laid on the floor and we slept on that. [Both cells] had a twenty-gallon metal garbage pail with a lid on it. And at night they locked us in, during the daytime the door was unlocked. But at night they locked us in and that twenty-gallon garbage can was our bathroom. If anyone had to do anything during the night they did it in the garbage can and put the lid back on. And in the morning the first thing we did was carry the garbage can out and dump it into a hole in the ground. And wash out the garbage can and set it in the sun.[163]

In Acre, the crew managed to converse with "numerous Jewish underground fighters who were doing 15 years to life";[164] Levitan later marveled that these men, some of whom knew English and Spanish in addition to Hebrew, "held regular classes in languages, economics, literature, philosophy."[165] Levitan recalled that all the Jews in the prison were political

160 Bethell, *Palestine Triangle*, 314; Wilson, *Cordon*, 263, 265.
161 Bethell, *Palestine Triangle*, 356.
162 "A M/V BEN HECHT Story."
163 Levitan Oral History, USHMM.
164 Nicolai, "I Ran Britain's Palestine Blockade," 35.
165 Levitan Oral History, USHMM.

prisoners . . . [and] all the Arabs in the prison were criminal prisoners. Now the Jews were young men [who were eighteen and nineteen years old or] in their 20s and they were allowed to go out of their jail cells every day and gather and talk. And they go off into private places that were available to them in the prison. And the older men were teaching the younger men tactics. Throwing hand grenades; make-believe rifles. And these men were sentenced to 20 and 30 years in prison and here they are learning tactics to fight. So they knew that they were not going to be in there for 20 or 30 years.[166]

The Irgun's underground newspaper celebrated the journey of the *Ben Hecht*: "The arrival of the ship of the 'Ben Hecht,' with 600 clandestine immigrants from all the streams, puts an end to the false accusation and slanders of the opposition [i.e., the Haganah] that they have a monopoly on clandestine immigration." However, unlike the Haganah, the Irgun did not think that the people could only blindly follow the slogan that the "clandestine immigrants will immigrate." Because "the truth is, they immigrate but do not ascend into the Land." They are brought into camps in Cyprus. "The clandestine immigration, whose organization we will continue, is a historical vision, that embodies and demonstrates the eternal quality of the masses of the people for the homeland." They also provided encouragement to those fighting forces within the Land:

> However, it is forbidden to deceive the people. In present conditions clandestine immigration is not free immigration and it is not in the power of the defenseless clandestine immigrants to break down the gates. The Gates will be broken and rebirth and redemption will come from war in stages of the inhabitants of Zion, its fighters and builders. The Clandestine Immigrants will Immigrate. And the Fighters will Fight. That is the path. Come and let us Go.[167]

Eitan Livni, commander of the Irgun prisoners, delivered a message which Menachem Begin had sent secretly to the prison, which Livni related to the *Ben Hecht* crew. It said

> We value greatly the work in which you abandoned your careers and volunteered for the holy purpose of bringing Jews in refugee ships to their

---

166 Levitan notes for synagogue presentation, 8.
167 National Military Organization (Irgun), "The Clandestine Immigration and the War," Adar 1947, MZ *Ben Hecht* (*Avril*) Newspaper Clippings file.

homeland. And even if they did not succeed this time to bring them by their hands, I promise that your sacrifice was not in vain and in the not too distant future we will be able to meet again, this time face to face as citizens of a free land. Your work has made us partners for this exalted purpose—the establishment of a free homeland for the Jewish people.[168]

---

168 Eitan Livni, *Personal Story of Operations Officer of Etzel* (Tel Aviv, Israel: Idanim Publishing, 1987), 224 (Hebrew, editor's translation).

Chapter 13

Breakout

Yet each man kills the thing he loves,
By each let this be heard,
Some do it with a bitter look,
Some with a flattering word,
The coward does it with a kiss,
The brave man with a sword! . . .

Some love too little, some too long,
Some sell, and others buy;
Some do the deed with many tears,
And some without a sigh:
For each man kills the thing he loves,
Yet each man does not die.

He does not die a death of shame
On a day of dark disgrace,
Nor have a noose about his neck,
Nor a cloth upon his face,
Nor drop feet foremost through the floor
Into an empty space.

—Oscar Wilde, *The Ballad of Reading Gaol*[1]

When the *Ben Hecht* crew arrived in Acre, the Irgun was feverishly planning a breakout from the prison to save Dov Gruner and three other condemned

---

1   *The Portable Oscar Wilde*, ed. Richard Aldington and Stanley Weintraub (New York: Penguin Books, 1981), 668–669.

men from the hangman's noose.[2] Dov Gruner had been captured and badly wounded during an Irgun raid of a British armory at Ramat Gan in 1946. After escaping wartime Europe on a refugee boat led by Eri Jabotinsky, Gruner had served in the Jewish Brigade in the British Army. Brought to trial in January 1947, Gruner refused to recognize the legitimacy of the British military tribunal to try him in Eretz Israel, the Land of Israel, which applied laws, he declared at his sentencing to death, that were "contrary to the fundamental rights of man, contrary to the wishes of the local population and contrary to international law. . . . And if your whole regime is one of unlawful occupation, how can I confer upon you the power to try me or any other citizen in this occupied country?" Cursing his captors in a biblical cadence, Gruner declared that "there is no force in the world that can break the link between the people of Israel."[3] Winston Churchill, who supported abandoning the Palestine Mandate as a useless waste of British blood and treasure, and noted Gruner's bravery in the House of Commons, nonetheless reprimanded the government for its softness in delaying the execution of Gruner.[4]

Gruner, who refused to appeal his sentence because to do so would have implicitly recognized the legitimacy of his captors, wrote to Begin while he awaited execution in a Jerusalem prison cell:

> I could use sonorous phrases like the famous Latin saying "Dulce et decorum est pro patria mori" ["It is sweet and proper to die for one's country," Horace's *Odes* III 2.13]. But at this moment it seems to me that such phrases sound cheap. . . . Of course I want to live. Who does not? I too could have . . . left the country altogether and lived securely in America. But that would not have given me satisfaction as a Jew and certainly not as a Zionist. . . . The right way, to my mind, is the way of the Irgun, which does not reject political effort but will not give up a yard of our country, because it is ours. And if the political effort does not have the desired result it is prepared to fight for our country and our freedom. . . . That should be the way of the Jewish people in these days; to stand up for what is ours and be ready to battle even if in some instances it leads to the gallows. . . .

---

2   Jan Gitlin, *The Conquest of Acre Fortress* (Tel Aviv, Israel: Hadar Publishing House, 1982), 55.

3   Begin, *Revolt*, 251–255.

4   Ibid., 259.

Gruner said, "I write these lines forty-eight hours" before the time set for his execution, and insisted that "at such a time one does not lie."[5] Gruner's refusal to allow appeals on his behalf because he did not recognize the authority of the British to try him struck his jailers as the act of "a very brave man."[6]

With time running out to save Gruner from being hanged, Eitan Livni put a halt to an ongoing effort to dig out the basement of the prison. Instead, his plan concentrated on an Irgun raiding party outside blowing out window embrasures, a weak point in the outer walls of the prison; while a group inside would blow out two interior iron gates so the prisoners could access the breach. Livni used Friday evening prayers as an excuse to enter into the condemned men's cell to tell them about the escape plan. Drums of oil, with double bottoms containing detonators and gelignite explosive materials, were smuggled into the prison. Bomb expert and poet Michael (Mike) Ashbel—who had in 1941 escaped from Vilna, then under Russian occupation, to Palestine—assembled these components into working explosives.[7] Ashbel had been wounded and captured in a daring Irgun raid for ammunition at Sarafand, the largest British camp in Palestine, in 1946.[8] Ashbel's death sentence had been commuted in exchange for the release of five British officers taken hostage by the Irgun.[9]

Ben Hecht crew members smuggled in contraband that aided the fateful escape of prisoners at the fortress, among them Irgun men as well as the Lochmai Herut Israel (Fighters for Israel's Freedom), known both by its acronym Lechi and as the Stern Group, after its founder Abraham Stern, and referred to pejoratively by the British as the "Stern Gang." Levitan had a small camera and Kaplan had film in luggage that had not been detected or confiscated by the British. Personal belongings of the *Ben Hecht* crew had not been thrown overboard by the British, as typically was done, probably because they had not physically resisted arrest. Before the crew was expelled from Palestine on March 30, 1947, Livni, the senior Irgun prisoner, asked Levitan to photograph prisoners who, unbeknownst to Levitan, had been selected to break out. Levitan was allowed into the main prison complex under the pretense of a visit for a shower. He smuggled the camera and the film into the shower in the main prison under a towel.[10] He photographed multiple Irgun and Lechi prisoners in each shot to save film. The photos were then smuggled out of the prison so that fake identification papers could be prepared, which was essential if the escapees were to evade capture after the breakout.[11] Matiyahu Shmulevitz, a Lechi member whose death sentence had been commuted without explanation, asked for the film after Levitan took the pictures.[12]

Over fifty years later, Henry Mandel recorded in a letter to the Israeli Defense Ministry his impressions of his arrest, confinement at Acre Prison, and his smuggling of contraband to imprisoned members of the Irgun and Lechi who without his knowledge were planning a prison break:

> When we were boarded by the English [March 8, 1947][13] the passengers were transported to Cyprus and the crew was held in Haifa lockup overnight. We were then transplanted to Acre Prison and charged with 'Aiding and Abetting Illegal Immigration.' At Acre as remanded prisoners we were held outside the main prison separate from the convicted prisoners. We were permitted to enter the regular prison for Shabbat services when a Rabbi would come in. One of the Irgun prisoners asked me if I had any electric batteries. Among my other duties aboard ship I served as Electrician and I had a box with about a dozen batteries with me. We were searched by the English before we were permitted to join the prisoners. I put three batteries in the bottom of each shoe and hobbled in. The British searched me but did not have me remove my shoe and I brought in the batteries. I did this twice and brought in a dozen batteries. About five weeks later on May 4, 1947 the Irgun, in one of its finest moments, blew out the side of Acre prison and many prisoners escaped. I feel proud that I have even the smallest part in this action. Anyway, the English realized that bringing us to trial would further reveal their perfidy to the entire world and to our great disappointment, released us without trial and expelled us from Palestine. However, there was

---

10 Levitan notes for synagogue presentation, 8.

11 Gitlin, *Acre Fortress*, 119; J. Bowyer Bell, *Terror Out of Zion: The Fight for Israeli Independence, 1929–1949* (New York: St. Martin's Press, 1977), 207–208; Hochstein and Greenfield, *The Jews' Secret Fleet*, 100; "A M/V BEN HECHT Story."

12 Jeffrey Weiss and Craig Weiss, *I Am My Brother's Keeper*, 36; see Jackie Headapohl, "Matityahu Shmulevitz Passes Away," *The Jewish News*, December 03, 2018, https://thejewishnews.com/2018/12/03/matityahu-shmulevitz-passes-away/.

13 Hochstein and Greenfield, *The Jews' Secret Fleet*, 99.

much publicity about the arrest of Americans opposing the British, and the incident served its purpose.[14]

Gruner and three other Irgun prisoners were hanged on April 16, 1947.[15] Although the breakout was delayed once Gruner and his comrades Yehiel Drezner, Mordechai Alkahi, and Eliezer Kashani were hanged, Begin ordered the operation to proceed on May 4, 1947, while the special session of the United Nations to decide the fate of Palestine was in process.[16] The breakout from Acre Prison would be the Irgun's response to Gruner's execution.[17] Napoleon had failed to capture the medieval crusader fortress of Acre;[18] the Irgun's successful assault on and breakout from Acre Prison took place on May 4, 1947 and shook the British resolve to retain its Mandate over Palestine.[19] Explosive material, ignition caps, and fuses were smuggled into the prison in barrels labeled as jam, which a British guard in fact sampled but did not realize anything was amiss.[20] Menachem Malatzky and Ashbel taped dynamite to the locks of two gates, lighted fuses, and blasted the gates. Perhaps only Ashbel would ever have known if the batteries smuggled in by Mandel helped him prepare these explosives, but he did not live to tell the tale. The prisoners also used grenades in the prison courtyard that made a great deal of noise and smoke, but were not lethal.[21] 41 of the 163 Jews in the prison escaped, and 214 of the 460 Arabs in the prison took advantage of the chaos to also escape. A detachment of British paratroopers happened to be in the area and killed eight Jews, four from the raiding party and four escapees, and captured thirteen Jews, eight of whom were severely wounded. British forces suffered eight wounded casualties.[22] Ashbel succumbed to wounds sustained in the immediate aftermath of the escape from Acre Prison. He might have survived but for the denial of medical attention after his capture.[23]

---

14 Mandel letter to the Israeli Defense Ministry.
15 Wilson, *Cordon*, 122.
16 Gitlin, *Acre Fortress*, 92.
17 Wilson, *Cordon*, 123.
18 McDonald, *Mission in Israel*, 165.
19 Wilson, *Cordon*, 123.
20 Livni, *Personal Story of Operations Officer of Etzel*, 228–230.
21 Gitlin, *Acre Fortress*, 135, 143.
22 Wilson, *Cordon*, 123, 125, 127.
23 "Ashbel, Michael ('Mike')," https://honorisraelsfallen.com/fallen/ashbel-michael-mike/.

Three captured Jews were sentenced to death for their participation in the operation.[24] On July 12, 1947, Sergeants Paice and Martin of the British Sixth Airborne were kidnapped and held hostage by the Irgun. The Irgun warned the British that if three Jewish prisoners sentenced to death for their part in the Acre Prison breakout were executed, the captured British soldiers would be killed in reprisal.[25] The lives of the three condemned Irgun prisoners in Acre were not spared; the Irgun executed the two British sergeants on July 31, 1947. Enraged, British soldiers and police killed five Jews and injured others soon thereafter. By the end of 1947, after these events, it was "clear that the problem was insoluble" from the British point of view, a British M15 agent recalled in a memoir.[26]

While the Haganah concentrated its resistance to British rule through means of illegal immigration of Holocaust survivors, which challenged the moral and political basis of British rule, Begin later explained to a historian that the Irgun wanted to convince the British that it faced an intractable armed revolt in Palestine that could not be defeated militarily and that withdrawal from Palestine was the wiser course. Begin argued,

> We had always regarded our fight for national liberation as a chain of military actions strictly combined for political aims. What we wanted to show was this: that we were capable of destroying the British Administration, and that the British could not rule this country. The fight in its purely military sense began only after the war ended, when the British proposed to turn Palestine into their chief Near East military base; well, we proved that Palestine could not be turned into a safe base, and a military base which is not safe is no base at all.

Begin felt that the political impact of the breakout was "[d]ecisive" because it showed the United Nations that Britain could no longer rule Palestine.[27]

---

24   Zadka, *Blood in Zion*, 77; Wilson, *Cordon*, 263.
25   Wilson, *Cordon*, 263.
26   Anthony Cavendish, "Inside Intelligence," *Granta* 24 (Summer 1988): 28–29.
27   Gitlin, *Acre Fortress*, 83–85, 92.

Chapter 14

Release

I the Lord have called thee in righteousness, and have taken hold of thy hand, And kept thee, and set thee for a covenant of the people, for a light of the nations. To open the blind eyes, to bring out the prisoners from the dungeon, And them that sit in darkness out of the prison-house.

—Isaiah 42:6–7[1]

The capture of the *Ben Hecht* was the lead story in the leading Yiddish-language newspaper in the United States, the *Forverts* (the *Forward*) on Monday, March 10, 1947. The *Forverts* published a slightly garbled list of twenty imprisoned *Ben Hecht* sailors in Yiddish, based on an American Broadcasting Company radio broadcast. A "Hank Moskovitz" is listed as a sailor, an apparent reference to Mandel.[2] More significant was the attention garnered in the general media.[3] A supporter of the American League for a Free Palestine (AFLP) later argued that given the value of the press coverage of the arrest of the *Ben Hecht* and its American crew "[a] hundred intercepted boats of unknown registry, with thousands of Jews forcing their way to Palestine, could not have done as much for the cause of Hebrew independence as that single converted yacht with its American sailors in a British prison."[4]

A Haifa attorney, Joseph Kaiserman, was retained by the Tyre Shipping Company to defend the sailors and to attempt to recover custody of the

---

1   *JPS Tanakh—The Holy Scriptures* (Philadelphia, PA: Jewish Publications Society, 1917).
2   *Forverts*, Monday, March 10, 1947, front page, and Tuesday, March 11, 1947, available at *Forward* website (Yiddish).
3   See "British Hold 20 U.S. Seamen in Zion Refugee 'Smuggling.'"
4   Zaar, *Rescue*, 219.

ship.[5] Kaiserman argued that the British had illegally seized the *Abril/Ben Hecht* when it was still in international waters.[6] At a press conference in Washington, Dean Acheson, then Under Secretary of State, said that neither the United States Consul in Palestine nor the American government had been asked to intervene in favor of the *Abril* sailors.[7]

After the seizure of the ship, the AFLP announced it had retained the law firm of Bennet, House and Couts, whose offices were at 40 Wall Street, to defend the arrested seamen. Professor Fowler V. Harper of Yale Law School, a vice chairman of the League, explained that "[t]his will be a test case. A British court will decide whether Mr. Bevin's foreign policy or international law is paramount." Harper argued that the American crew of the *Ben Hecht* had violated neither American nor international law. Aaron Kope, a spokesperson for the Hebrew Committee for National Liberation (HCNL), told journalists that the *Ben Hecht's* crew were cautioned that they could be captured by the British and that they were not to resist arrest or try to escape from custody.[8] Professor Harper said "that the case will establish the illegality of any law preventing Hebrews from going to Palestine in an orderly manner." At the same press conference Maurice Rosenblatt, also a Vice-Chairman of the AFLP, said that the AFLP had wanted a test case to challenge the deportation of immigrating Jews to Cyprus.[9] The AFLP published an advertisement asking:

> Did the Ben Hecht Crew violate the international pact of 52 nations? Did they slam the gates of Palestine, violating the world's mandate? Did they reduce Palestine to an armed camp? OR DID THEY EFFECTIVELY FULFILL PRESIDENT TRUMAN'S REPEATED DEMAND THAT PALESTINE'S GATES BE OPENED AT ONCE. . . . The only "law" in Palestine is British might. Against this might U.S. veterans volunteered in the American tradition.[10]

The passenger on the *Ben Hecht* who garnered the most press attention in Palestine itself was Henrietta Goldenburg, the seventeen-year-old French

---

5   Horev, *I Will Gather Them*, 191.
6   Nicolai, "I Ran Britain's Palestine Blockade," 26.
7   "At the Last Moment," *Davar*, Wednesday, March 12, 1947, front page (Hebrew).
8   Helen Salmon and Robert Roth, "Many Sign Here to Man Jews' Ships," The Hebrew Committee for National Liberation, found in Bob Levitan collection, USHMM.
9   Zarr, *Rescue*, 221.
10 Quoted in Zaar, *Rescue*, 219.

Jew engaged to a Palestinian Jew who had served in the British Brigade of the British Army. She only spoke French.[11] Goldenburg claimed to possess press credentials from a French newspaper. Her case drew the interest of the Jewish press in Palestine due to her young age and her romantic quest to reunite with and marry her fiancé, Bert Stow. In response to an appeal published in the local Hebrew-language newspapers, after many volunteered the bail for Goldenburg, Ephraim Katz from Sivina (Haifa Bay) put up bail of 1000 Palestinian pounds, allowing her to marry her fiancé in a Jewish ceremony in Haifa after Stow had been given special permission to leave Tel Aviv despite the military curfew. She was ultimately given the choice either to return to France or to accept expulsion to Cyprus, and she chose to go to Cyprus and await admission into Palestine to be reunited with her new husband.[12]

The American crew of the *Abril / Ben Hecht*, and the captured journalists and Goldenberg made two separate motions at the end of March requesting bail. It was reported that the "judge told the passengers that he had no jurisdiction over their cases and that 'so far no charges were intended to be filed' against them." The crew was informed that there were "strong and reasonable" grounds for keeping them in prison.[13]

Esther Kaplan, the mother of *Ben Hecht* radioman David Kaplan, organized a campaign to free the imprisoned sailors among Brooklyn synagogues, the Woman's League of Torah Vodaath, the yeshiva that David had attended, and by personally lobbying Congressmen.[14] Her pleas soon bore fruit. Congressman John D. Dingell of Michigan, on March 20, 1947, in an address at the House Representatives, said that

> [t]he civilized nations of the world clearly set forth in the League of Nations Mandate their intent that Palestine become a Hebrew homeland. Britain concurred in that intent and eagerly accepted the Mandate. She has, in fact, been extremely loath to relinquish the powers the Mandate gave her and

11 Rifkin, *What Ship*, 219.
12 "Bride Will Wait in Cyprus," *The Palestine Post*, Monday, March 24, 1947, 3, Palestine Post Bureau, dateline, Haifa, Sunday, March 23, 1947; "Court Refuses Bail," *The B'nai B'rith Messenger,* Friday, April 4, 1947, 15; "Three Journalists Came on the Abril," *Al Hamishmar*, Wednesday, March 12, 1947, 4 (Hebrew); "Boy Meets Girl in Haifa Jail," *The Palestine Post*, Friday, March 14, 1947, 3, Palestine Post Bureau, dateline Haifa, Thursday, March 13, 1947; "Came 'Illegally', and Married according to Custom and Law," *Al Hamishmar*, Tuesday, March 25, 1947, 4 (Hebrew).
13 "Court Refuses Bail."
14 Medoff, *Militant*, 161–162.

unbecomingly assiduous in extending those powers. . . . The freedom of the seas has a long history in American interest from the shores of Tripoli to Leyte Gulf. I should not like to see that freedom abandoned under circumstances in which every precept of law, honor, and humanity asserts its dignity.

On March 21, 1947, Congressman Andrew L. Somers of New York said on the floor of the House of Representatives:

I want to emphasize then, Mr. Speaker, that the seamen in the crew of the *Ben Hecht* are not now in prison as a result of their irresponsibility or willful violation of any recognized agreement. Those men are in prison because they carried out what we—again and again—told them we wanted carried out. In perfect good faith, every one of those seamen had reason to believe, and I am sure they were right, that they were serving their country's interest in embarking upon such a merciful venture. It was our policy they executed, and their present incarceration is our responsibility. We cannot, in justice to them and to ourselves, allow them to remain behind British bars.

Representative D. Scott, Jr. of Pennsylvania, said that

[A]fter repeated statements of the President of the United State that this country desires the admission to Palestine of Hebrew refugees now in displaced person camps in the Western zone of Europe . . . a group of American citizens have been arrested by the British for trying to do their part in implementing American policy. . . . The fact that the British have delayed releasing or trying the crew members for another two weeks pending investigation, strongly indicates that they, too, are aware of the critical test nature of the case. . . . Inasmuch as American men manned the *Ben Hecht* under the impression – hardly to be disputed—that it was in furtherance of American interest and policy, as stated by President Truman, as well as a daring and humane venture, I strongly urge that the Government of the United States spare no effort to protect the young seamen and secure their immediate release.[15]

Historian Rafael Medoff has observed that "every telegram or phone call that the British received from a congressman about the *Ben Hecht* contributed further to the pressure on England to withdraw from Palestine altogether."[16]

---

15   Zaar, *Rescue*, 221–223.
16   Medoff, *Militant*, 163.

On March 13, 1947, American Vice Consul R. Roberts visited the crewman in Haifa lock-up and Acre prison, accompanied by a lawyer, Mr. Rutberg. Wallace Litwin and Shepard Rifkin, who had been hospitalized, were transferred that day to Acre prison. Unlike the other prisoners, no charges were brought against Hirschkoff, and he was returned to Haifa lock-up to await deposition. The Palestine Post reported that "[s]everal of the crew held at Acre are ill, and have been transferred to the sick-bay."[17]

On Thursday, March 20, 1947, photojournalist and crewmember Wallace Litwin, Albert Hirschkoff (who was claiming to be an accredited string writer), and French journalist Jacques Méry were expelled from Palestine on the grounds that they had entered into the country without visas, leaving aboard the SS *Providence*.[18] Following the Congressional protests and diplomatic interventions, the British decided that the *Ben Hecht* sailors would also be expelled from Palestine. The *Ben Hecht* crew were warned that if they served on another illegal immigrant ship they could be sentenced to an eight-year prison term under British law.[19] Kaiserman cabled Stanley B. Kurta, Executive Director of the American Sea and Air Volunteers for Palestine on March 24, 1947 that he had obtained a ruling that the British Mandate's Attorney General was "not to prosecute crew, hope to sail around March 30th."[20] On March 23, 1947, the *New York Times* ran a short dispatch from its Jerusalem correspondent that the *Ben Hecht* crew would be expelled in order to avoid a public trial on the legality of the bringing of Jewish immigrants to Palestine.[21] On March 27, 1947, the US State Department was informed by the British government in Palestine that the *Ben Hecht* crew would be deported to the United States. A State Department spokesman noted that eighteen of the prisoners "seemed to be American citizens" and that two others were Norwegians who had already initiated the American naturalization process.[22] The Norwegian engineers had not been to their homeland since 1940, when they left occupied

---

17　American Consul Visits Abril Crew," *The Palestine Post*, Friday, March 14, 1947, 3, Palestine Post Bureau, dateline Haifa, Thursday, March 13, 1947.

18　"Journalists Saw Enough," *The Palestine Post*, Friday, March 21, 1947, 3; "Immigrants," *Davar*, Friday, March 21, 1947, front page (Hebrew).

19　Halkenhauser, "Ben Hecht Seamen Tell of Seizure."

20　Cable from Stanley B. Kurta to Hyman Robert Levitan, March 24, 1947, 3:07 p.m., file 5, Bob Levitan collection, USHMM.

21　Lazar, *Immigrant Ship "Ben Hecht,"* 14.

22　"20 Off the Ben Hecht Will Be Sent to U.S.," AP, dateline Washington, March 27, 1947, found in Newspaper Clippings file, Bob Levitan collection, USHMM.

Norway.[23] Levitan was told by his British captors that if he ever returned to Palestine, they would jail him.[24]

The nineteen *Ben Hecht* sailors were expelled from Palestine on March 30, 1947. The Tyre Shipping Company in New York provided for the expenses of the journey of the exiled American sailors. The sailors told a Jewish journalist in Palestine that they did not regret volunteering on their mission despite their imprisonment. The journalist "found them in the dining room eating with appetite the first proper meal" from when they were arrested on March 8, the time the ship reached Haifa.[25] The day before the sailors' release, the British permitted the permanent prisoners in Acre to provide a farewell dinner of meat stew, with singing and speeches, which concluded with a traditional Hora circle dance.[26] The crew asked their lawyer Kaiserman to thank the Jewish community of Haifa for "having made their stay in prison more comfortable"; the community also provided *matzos* to the crew as Passover would fall during their voyage.[27]

Kaplan recalled that the American prisoners were taken

> to the ship from Acco in irons, on the ship in irons and the captain of the *Marine Carp* came down and said to us, "I don't want any trouble with you guys or I'm gonna throw you in the brig. Any problems and I'm gonna put you in—" as if we were, you know, condemned criminals. And this is an American ship, an American captain, so he was also under the British; controlled by them, and he was a *mamzer*. In fact, we came on the ship and he kept us in irons on the ship for a while until they took us out. We couldn't eat; the first meal we had . . . we were sick.

But after that they recovered very quickly, and Kaplan "was bored stiff" on the return voyage to the United States.[28] Mandel used his sailor papers and was able to join the crew of the *Marine Carp* when the ship became short-handed in Alexandria, Egypt, the *Marine Carp*'s next stop after leaving

23   See Rifkin, *What Ship*, 181.
24   "Hyman R. Levitan, Tried to Help Jewish Refugees," *Sun-Sentinel*, August 13, 1998, found in Newspaper Clippings file, Bob Levitan collection, USHMM.
25   "Exiled to America 19 Sailors of the 'Ben Hecht,'" *Haboker,* Monday, March 31, 1947, 4 (Hebrew).
26   Nicolai, "I Ran Britain's Palestine Blockade," 35.
27   "Spent Three Weeks in Acre Prison," *The Palestine Post*, Monday, March 31, 1947, 3, Palestine Post Bureau, dateline Haifa, Sunday, March 30, 1947.
28   David Kaplan Oral History, part 1, MZ.

Palestine.[29] The Norwegian sailor Lilliby remained in Haifa prison until his departure by plane to Norway, where his mother had recently died. The Tyre Shipping Company paid for his ticket.[30]

On Wednesday, April 16, 1947, the *Ben Hecht* crew arrived aboard the *Marine Carp* at Pier 88, North River at Forty-Eighth Street in New York City.[31] The Justice Department decided not to prosecute the crew.[32] The *Ben Hecht* crew was interviewed by the press as a group upon their arrival in New York on the *Marine Carp*. The crew revealed in the interview the previously secret information that the *Ben Hecht* sailed from Port-de-Bouc near Marseilles. The interviewees talked more about the capture and martyrdom of Dov Gruner than of their own story.[33] Members of the crew, upon their arrival in New York, hinted of the plans of the Acre prisoners. Kaplan told reporters that "I feel sorry for a couple of hundred British over there. By tomorrow they're going to see more action than they ever bargained for."[34] The members of the crew were honored along with Ben Hecht at an AFLP dinner, to which the families of the crew members were invited too.[35]

Regarding his short imprisonment with other crew members after the British capture of the *Ben Hecht*, the ship's cook Walter Cushenberry said "I don't regret it a bit. I think I learned more than history can teach. The terrorists we talked to in prison impressed us more than anything else" that the ALFP had told Cushenberry about Palestine. Cushenberry, like the other imprisoned sailors, received a wooden medal from the Irgun prisoners in Acre Prison inscribed "To a brave sailor from his comrades, members of the 'Irgun Zevai Leumi.' Acre Prison." Cushenberry explained to a reporter that the Irgun prisoners "sneaked the wood in and carved it out in prison. I think that's a wonderful thing. The biggest thing in the world, that makes me want to go back again now, after talking to those guys in prison and learning the truth. The only way it's gonna be stopped is for us to try and go and give them their freedom." Cushenberry, an African-American who had been raised in the Jim Crow era segregated South, whispered, "I happen to know just what freedom means, you know."[36]

---

29 Mandel interview by Shuster, 2000.
30 "Exiled to America 19 'Ben Hecht' Sailors."
31 "Hecht Sailors Back; British 'Fair,' Says One."
32 Medoff, *Militant*, 163.
33 Edel and Parlaton, "Ben Hecht Seamen Talk of Dov Gruner."
34 Halkenhauser, "Ben Hecht Seamen Tell of Seizure."
35 Jeffrey Weiss and Craig Weiss, *I Am My Brother's Keeper*, 37.
36 "How Ship's Cook Walter Cushenberry."

In his previous position as head of the War Refugee Board, New York City Mayor William O'Dwyer had urged the United Nations to intervene to solve the Jewish refugee problem.[37] Mayor O'Dwyer's brother Paul O'Dwyer may have been an influence on the Mayor: Paul was on the board of the AFLP[38] and was a liberal lawyer who defended Jewish Zionist gun runners in court.[39] However, Mayor O'Dwyer may have been under some British pressure as he did not attend the ceremony with the *Ben Hecht* sailors himself, and instead delegated an assistant mayor to the task.

On April 18, 1947, Deputy Mayor Vincent R. Impellitteri, serving as acting Mayor in Mayor O'Dwyer's absence, presiding at a welcoming ceremony at City Hall, said,

> I am honored to welcome to the City of New York the brave crewmen of the *Ben Hecht*, who symbolize American determination to save the Hebrews of Europe and to help transport them to Palestine. As a war veteran myself, I can understand how you, war veterans, volunteered for this hazardous voyage with no reward for yourselves, except the satisfaction of helping to attain American war aims, including justice and freedom for all deserving peoples.[40]

The same day that the *Ben Hecht* crew was honored at City Hall, some *Ben Hecht* crew members led the temporary takeover of the British Consulate in New York by forty members of the Betar youth group for a memorial service for the execution of Dov Gruner.[41]

The power of the American League for a Free Palestine's rhetoric and the League's use of the story of the *Ben Hecht*'s voyage is demonstrated in the following advertisement that appeared shortly after the capture of the ship in the New York Post:

> More men—women—children SAVED from the rot of DP Camps . . . WITH YOUR DOLLARS DO IT AGAIN! AND AGAIN! And AGAIN! Your American dollars paid for the Hebrew Repatriation ship, "S.S. Ben Hecht" . . . and for other ships we need. American crews man those ships.

---

37   Erbelding, *Rescue Board*, 271.
38   Memorandum on the status of the claim against the state of Israel for compensation arising out of requisition of the M/V Abril ("Ben Hecht"), June 30, 1952, Ben Hecht file no. 1, file 1816/6, Attorney General, the Ship "Ben Hecht," vol. 1, ISA.
39   Caro, *Power Broker*, 757–763; Slater, *Pledge*, 115.
40   Zarr, *Rescue*, 223; Medoff, *Militant*, 177.
41   Baumel, *Bergson Boys*, 234.

American food sustains the passengers. The British try to call it "illegal." But Americans say there is no such thing as an ILLEGAL Hebrew life. If it's legal for the British to live, IT'S LEGAL FOR HEBREWS TO LIVE. In dignity. In safety . . . instead of DP camps. YOUR money does it! [Picture of little boy in life preserver on *Ben Hecht*, captioned "Yesterday existing insecurely in a European hellhole. Today, on the threshold of happiness and freedom in Palestine."] THE SHIPS ARE READY . . . THE CREWS ARE READY . . . BUT THE PASSENGERS ARE WAITING . . . WAITING! NOW IS THE TIME TO THROW ANOTHER PUNCH, THE STRONGEST ONE YOU CAN. $250 saves a life—repatriates a Hebrew man, woman, or child on the way to Palestine. Send us $250,—$50—$5 to speed the Hebrews home on an Armada of Mercy Ships. The need is now—the time is now—the victory can be now. Hit hard to save more lives. You must send all you can—NOW. Get your friends to send money too! SAVE MORE "ILLEGAL" LIVES— TODAY! [Picture of overcrowded bow of *Ben Hecht*, captioned "THEY are lucky. THEY are saved. But there are tens of thousands more still locked in Europe. Conferences won't save them. Words won't save them. Ships will. More ships. And the ships are ready. ONLY YOUR MONEY IS NEEDED!"] Repatriation Supervisory Board. Ben Hecht Louis Bromfield Will Rogers, Jr. American League For a Free Palestine, Inc. give us the money . . . we'll get them there![42]

On Tuesday, September 2, 1947, the *Abril / Ben Hecht* was among the illegal immigrant ships that the Attorney General of the British Mandate Palestine requested to be confiscated in Haifa along with the *Exodus 1947*, the *Tradewinds*, and the *Fighters of the Ghetto*.[43] Attorneys Kaiserman and Rothenberg, who had been retained by the Tyre Shipping Company, the official owners of the ship, claimed that the presiding judge in the Haifa District Court, Judge Orr, did not have jurisdiction and this suit could only be adjudicated in an international court or an admiralty court.[44] Their claim was overruled by Judge Orr, who began to hear testimony of a few officers of the Haifa harbor police who testified how the *Ben Hecht* was captured at sea by the destroyer *Chevron*. They claimed that after the Royal Navy took control of the ship, they found 600 people who had in their possession illegal

---

42 "More Ships Are Coming."
43 "Proceeding to Confiscate 4 Immigration Ships," *Al Hamishmar*, Wednesday, September 3, 1947, 4 (Hebrew).
44 "Suit to Condemn the Ship 'Ben Hecht,'" *Hamashkif*, Wednesday, December 3, 1947 (Hebrew).

travel visas issued by the Hebrew Committee for National Liberation. After the lawyers for the Tyre Shipping Company asked that the judgment be delayed until written testimony of the American crew of the ship that were expelled to the United States could be obtained, the Judge overruled the request and informed that the judgment would be issued to them that day.

Judge Orr accepted the Royal Navy's account and rendered the judgment confiscating the *Ben Hecht* on December 3, 1947.[45] According to a press account, Judge Orr ordered, for the first time in an action confiscating a Jewish illegal immigrant ship, that costs of thirty Palestinian pounds be paid to the British Mandatory Government. Judge Orr also "declared that he was satisfied that the ship was in the territorial waters of Palestine [on March 8, 1947] with 565 illegal immigrants on board, so it must be deemed as having aided and abetted illegal immigration into Palestine."[46]

As summarized later by attorneys involved in later litigation about the fate of the *Ben Hecht*, "While admitting that the vessel was boarded on the high seas, the Attorney General of the Mandatory Administration nevertheless applied for an order of confiscation. The District Court granted such an order, holding that the vessel was within Palestinian waters when the order of confiscation was made; and holding in effect that how the vessel reached territorial waters was beyond its jurisdiction."[47]

David Ben Gurion declared the establishment of the State of Israel on May 14, 1948 "by virtue of our natural historic right and in the strength of the resolution of the UN General Assembly."[48] The *Abril / Ben Hecht* had been laid up next to other captured former illegal immigrant ships;[49] in late July 1948, soon after Israel declared its independence, the new Government of Israel confiscated the ship,[50] and it was fitted out by the Israeli Navy as the INS *Maʻoz* K-24.[51]

---

45 "'Ben Hecht' Confiscated in Judgement," *Haboker*, Thursday, December 4, 1947, 3 (Hebrew).

46 "Abril Awarded to Government," *The Palestine Post*, Thursday, December 4, 1947, 3, Palestine Post Bureau, dateline Haifa, Wednesday, morning of December 3, 1947 (Hebrew); "'Ben Hecht' Confiscated and the Owner of the Ship Penalized," *Al Hamishmar*, Thursday, December 4, 1947, 4 (Hebrew).

47 Memorandum on the status of the claim against the state of Israel.

48 "Proclamation of Independence," *Official Gazette of the Provisional Government of Israel*, no. 1, May 14, 1948 / 5 Iyar 5708, https://www.knesset.gov.il/docs/eng/megilat_eng.htm.

49 Wandres, *The Ablest Navigator*, 62.

50 "Government Confiscates 'Ben Hecht,'" *Hamashkif*, Tuesday, July 27, 1948, 4 (Hebrew).

51 Silverstone, *Our Only Refuge*, 23, 36.

Chapter 15

Machal

The Diaspora's most important contribution to the survival of the Jewish state.
—David Ben-Gurion[1]

After the capture of MV *Ben Hecht*, its namesake author shifted to advocacy for the Irgun's guerilla war in Palestine, rather than the Bergson Group's preferred approach of attempting to galvanize public opinion to support a government in exile, or the mainstream Zionist tactic of mass illegal immigration to Palestine.[2] *Ben Hecht* crew members Dave Gutmann, Walter "Heavy" Greaves, and Lou Brettschneider all volunteered for the Haganah-organized illegal immigrant ship *Paducah* upon their return to the United States.[3]

Mandel related in his 1998 letter to the Israeli Defense Ministry that:

When I came back home I returned to college and graduated in January, 1948. When Mr. Stavsky called me to join the *Altalena* I was not available.[4] I was involved in a project to set up a bazooka shell manufacturing plant to be shipped to Israel. I participated in obtaining and setting up the machines and preparing the tools and dies. After we had the equipment producing here in the U.S. we shipped the machines and tooling out. We had to ship everything first to Brazil, then to Israel, as the U.S. had an embargo against

---

1   Judy Maltz and Yaniv Kubovich, "What's Killing Israel's Lone Soldiers?," *Haaretz*, August 25, 2019, https://www.haaretz.com/world-news/MAGAZINE-israel-army-idf-lone-soldiers-suicide-military-1.7729693.
2   Hoffman, *Fighting Words*, 179; Gorbach, *Notorious*, 239.
3   Jeffrey Weiss and Craig Weiss, *I Am Brother's Keeper*, 38.
4   See Wyman and Medoff, *Race against Death*, 251 n.10; Ben-Ami, *Years of Wrath*, 452, 454.

exporting military equipment to either side at the time. Our group went to Israel and set up the plant and produced bazooka shells. The plant still exists—it is located in Kurdani. We became part of the Zahal in Chemed [Mandel adds "Chayl Madda" in Hebrew letters] Base Gimmel. The head of Chemed was Professor Katchalski (who changed his name to Katzir when he became President of Israel) [Efraim Katzir was President of Israel from May 24, 1973 to May 24, 1978]. I was a lieutenant, my number was 67674 in Zahal. I never received a number from Irgun.[5]

Abrasha Stavsky's next project after the *Ben Hecht* was organizing the purchase and outfitting of the *Altalena*, with the assistance of Gershon Hakim, during the summer of 1947.[6] Originally the *Altalena* was intended to be another illegal immigration ship like the *Ben Hecht*, but it was decided that the ship would transport recruits and arms instead.[7] Hakim worked on recruiting a crew;[8] the AFLP tried to recruit experienced sailors for the *Altalena* who wanted to help the Jewish cause, irrespective of Haganah or Irgun affiliations.[9] Stavsky had attempted to recruit Mandel, but he demurred because he was otherwise engaged in the clandestine bazooka factory. Instead, Mandel suggested a friend, who ultimately died on the *Altalena*.

Stavsky sustained mortal wounds as the *Altalena* went up in flames[10] on June 22, 1948 in the same area of the Tel Aviv beach where Chaim Arlosoroff had been killed on June 16, 1933.[11] Stavsky was fatally wounded attempting to reach the shore of Tel Aviv beach from the burning *Altalena*, among the sixteen men killed that day from the ship by Israeli Army and naval forces who believed they were preventing a coup by the Irgun,[12] fratricidal deaths that forever haunted Henry Mandel. Stavsky died of his wounds in a Tel Aviv hospital.[13]

***

5   Mandel letter to the Israeli Defense Ministry.
6   Wyman and Medoff, *Race against Death*, 251 n.10.
7   Baumel, *Bergson Boys*, 241.
8   Ben-Ami, *Years of Wrath*, 452, 454.
9   Barahona, *Odyssey*, 90–91.
10   Horev, *Dawning Ships*, 25.
11   Heckelman, *American Volunteers*, 41, 69.
12   See Ned Temko, *To Win or To Die: A Personal Portrait of Menachem Begin* (New York: William Morrow and Company, Inc., 1987), 121–122; Baumel, *Bergson Boys*, 241, 249.
13   Begin, *The Revolt*, 175.

Ten credits short of an undergraduate degree when he returned to New York after being deported, Mandel graduated from City College in January, 1948.[14] After the *Ben Hecht*'s journey, Mandel went on to work in a clandestine bazooka shell plant in Manhattan.[15] In January 1948, while working at the Brooklyn Navy Yard during the day, Mandel began devoting his nights to the Eastern Development Company at 119 Greene Street in New York City. The factory occupied a loft on the second floor of a building that was then part of the lower Manhattan electrical and hardware district. The Eastern Development Company was a secret front for Haganah operatives in New York.[16] There, Mandel, a machinist by trade, assisted his superior, Mota Teumim, an Israeli engineer, in the setup of a clandestine bazooka shell plant.[17]

When asked why he thought his personal service and that of other volunteers contributed to Israel's 1947–1949 war effort, Mandel responded "Aliyah Bet together with other acts in Israel helped England decide to leave [Palestine], and providing a bazooka shell plant producing shells certainly helped with the war. Having American volunteers boosted the morale of the Israelis, and the Americans in the Israeli Air Force played a significant part in the ultimate victory."[18] The overseas Machal volunteers, with their technical knowledge and skills developed during World War II service, were indeed essential to the Israeli Air Force, Navy, and other technical branches of the Israeli forces during the Israeli War of Independence.[19] Mandel helped to transfer the bazooka shell plant to Israel as a foreign Machal volunteer in the Chemed arms scientific research branch of the Israeli Army.[20]

The United States' Neutrality Act, whose origins went back to an outbreak of anti-French feelings in the wake of the French Revolution in 1794, forbids an American to "enlist or hire himself" in the United States, or to leave the United States with the intent to enlist in the service of a

14   Mandel *Jewish Week* interview, 1998.
15   Mandel interview by Shuster, 2000.
16   Slater, *Pledge*, 181.
17   Mandel interview by Shuster, 2000.
18   Aliyah Bet questionnaire, Mandel file, Machal and Aliyah Bet Records, undated, 1930–2010, I-501, American AJHS, Center for Jewish History, New York.
19   Wandres, *The Ablest Navigator*, 87; Nir Arielli, "When Are Foreign Volunteers Useful? Israel's Transnational Soldiers in the War of 1948 Re-Examined," *Journal of Military History* 78, no. 2 (2014): 703–724, in particular 719 and 721.
20   Mandel interview by Shuster, 2000.

foreign state, upon threat of imprisonment and fines.[21] The 1937 update of the Neutrality Act, adopted in the midst of the Spanish Civil War, where Americans had volunteered to defend the Spanish Republic in the Abraham Lincoln Brigade organized by Communists, prohibited serving in the civil wars of foreign countries.[22] The Nationality Act provided that an American citizen "shall lose his nationality by: . . . (c) Entering, or serving in, the armed forces of a foreign state unless expressly authorized by the laws of the United States. . . ."[23] The Israeli government's special oath for Machal, which required pledging to follow orders in the Israeli Army, rather than allegiance to the Israeli Government, was apparently designed to avoid violating the Neutrality Act.[24] Still, as a naturalized American citizen Mandel acknowledged he was at risk of losing his citizenship when he volunteered and yet he still did so.

***

Mandel was disappointed when he learned in later years of the lack of unity within the Jewish forces. The Haganah, Irgun, and Lechi had belatedly begun an attempt to recapture the Old City of Jerusalem on July 15, 1948, just as it was agreed that a cease-fire would take place a few days hence.[25] On July 17, 1948, shortly before the start of a cease-fire, the Irgun succeeded in breaching the Old City walls, but lack of reinforcement and coordination from the Haganah led to the division of the city. If the Jews had succeeded in capturing the city, the future borders and character of the State of Israel would have been different.[26]

The second truce between Israel and the Arab armies began on July 19, 1948, and Israel took the opportunity to secretly strengthen and rearm its

---

21   18 US Code § 959; Slater, *Pledge*, 209.

22   Wandres, *The Ablest Navigator*, 37, 77; Lucy S. Dawidowicz, *From That Place and Time: A Memoir 1938–1947* (New York: Bantam Books, 1991), 22.

23   The Nationality Act, Seventy-Sixth Congress, Third session, ch. 876, sec. 401, October 14, 1940.

24   Wandres, *The Ablest Navigator*, 80; Doron Almog, *Weapons Acquisitions in the United States, 1945–1949* (Tel Aviv: Ma'arakhot / Tseva haganah le-Yisra'el, 1987), 92 (Hebrew); Eliezer Tal, *Naval Operations in the War of Independence* (Tel Aviv: Ma'arakhot, 1964), 170.

25   Albert N. Williams, *The Holy City* (New York: Duell, Sloan and Pearce / Boston: Little, Brown and Co., 1954), 404.

26   Collins and Lapierre, *O Jerusalem*, 553, 556, 558.

army.[27] Mandel sailed from New York on October 15, 1948, the day before the second truce ended,[28] as a passenger on the SS *Nieuw Amsterdam* with a destination of Le Havre, France. (On July 23, 1948 James G. McDonald, the first American Ambassador to Israel, had sailed on the *Nieuw Amsterdam* from New York on the first leg of his journey to Israel.)[29] Once in Israel, Mandel helped set up the bazooka factory in Koordani, near Haifa.

Though Mandel did not serve in the Israeli Navy, it is noteworthy that the *Ben Hecht* was incorporated into the Israeli Navy and renamed the K-24 *Ma'oz* ("Stronghold"). The most lightly armed ship in the tiny fleet, it was chosen to be the mothership of the Israeli Navy's secret weapons: explosive torpedo motor boats, manned by commandos that ultimately sank the Egyptian Navy's flagship, the sloop *Emir Farouk*, off the shore of Gaza on October 22, 1948, along with hundreds of Egyptian troops on board.[30] The *Abril / Ben Hecht* was refurbished for naval service along with three other salvaged illegal immigrant ships at an Israeli naval dry dock overseen by Haim Gershoni (Gershenow), an American volunteer.[31] Gershenow was a veteran of the US Navy who established Israel's first naval shipyard.[32] The *Maoz* sailed in October 1948 with four torpedo motor boats, which had been fastened on deck the night before, and covered with tarpaulins for secrecy.[33] The third truce between Israeli and Arab forces was to take effect on 2 p.m. on Thursday, October 22, 1948.[34]

Paul N. Shulman, a graduate of the United States Naval Academy, who had commanded the Israeli government ships that had pursued and ultimately fired upon the *Altalena* in obedience to the orders of Ben Gurion,[35] was the Commander of an Israeli squadron of four former illegal immigration ships including the K-24 *Ma'oz*.[36] Though the lightly armed *Ma'oz* was not usually the Israeli flagship, it assumed this role during the operation

---

27 Heckelman, *American Volunteers*, 41.

28 Priscilla Roberts, ed., *Arab-Israeli Conflict: The Essential Reference Guide* (Santa Barbara, CA: ABC-CLIO, 2014), 330.

29 McDonald, *Mission in Israel*, 20.

30 Tal, *Naval Operations*, 163–169; Heckelman, *American Volunteers*, 30; Morris, *1948*, 329; Wandres, *The Ablest Navigator*, 123.

31 Haim Gershoni, *Israel: The Way It Was* (Cranbury, NY / London / Mississauga, Ontario: Herzl Press, 1989), 79–80.

32 Wandres, *The Ablest Navigator*, 62.

33 Gershoni, *Israel*, 79–80.

34 Lorch, *Edge of the Sword*, 367.

35 Wandres, *The Ablest Navigator*, 70.

36 Lorch, *Edge of the Sword*, 367.

because it was the mothership of the torpedo motor boats.[37] The *Emir Farouk*, a 1,440-ton sloop, and an Egyptian minesweeper were detected offshore of Gaza, and the *Ma'oz* sailed there along with the rest of the Israeli squadron. The *Emir Farouk* had 500 Egyptian troops onboard, intended as reinforcements for the Egyptian forces in Gaza. The Israeli naval forces received orders to attack as the third truce went into effect. Shulman had radioed Israeli Defense Forces High Command and asked that Ben Gurion be told that the four Israeli ships outnumbered the two Egyptian vessels in Gaza Bay. Ben Gurion radioed back himself, around 10:30 p.m, and speaking in English, said "Paul, if you can sink them, shoot. If you can't, don't."[38] The final command was to attack the enemy with full strength.[39]

Late in the evening of October 22, 1948, two explosive motor boats which had been launched from the *Ma'oz*, one piloted by Yitzhak Brockman and the other by Yaacov Reitov, attacked the *Emir Farouk*, which was rammed by two torpedo boats and sunk by their explosives, but due to a faulty mechanism the commandos piloting the boats only with difficulty escaped before impact. The minesweeper was still untouched and now directed its searchlight and machine gun fire at Yochai Ben-Nun, the leader of the Naval commandos who continued on the attack. Due to a faulty release mechanism Ben-Nun was able to escape his motor torpedo boat a mere twenty meters from the minesweeper, which was badly damaged but did not sink.[40] The commandos swam among the cries for help of drowning Egyptian soldiers on the *Emir Farouk*.[41] These commandos had been equipped with infra-red lights that enabled them to be picked up by the remaining torpedo boat, which brought them back to the *Ma'oz*, which had traveled closer to the area of the battle than had been planned.[42]

The nascent Israeli Navy's success at neutralizing the Egyptian Navy with the sinking of the *Emir Farouk* prevented the Egyptians from reinforcing their forces in Gaza and the Negev, which significantly aided the Israeli conquest of the Negev region.[43] The defeat of the Egyptian Navy's attempt to cut off Israel from overseas supplies and reinforcement was also a major

---

37   Almog, *Weapons*, 92; Tal, *Naval Operations*, 163.
38   Lorch, *Edge of the Sword*, 367; Wandres, *The Ablest Navigator*, 1–2.
39   Tal, *Naval Operations*, 163.
40   Gershoni, *Israel*, 82–83.
41   Tal, *Naval Operations*, 166.
42   Morris, *1948*, 329.
43   Rosen, *In Quest of the American Treasure*, 392.

strategic contribution of the Aliyah Bet ships. Insurance rates for shipping to Israel dropped dramatically after the sinking of the *Emir Farouk*, which indicated the naval victory helped prove to American and British insurance brokers that Israel was an established fact.[44] Yochai Ben-Nun received Israel's highest military decoration for his leadership and exploits: selection as one of only twelve "Heroes of Israel" of the 1948 War.[45] Shulman was appointed commander of the Israeli naval forces with the rank of *aluf* (general or admiral).[46]

Mandel never discussed with his family his old ship's role in the sinking of the *Emir Farouk*. Probably he did not know the details of the action, in which he did not participate and which remained secret for years. Certainly the fiery drowning of hundreds of Egyptian sailors and soldiers aboard the *Emir Farouk* is painful to relate, even if justified and necessary for Israel's survival. The following mystical perspective may help the reader process the fate of the *Emir Farouk*:

Rabbi Kalonymos Kalman HaLevi Epstein, known by the Hasidic Torah commentary *Maor VaShemesh* that was published after he passed away in 1827, grappled with the parallel biblical story of the drowning of the Egyptian army in the sea by humanizing the Egyptians, and mystically contextualizing their deaths. *Maor VaShemesh* relates that:

> I heard in the name of the Rabbi [Shmuel Shmelke Halevi Horowitz of Nikolsburg, founder of the Bostoner Rabbinic dynasty] on the homily on the ministering angels who requested to sing a song [upon the drowning of the Egyptian army in the sea] and the Holy One Blessed Be He said "the works of my hands are drowning in the sea and you are singing a song?" [The angels explained that they were singing] so that Egypt would hear the pleasant voice of [the angelic voices] and their souls would leave [their bodies suddenly and painlessly] like Sennacherib and his soldiers that would [later] hear the song of the ministering angels and their spirits would leave. The Holy One Blessed Be He replied "the works of my hands drown in the sea, that is to say that Egypt drowned the works of my hand, Israel, in the sea when they threw them in the Nile, and I need to pay them back measure to measure so that they will drown in the sea."

---

44   Almog, *Weapons*, 92.
45   Lorch, *Edge of the Sword*, 367.
46   Wandres, *The Ablest Navigator*, 3.

The *Maor VaShemesh* expanded upon this theme by explaining the verses "And Moses stretched forth his hand over the sea, and the sea returned to its strength when the morning appeared; and the Egyptians fled against it; and the LORD overthrew the Egyptians in the midst of the sea. And the waters returned, and covered the chariots, and the horsemen, even all the host of Pharaoh that went in after them into the sea; there remained not so much as one of them"[47] as follows:

> The explanation is the Holy One Blessed Be He reminded the sea . . . of the light that illuminated them [the waters] on Sabbath eve at twilight [after the six days of creation, which was then hidden on the eve of the first Sabbath, a mystical doctrine alluded to in the Talmudic statement that the first fire was lit on Saturday night upon the conclusion of that Sabbath],[48] and since they [the waters] were reminded, they were silent and they did the will of the Creator and they split before the Children of Israel, and even as morning approached and it [the sea] returned to its strength, to its original condition, there was still an impression of that illumination of light, and Egypt fled to meet it. The explanation being that the Egyptians were silenced and ran to greet that light, even though they were not able to tolerate even the impression of the light, it negated them from material reality. And the "LORD overthrew the Egyptians in the midst of the sea" means that they were negated from existence and their souls left as they were unable to tolerate the light that that the Holy One Blessed Be He influenced [kindled] in the sea, it appears to me.[49]

Thus the *Maor VeShemesh* thought of the drowned Egyptians as flawed human beings who sought the illumination of the holy primordial (perhaps infra-red) light and ran towards it and their fate. Like us.

---

47 Exodus 14:27–28 (quoted after *JPS Tanakh—The Holy Scriptures*).
48 Talmud Bavli *Pesachim* 54a.
49 *Maor VaShemesh* commentary for the seventh day of Passover, in Kalonymos Kalman HaLevi Epstein, *Sefer Maor VaShemesh HaShalem*, ed. Menachem Avrohom Braun (Israel: Machon Or L'Sefer, 2012), vol. 3, 222–225 (Hebrew); Kalonymus Kalman Epstein and Aryeh Wineman, *Letters of Light: Passages from Ma'or va-shemesh*, trans. Aryeh Wineman (Eugene, OR: Pickwick Publications, 2015), 83–88.

Chapter 16

A Mercy Ship's Legacy

Save, O Lord, Your People, The remnant of Israel. I will bring them in from the northland, Gather them from the ends of the earth—The blind and lame among them, Those with child and those in labor—In a vast throng they will return here. They will come with weeping, And with compassion I will guide them. I will lead them to streams of water, By a level road where they will not stumble. For I am ever a Father to Israel . . .

—Jeremiah 31:7–9[1]

Abraham Tiar, who had been a Betar leader in Tunisia before becoming a passenger on the *Ben Hecht*, was able to escape his detention camp in Cyprus and arrived in Palestine in April 1948 (Tiar later became a member of the Israeli Knesset).[2] The British only permitted unfettered immigration from the Cypriot detention camps for two weeks after Israel declared its independence on May 15, 1948. Then, when the United Nations Security Council passed a resolution calling for the embargo of people of age for military service from entering Israel, the British did not permit refugees, including the *Ben Hecht* passengers, aged eighteen to forty-five to immigrate until February 1949.[3] The British released the Cyprus refugees in the aftermath of an embarrassing incident in which five Royal Air Force fighter planes who were flying over Israeli territory and appeared to attack Israeli troops fighting in the Negev were shot down by the Israeli Air Force.

---

1   *JPS Hebrew-English Tanakh: The Traditional Hebrew Text and the New JPS Translation,* 2nd ed. (Philadelphia: The Jewish Publication Society, 2003 / 5764), 1087.
2   "Knesset Member Abraham Tiar," https://main.knesset.gov.il/mk/Pages/MKPersonal Print.aspx?MKID=432.
3   Lorch, *Edge of the Sword,* 329.

The Israeli pilots, who were American and Canadian volunteers, initially thought they were Egyptian planes.[4]

Hillel Kook (Peter Bergson) was a member of Israel's first Knesset, but he resigned when Israel failed to adopt a written constitution. In 1951, he went to the United States and pursued a private business career. He returned to resettle in Israel in 1970, where he passed away in 2001. In retirement, Kook advocated for the recognition of the national aspirations of Palestinians to their own state and the division of religion and state in Israel.[5]

Hyman Robert ("Bob") Levitan served for fifteen years in the Miami Fire Department; at retirement he had attained the rank of Captain.[6] Bob Levitan returned to Israel five times to work in Kibbutzim. His stepson, Allen Cowan of Charlotte, NC was grateful to him as a beloved stepfather. "When he married my mother, she had three children . . . We had grown up without parental supervision. When Bob came into my life, I didn't like him because he tried to discipline me. The first person to spank me was Bob Levitan. The first person who ever took me to a baseball game was Bob. He was my hero." Levitan had a daughter Barbara Dennis, stepsons Randy and Steve Klein and Allen Cowan, and three grandchildren.[7] Levitan died on August 10, 1998, at age seventy-six, due to a sudden heart attack.[8]

After returning to the United States, Shepard Rifkin became Executive Director of the American Friends of the Fighters for the Freedom of Israel (Lechi). When he wrote to Albert Einstein asking for his support, Einstein replied angrily "When a real and final catastrophe should befall us in Palestine the first responsible for it would be the British and the second responsible for it the Terrorist organizations built up from our own ranks. I am not willing to see anybody associated with those misled and criminal people."[9] While dedicated "To the crew of the *Abril*, wherever they are,"

---

4 McDonald, *Mission in Israel*, 124–127; Jeffrey Weiss and Craig Weiss, *I Am My Brother's Keeper*, 262–263.

5 Louis Rappoport, *Shake Heaven and Earth: Peter Bergson and the Struggle to Rescue the Jews of Europe*, (Jerusalem: Gefen, 1999/5759), 202.

6 Joyce Moed, "Boat Captain that Brought People to Israel, Dies," *Broward Jewish Journal*, zone C, 4A, Bob Levitan collection, USHMM.

7 Christine Walker, "Hyman R. Levitan, Tried to Help Jewish refugees," Bob Levitan collection, USHMM.

8 Moed, "Boat Captain that Brought People to Israel, Dies"; "A M/V BEN HECHT Story."

9 Albert Einstein letter to Shepard Rifkin, April 10, 1948, https://lettersofnote.com/2010/03/04/when-a-real-and-final-catastrophe-should-befall-us/.

Rifkin's novelization of the *Ben Hecht*'s journey revealed that he had mixed feelings about the experience, often unfavorably comparing the ship's haphazard organization and lack of secrecy to that of Haganah operations.[10] However, it is not surprising that Rifkin, who was inspired by the radical Lechi members he met in Acre Prison, would not be fully comfortable with the Bergson Group's idiosyncratic combination of the advertising methods of Madison Avenue, non-violent civil disobedience, and political theater. Notably, his novel ends with the ship's arrest; the crew's unanticipated key assistance to the breakout from Acre Prison, which struck a major blow to British prestige and resolve, is left out of the story. Throughout the 1950s, Rifkin traveled the country and worked as a taxi driver, bartender, moving man, tugboat captain, ambulance driver, manager of a paperback book store, and occasionally went back to sea. In July 1961 he was married and living in New York, and embarked upon a career as a writer, mostly of crime novels. He died in Washington, D.C. on July 4, 2011.[11]

After volunteering to serve on the Haganah ship *Paducah*, and his internment in Cyprus after the *Paducah*'s capture by the British in October of 1947,[12] Walter "Heavy" Greaves served in the infant Merchant Marine of Israel, where, as a bosun, he trained young sailors. He eventually returned to the United States, where he was living when he passed away.[13]

After the voyage of the *Ben Hecht*, Dave Gutmann likewise volunteered again as an oiler on the *Paducah*. Lawrence Kohlberg, a crew-mate on the *Paducah*, who later became a famous psychologist of moral development, convinced him to enroll at the University of Chicago because a high school degree was not necessary for admission there. Gutmann became a professor of psychology at Northwestern University who specialized in the effect of parenting styles on the aging process. He died on November 3, 2013.[14]

Marvin Liebman held various posts in the federal government during the Reagan Administration after decades as an activist and fundraiser for conservative causes.[15] In his memoir *Coming Out Conservative*, Liebman discusses his conversion to Catholicism, but he no longer was a practicing

---

10   See Rifkin, *What Ship, passim.*
11   Author's biographical note, in Shepard Rifkin, *Desire Island* (New York: Ace Books, 1960); "Shepard Rifkin," US Social Security Death Index, 1935–2014.
12   Wilson, *Cordon*, 265.
13   Patzert, *Running the Palestine Blockade*, 217.
14   Rose, Huyck, and Grunes, "David L. Gutmann (1925–2013)."
15   "Marvin Liebman, 73, Dies; Conservative for Gay Rights."

Catholic at the time of his death. In 1990, he came out as gay in a public letter to his friend William Buckley, in which he decried "political gay bashing, racism, and anti-Semitism" in the American political right wing. Liebman wrote that "Today, bigotry masquerades in many guises—conservatism, morality, religion, family—but it is the same as the barbarian's knout or Mengele's surgical blade."[16]

Harry N. Schatz died at age fifty-eight on September 25, 1958 in Indiana, and was remembered as "a member of the crew of the famed Ben Hecht ship."[17] Walter Cushenberry was shot and killed in 1960 at a New York hotel where he worked as a night clerk, while attempting to fight off robbers.[18]

David Kaplan became a dentist and served on the faculty of the Columbia University School of Dental and Oral Surgery for more than thirty-five years until his death in 2002.[19] Ed Styrak, who along with Dave Kaplan was one of the two radio operators on the *Ben Hecht*, went on to volunteer for the Israeli Air Transport Command as a radio operator with Israel's clandestine Air Transport Command, bringing vital arms from Czechoslovakia to Israel.[20] Styrak, as a non-Jewish volunteer, was described by a friend in the Air Transport Command as "more idealistic than any of us Jews whose 'duty' it was to serve."[21] As mentioned earlier, Styrak survived a crash landing of a cargo airplane packed with a fighter plane and other weapons when the Israeli air base declined to light the runway because the first truce with the Arab forces had been declared. Israeli ground control did not want to turn on the lights in the air field because it would have alerted UN observers of the cease-fire. Attempting an emergency landing, the carrier plane crashed into a hill near Latrun. Styrak survived the plane

---

16 Liebman, *Coming Out Conservative*, 223, 236.

17 *The Jewish Post and Opinion*, Indiana edition, September 26, 1958, 5.

18 Kaplan Oral History, part 1, MZ; Associated Press Name Card Index to AP Stories, 1905–1990, Ancestry.com, original data: Name Card Index to AP Stories (series 4), Associated Press File Drawers of National, International, News Feature Name/Subject Cards, 1937–1985, microfilm, Associated Press Corporate Archives, New York, NY; "Walter Rex Cushenberry," Newspapers.com Obituary Index, 1800s–current; Walter R. Cushenberry in the Kentucky Birth Index, 1911–1999, Ancestry.com, original data: Kentucky Department for Libraries and Archives, Kentucky Birth, Marriage, and Death Databases: Births 1911–1999, Frankfort, KY, Kentucky Department for Libraries and Archives.

19 "Obituaries," *AVI Newsletter*, Spring 2002, 4, https://www.sas.upenn.edu/~sklausne/Spring02.html/Spring02.htm.

20 Ed Styrak," *AVI Newsletter*, Summer 2013, 10.

21 Livingston, *No Trophy*, 88.

with a broken leg but he had to be carried unconscious through a shattered windshield by the pilot and co-pilot. Another crew member died in the hold of the crashed plane.[22]

After service in the 1956 Sinai campaign, Israel sold the *Ma'oz*. In 1957, after the ship left Israeli service, the ship was renamed the *Maria del Mare* and was still in active use as a ferry ship in the Bay of Naples as of 1999.[23] It was in the process of being rebuilt in 2009, and was under repair in 2013.[24]

Royal Naval officer Alan Tyler recounted that "the only time I felt ashamed to be taking part in such a heartless and insensitive operation" was when he saw a group in *tallitot* reciting Sabbath prayers on one of the prison ships carrying the passengers of the *Exodus 1947* as prisoners to Germany. He retired from the Royal Navy in 1964, and worked in his family's textile importing firm. He joined Wimbledon Synagogue, where he eventually served as chairman.[25]

I. F. Stone became a leading left-wing independent journalist. He was ostracized by the mainstream Zionist movement due to his support of a binational Jewish-Arab state. Stone argued in 1978 that "the two peoples must live together either in the same Palestinian state or side by side in two Palestinian states." He wrote then that "I remember, as if it were yesterday, the horror of statelessness in the thirties for those who fled Fascist and Nazi oppression. I feel for the scattered Palestinians who would like a state and a passport too."[26]

***

Mandel did not experience any problems reentering the United States after his time in the Israeli Army, and his American citizenship was never questioned as a result of his service with Israel. The first American Ambassador

---

22   Robert Gand, *Angels in the Sky: How a Band of Volunteer Airmen Saved the New State of Israel* (New York: W. W. Norton & Company, 2017), ch. 16.

23   Silverstone, *Our Only Refuge*, 23, 36; "Maoz," http://www.navypedia.org/ships/israel/isr_es_maoz.htm.

24   "The rebuild of superyacht Santa Maria Del Mare (1931)," https://www.superyachttimes.com/yacht-news/the-rebuild-of-superyacht-santa-maria-del-mare-1931 (December 15, 2009); "Santa Maria Del Mare," shipspotting.com, http://www.shipspotting.com/gallery/photo.php?lid=1733460 (January 29, 2013).

25   Alan Tyler, "The View from a 'Brit.'"

26   I. F. Stone, *Underground to Palestine and Reflections Thirty Years Later* (New York: Pantheon Books, 1978), 229–233, 260.

to Israel, James McDonald, would describe "dual allegiance" as an "old bogey" as early as 1951. McDonald thought this problem to be "inherent . . . in the very nature of man as a complex being with diverse ends. All men have not single or dual but multiple allegiances. If a Jew has an emotional sympathy for another State because in that State live other Jews, his attitude is no different from that of an American of Irish descent who has an affection for Ireland and an interest in its welfare."[27] Mandel was loyal and deeply committed to both the United States and to Israel.

After returning from the war, Mandel lost touch with many of his former comrades in the Aliyah Bet and Machal who lived in the United States. As he explained in a letter written to the Israeli Defense Ministry decades later requesting membership in the Irgun veteran's organization, even though he had not formally been a member of the organization:

> . . . I really have no knowledge of anyone I can get to fill out Paragraph Vov [of a form, requesting the name of his commander]. Avraham Stavsky, who was my Mefaked [commander], was killed in the *Altalena*. I have no idea where I can reach Peter Bergson or even if he is still alive. [Bergson (Hillel Kook), who passed away August 18, 2001, was in fact still alive at the time Mandel wrote this letter.] I am 77 years old and do not have total recall. It is more than fifty years since I participated. I would greatly appreciate any assistance you can give me. Perhaps a veteran of Acre Prison can remember my action there. I am enclosing a copy of a pin award that I received from the Irgun members in Acre.[28]

Subsequent to the writing of this letter, Henry Mandel was awarded the Irgun service membership award and was admitted into the Irgun veteran organization.

Mandel maintained contact with other veterans of the 1947–1949 struggle for Israeli independence, and he belonged to American Veterans of Israel (AVI). His stints in Israeli service did not seem to him to have changed his life or the way he raised his two daughters. He had "hoped," he later wrote in response to a questionnaire in 1995, "that Israel would have a higher standard than other countries. Unfortunately it has the same dirty politics, dirty politicians, and placing personal advantages over common good as the rest of the world."[29]

---

27   McDonald, *Mission in Israel*, 289.
28   Mandel letter to the Israeli Defense Ministry.
29   Mandel Machal questionnaire.

As of 1995, Mandel had visited Israel twice (he would visit again for his grandson Benjamin Leinwand's bar mitzvah in 2003). Mandel reported that "My two daughters each spent a year in Israel after High School with Bnei Akiva." Mandel described the benefit he personally derived from his experiences volunteering for Israel as "personal satisfaction that I helped in the formation of Israel (the state)." After his volunteering for Israel, he did not actively affiliate with pro-Israel organizations. However, Mandel remained tremendously dedicated to assisting the State of Israel. He always made a point of using Israeli products for religious rituals. When his daughters spent post-high-school years in Israel at a time of runaway inflation, he insisted that they change their money legally at lower rates to support the state. As president of his synagogue, he voted to fund an Israeli ambulance and two motorcycle ambulances in Israel with proceeds on the sale of the synagogue building. His favorite personal charity supported disabled Israeli veterans. His grandson Keith Flaks followed in his footsteps by serving as an overseas volunteer in the Israeli Defense Forces Machal program, and Amichai Steinmetz, a grandnephew, served for three years in the Israeli Defense Force's elite and hazardous Duvdevan counter-terrorism unit.

When Eliyahu Lankin, the former European Irgun chief who sought to bridge the divide between the Bergson Group and Menachem Begin, asked Mandel's friend and *Ben Hecht* crewmate David Kaplan why he and his crewmates risked their freedom to bring Holocaust survivors to Palestine, Kaplan reflected:

Everything has a rationale, except a miracle because a miracle I accept. Because I am a miracle. This land is a miracle. I mean, you and I sitting here now. We should have both been dead a long time ago. This country [Israel] shouldn't exist. No one's arguing the point, what I'm saying is that this has all been to this point of view because if you take a child and you bring them up to recognize that this is right, this is wrong, with a sense of moral judgment and he sees an injustice being done he will do what he can to correct that injustice if you bring them up that way. If . . . everybody does it so you do it too. *Agenavenor gornisht.* Nothing is going to happen. And here are people. Talk about Walter Cushenberry, he was once interviewed, a black man, and he said, "I know what it is to be persecuted." That was his answer. Why are you here? "Because I know what it's like to be on the other side." So—and listen, we lived in the lap of—America was luxury and we lived in—these guys didn't have to do anything and we were—and nobody knew anything about . . . By the way, people were, "What are you doing? Are you crazy? What kind of—you're never gonna be this. You're never gonna be that." People of little faith, but the faith wasn't a blind faith; it was something that you just felt, a feeling. But it had to be there to start. In my own [yeshiva] education I went away from—I turned away completely by the time I was at sea and all that. It took me a long time to know what I'm studying now. That's all. . . . I'll tell you this story, one sentence to clean it all up.... "Most Jews themselves don't know what their role is." Now that's the truth. Very few of us are privileged to know [that]—even we who think we know it don't know it, but it [the story of the *Ben Hecht*] has a piece of this [knowledge] that makes me and you sit here and talk to each other like this.[30]

***

The publicity strategy of the *Ben Hecht* was controversial at the time and dismissed by Mossad L'Aliyah Bet activists who believed in the efficacy of a purely clandestine approach to illegal immigration to Palestine, but such tactical disagreements have recurred frequently in the history of immigration of oppressed Jews to Israel. Similarly, decades later it was argued that public pressure and advocacy by the American Association for Ethiopian Jews was counterproductive and threatened clandestine Mossad operations to bring Ethiopia's Jews to Israel.[31] Until 1969, Shaul Avigur, who had headed Mossad Aliyah Bet, directed Israeli clandestine efforts to help Jews emigrate from the Soviet Union and he eschewed public protests, but soon after, Israeli policy shifted towards a public campaign to free Soviet Jewry.[32] In the late 1940s, the Aliyah Bet clandestine immigration movement not only put political pressure on Great Britain to abandon Palestine and to allow the establishment of a Jewish state to welcome those of the remnant of European Jewry that wished to live in Israel, but it also made it possible for others to immigrate to the United States. If the bulk of Jewish displaced persons had not gone to Israel, the United States probably would not have

---

30   Kaplan Oral History, , interview by Eliyahu Lankin, July 17, 1987, Jabotinsky Institute, part 2, tape CS-0328, Metzudat Ze'ev (MZ) (Jabotinsky Institute), Tel Aviv, Israel.

31   Batia Makower, *The Power of One: The Story of the Man who Opened the Route to Israel in Sudan for the Ethiopian Jews. Ferede Yazezew Aklum 1949–2009*, trans. Heidi Gleit, ed. Shmuel Yilma (n.p., Israel: Yerusalem Forum, 2019), 96.

32   Sachar, *Diaspora*, 415–417.

loosened immigration enforcement to allow other displaced persons into the United States, the majority of whom were not Jews.[33]

The Jews of the Diaspora have been sustained by the visible influence of Israel on both potential enemies who fear Israel and friends who admire it. Most significantly for the Jewish Diaspora, Israel has bolstered the pride and culture of Diaspora Jews themselves.[34] For our part, as long as the *Ben Hecht*'s and Henry Mandel's journey continues to challenge and inspire, it is not over.

The voyage of the *Ben Hecht* was a turning point in the Bergson Group's trajectory from activist political pressure group to an adjunct of the Irgun's military struggle. Quite unexpectedly, the ship's crew would aid a prison break that helped undermine the British will to rule Palestine. Ultimately, the journey of the *Ben Hecht* illustrates the power and limits of civil disobedience in a battle against injustice. Like contemporary unauthorized immigrants in the United States, the *Ben Hecht* passengers had been defined by their "illegal" status, not by the past traumas they had survived or their future potentials.[35] The story of the *Ben Hecht* has renewed resonance in a world, such as ours, rent by debates on the practicality and morality of attempting to stop "illegal" immigration and migration of refugees in both the Old and New Worlds. The *Ben Hecht* provides one historical model for undertaking such immigration: a bold attempt to put the gatekeepers on trial. The travails of the refugees and crew of the *Ben Hecht* can also serve as a reminder that the establishment of Israel was a humanitarian cause. Yet, even as their tale illustrates the potential of non-violent protest and civil disobedience, the imprisonment and exile of the passengers and crew from the Promised Land highlights its potential limits.

Albert Camus, in a preface to an account of the *Ben Hecht*'s voyage, hinted of freedom fighting to come and the moral dilemmas inherent even in justified violence, by commenting that

> [t]he idea that these persecuted people are tired of being so will make them
> much more interesting and finally make some friends. They no longer want
> the mass grave and they want the right to have a grave like everyone else,

---

33 See Leonard Dinnerstein, *America and the Survivors of the Holocaust* (New York: Columbia University Press, 1982), 268.

34 Sachar, *Diaspora*, 479.

35 Lydialyee Gibson, "'From Neither Here Nor There': Sociologist Roberto Gonzalez Interprets the Lives of Undocumented Immigrants Growing Up in America," *Harvard Magazine* 122, no. 6 (July/August 2020): 32.

because they have a life like everyone else. It's a good start, and then there's no reason not to listen to them. Think, then, if they understood the lesson and if one day they became persecutors? They would return to the community in the midst of general relief. Everything would be in order, finally. It would be with us the feast of the prodigal, the day of joy.[36]

As Amos Elon has noted, in a passage that Mandel underlined in his copy of Elon's account of the founding generation of the State of Israel, if allowing the Jews into "Palestine was an injustice to the Arabs, not allowing them in was an even greater injustice to the Jews. If two rights were clashing in Palestine, . . . surely the satisfaction of Jewish rights involved a smaller measure of suffering and injustice."[37]

At a time when the world was allowing the Holocaust survivors to despair without permanent refuge in displaced persons camps in Germany and internment camps in Cyprus, a resolute few were determined to save the Jewish people, fully aware of the sacrifices and even the potential harm to others that might be necessary to fight oppression.[38] Mandel's *Ben Hecht* shipmate David Gutmann, who also volunteered on an Haganah illegal immigrant ship, in response to ethicist Carol Gilligan's argument in a review of his daughter Stephanie Gutmann's book *The Kinder, Gentler Military*[39] that the elder Gutmann's experiences as a non-violent blockade runner did not justify traditional military strength, wrote:

> my experience with unarmed resistance to the British crown only confirmed for me the need for real warriors. Lacking guns, we Haganah sailors were helpless when Royal Navy marines seized our unarmed ships and hauled young Jewish survivors off to yet another stinking prison camp, this time on

36 "[L]'idée que ces persécutés en ont assez de l'être va les rendre beaucoup plus intéressants et leur faire enfin quelques amis. Ils ne veulent plus de la fosse commune et ils veulent qu'on leur reconnaisse le droit d'avoir une tombe comme tout monde puisqu'ils ont une vie comme tout le la leçon et si, un jour ils devenaient persécuteurs ? Ils reviendraient ainsi dans la communauté, au milieu du soulagement général. Tout serait en ordre, enfin. Ce serait chez nous le festin du prodigue, le jour de l'allégresse. Il faudrait alors tuer le veau gras . . . Encore tuer! diront les délicats." Albert Camus, préface to Méry, *Let My People Go*, 10.

37 Amos Elon, *The Israelis: Founders and Sons* (New York: Holt, Rinehart and Winston, 1971), 177, 279.

38 See Elie Wiesel, *Dawn* (New York: Hill & Wang, 1961).

39 Carol Gilligan, "Make War, Not Nice!," *New York Times*, May 7, 2000, review of *The Kinder, Gentler Military: Can America's Gender-Neutral Fighting Force Still Win Wars*, by Stephanie Gutmann (New York: Scribner Book Company, 2000).

Cyprus. Love was not enough: it took guns, warriors and killing to complete the rescue mission that our voyages of peaceful resistance could only begin. Before the orphans of the Holocaust could finally reach haven in the new state of Israel, Jewish warriors had to fight a bloody battle for Haifa Port, they had to hold the country against invading Arab armies, and Jewish warships had to secure the sea lanes from Europe to Cyprus. Stephanie Gutmann is right that love and war are not inevitably in conflict, but form a paradoxical unity. Until all the lions lie down with all the lambs, the ports of refuge and islands of decency have to be secured by disciplined soldiers who are prepared to kill as well as to die.[40]

---

40   David Gutmann letter, *New York Times Magazine*, June 4, 2000, found in David Gutmann file, Machal and Aliyah Bet records, undated, 1930–2011 collection, AJHS, Center for Jewish History, New York.

Part Three

Henry Mandel Reflects

A person's life purpose is nothing more than to rediscover, through the detours of art, those one or two great and simple images in whose presence his heart first opened.
—Albert Camus, "Between Yes and No" ("Entre Oui et Non," 1937)

Chapter 17

Family and Brotherly Love

Eternal delight and deliciousness will be his, who coming to lay him down, can say with his final breath—O Father!—here I die. I have striven to be Thine, more than to be this world's, or mine own. Yet this is nothing; I leave eternity to Thee; for what is man that he should live out the lifetime of his God?

—Herman Melville, *Moby Dick*, chapter 9

Henry Mandel delivered the following eulogy of his younger brother, Moshe Mandel:

Moish and I didn't really grow up together. We both went to Salanter yeshiva, but I graduated in June 1932, while he began in September 1932. We really didn't get together until he was grown, and then we couldn't always be together. We were both in the Merchant Marine at the same time, but ironically I was in the National Maritime Union (the NMU) while he was a member of the Seamen's International Union (the SIU). He was on a ship going back and forth to Puerto Rico when he met Polish and German refugees who had reached P.R., and were in bad shape financially. He raised cash and collected clothing which he brought to them in the next trip. A typical thing for Moish.

Our father was not well, and although he was a member of Rabbi Bick's *shul*, he had all he could do to go to the Bais Yaakov *shul* that was on the same block. I would walk with him there in the morning, and Moish, who davened in Rabbi Bick's *shul*, which finished early, would pick Pa up after davening. Moish was a Rabbi Bick *chasid* and would go to sit at his table after we finished the Pesach *seder* (I trust that Rabbi Bick had just about started), and Moish was always there to hear a *D'var Torah* from the Rabbi. He also went to Rabbi Bick's *sukkah* after we finished our meal in our *sukkah*.

He would listen to the Rabbi's speaking. We would always ask him for any interesting points or items that the Rabbi elucidated. One Sukkos evening he came home with a very interesting story. The Rabbi always had several Jews at the *sukkah* whom he fed. This Sukkos evening the Rebbitzen brought some dessert to the window of the *sukkah*. One Jew, anxious for his dessert, leaned over the table to get to the window. Unfortunately, he also leaned over the candlesticks, and his beard caught on fire. The Rabbi, without consulting any of the books discussing what is or is not permitted on the holidays, immediately made the decision and cried "*Mon meg farlesen, mon meg farlesen*." It is permitted to put out the fire. We all had a good laugh, though the man had a shorter beard for several months.

One interesting incident happened to us when he was little. He was about three years old, sitting on a curb. A Global moving van, which was a huge truck, ran over and crushed his left foot below the ankle. He was taken to Lincoln Hospital, which was brand new at the time. Until then we had used Lebanon Hospital. Pa rushed to Lebanon Hospital, and was redirected to Lincoln Hospital. There he was told that Moish's foot was completely mangled and should be immediately removed or an infection could set in and the leg would have to be amputated at the knee. We had an excellent physician, Dr. Mayantz, who had a pre-communist education. Pa called him to the hospital, and he advised not to permit the operation. The hospital doctor warned of the complete amputation possibility. Dr. Mayantz said "Amputated at the ankle or amputated at the knee, he will be a cripple the rest of his life." Pa did not sign for the operation. I will now add that in the Army he was a M.P.—a military policeman and afterwards, a port authority policeman with his so-called crushed foot.

I hate to concede this, but he was everybody's favorite brother. He was always readily available to help any one of us. If someone needed help, Moish was the first one to call and he always was the last because he never said no.

After he got married he and Cidelle were one. They had one mind, and were one person. They always were together, and in their entire married life I never saw them argue. It was an ideal marriage, and it's regrettable it did not last longer. Cidelle always entered contests and sometimes won. But Moish was the greatest prize of all. In his last years Moish was sick, and Cidelle cared for him and nursed him beyond human endurance. When we called her she never complained of all the care and labor bestowed upon Moish. She was a ministering angel. We are all grateful and appreciative to her. May she have pleasant memories, and may she enjoy a healthy life.

Moish, we all miss you. May you look down upon us and bless us.

Henry Mandel grew up near the family of the author Herman Wouk in the Bronx. He recalled that in the late 1940s he attended a Simchat Torah service at the synagogue where Wouk's grandfather was the Rabbi, because it was easier for Mandel's father to walk there. Wouk's grandfather got into a bidding war with a woman in the ladies' section over the right to name the *Chatan Torah*. It turned out the woman was Wouk's mother, and they were both trying to purchase the honor for Wouk.

After he got married, Leo Mandel, Hank's elder brother, attended non-Hasidic synagogues in the Bronx where the Ashkenazic rite was prayed, led by Rabbi Eliyahu Rusoff, the author of responsa, at 2067 Vyse Avenue,[1] and by Rabbi Yechiel Michel Charlop (1889–1974), at the Bronx Jewish Center.[2] Rabbi Bick officiated at Henry and Libby Mandel's wedding, where he went to great lengths in praising Mandel, but only said in Yiddish that the bride came from "a good family." This amused the groom because the Dershowitz family was much more important and well-known than the Mandel family. Zechariah Dershowitz, from Pilsner in Galicia (which later became part of Czechoslovakia), had immigrated to the United States. He initially left four children with his wife Leah in Europe, Leibish (Louis, age five), Schmiel (Sol, age four), Shulem (Sam, age two), and newborn Sima (Sadie), and a few years later his family joined him on the Lower East Side. A tailor, Zechariah at one point worked at the Triangle Shirt Factory. The notorious Triangle Fire of 1911 took place on a Saturday, and he felt that his life was spared because in observance of the Sabbath he had not gone to work that day.

The family were among the founders of Yeshiva Torah Vodaath, the first yeshiva in Brooklyn. In 1918, Torah Vodaath's founders planned a religious Zionist school that combined Hebrew language, religious studies, and secular studies.[3] Sam Dershowitz, Libby's father, years later pawned his wife Ida Mehr Dershowitz's engagement ring to help pay the rent for the struggling elementary school, which had instruction in both Jewish and secular

---

1   Yisrael Mizrachi, "Rabbi Eliyahu Rusoff of the Bronx and His Beating on the Subway," July 10, 2014, http://judaicaused.blogspot.com/2014/07/rabbi-eliyahu-rusoff-of-bronx-and-his.html.

2   Mandel interview by Esther Mandel, Aaron Mandel, and Chana Liba Mandel, 2012; "Charlop, Yechiel Michel," https://www.jewishvirtuallibrary.org/charlop-yechiel-michel; "Charlop, Yechiel Michel," Tiktin collection, YIVO Archives, New York.

3   Jeffrey S. Gurock, *The Men and Women of Yeshiva: Higher Education, Orthodoxy and American Judaism* (New York: Columbia University Press, 1988), 108–109.

studies. Zechariah Dershowitz's family started the first Nusach Sfard *shtiebel* in Williamsburg, called the Dershowitz Family Congregation.[4]

The Immigration Act of 1924 severely limited immigration into the United States by imposing quotas, but it did permit the immigration above the quota limitations of "[a]n immigrant who continuously for at least two years immediately preceding the time of his application for the United States has been, and who seeks to enter the United States solely for the purpose of, carrying on the vocation of minister of any religious denomination. . . ."[5] The small Dershowitz synagogue hired a new rabbi and other religious functionaries every month, allowing them to immigrate to the United States in the "Rabbi of the Month Club" and saving them from the Holocaust. The Dershowitz family also saved many cousins in Czechoslovakia by signing affidavits pledging to support them financially, which the United States government required to allow them to immigrate. Libby's mother, Ida, took care to arrange for apartments for these families, which she personally owned and maintained.

FS: I would like to ask you when you got married . . .

HM: I . . .

FS: If you did?

HM: I married in 1952, and my first daughter was born in . . .

FS: What is your wife's name?

HM: My wife's name is Libby. Her maiden name is Dershowitz.

FS: And do you have children?

HM: I have two daughters. My older daughter Bethsheba was born in 1953. My younger daughter Susan was born in 1958. Bethsheba is married to Robbie Leinwand and she has three sons. And Suzy is married to Michael Flaks, and she has two sons. No granddaughters. I'm stuck with only grandsons. [*HM smiles*].

FS: And what are your grandsons' names?

---

4   Sylvia Dershowitz Fuchs, "Dershowitz Family Centennial," *The Jewish Press*, Friday, April 7, 1989, 28B.

5   *Laws Applicable to Immigration and Nationality*, ed. Edwins Austin Avery, under direction of Carl B. Hyatt (Washington, D.C.: US Department of Justice, 1953), 413, quoted in Rakeffet-Rothkoff, *Silver Era*, 192.

HM: Well, the Leinwands are Joshua, Gabriel, and Benjamin. The Flakses are Sam and Keith. . . . This is a picture of my family taken recently at the Bar Mitzvah of Sam. I am seated. Alongside me is my wife Libby. Starting from the upper left is my daughter Bethsheba, her husband Robbie Leinwand, their son Joshua, then is Sammy Flaks who was Bar Mitzvah'ed, my daughter Susan and her husband Michael Flaks. In the middle row on the left is Gabriel Leinwand, and next to him is his brother Benjamin Leinwand, and then on the other side we have Keith Flaks.

FS: How did the war affect your children, your two daughters?

HM: I don't know if it affected them, because I really don't know how I would have raised them otherwise [*HM smiles*] because I did not have any children before. For me it was the only way to raise them. I sent them to yeshivas through high school and to college, they both went to Brooklyn College. And Bethsheba got her master's from NYU and Susan got her JD from Hofstra.

FS: Is there anything that you would like to add that I have not asked you?

HM: Well, I can only add that I am proud to be a Jew and I am proud to have had the opportunity to help participate in the liberation of Palestine so that the Jews can have their own land. And I am grateful that I had that opportunity because I think that was an important thing for not only for the Jewish people, but for my own mental satisfaction. I think that I am happy that I did it and I am grateful for the opportunity because there are so many people that never had such an opportunity. And I think that is what I would say. I am proud to be a Jew. I don't think being Jewish is different from any other nation. If I were Irish I would be proud to be Irish. If I were Italian I would be proud to be Italian. But I am not, I am Jewish. [*HM smiles*]. And I am proud to be a Jew.

FS: I would like to thank you very much for participating in our project.

HM: Well . . . [fades to black][6]

*** *

HM: I am going to have to cut this short because it is Friday afternoon and I have a lot of things to do. You can call me another time, if you have any more questions.

---

6   Mandel interview by Shuster, 2000.

AGM: OK, thank you very, very much Mr. Mandel.

HM: And what is your name?

AGM: Alyssa.

HM: Alyssa what?

AGM: Goldschmidt.

HM: All right, Alyssa.

AGM: Thank you, very, very much. I appreciate all your time, you have been very, very helpful. And have a Shabbat Shalom.

HM: Thank you, you too.

AGM: Take care. Good bye.[7]

***

For Mandel, civic and religious freedoms were intertwined. Soon after moving with his young family to Coney Island to live in a middle-income housing development sponsored by the Amalgamated Clothing Workers Union of America, he spearheaded an effort to build a communal ritual tabernacle, a *sukkah*, for the development and a synagogue in the community. The following petitions and letters advocating for permission to erect a *sukkah* illustrate Mandel's faith in the democratic and union values of equity, equality, solidarity, and persistent advocacy as much as to faithful adherence to religious laws:

> We the undersigned hereby petition Amalgamated Warbasse Houses, Inc. to permit the erection of a Succah (Tabernacle) for the holiday of Succoth. We agree to pay all costs of purchase, erection, maintenance and removal after the holiday. We agree to provide the necessary insurance coverage (estimated cost $25.50 per family).
>
> A delegation of Rabbis and laymen, residents of Amalgamated Warbasse Houses, are interested in having a Sukkah. Permission to erect this Sukkah has not been granted by the housing management.
>
> It is not conceivable that a development sponsored by and carrying the name of the democratic Amalgamated Clothing Workers of America union

---

7   Mandel interview by Goldschmidt Magid, 2006.

would inhibit the free practice of religion. It is earnestly requested that you, as a member of the Board of Directors, use your responsibility and influence to instruct the development management to permit erection of a sukkah to enable the cooperators to follow their religious tenets and beliefs. We hope that you react favorably to this request.

***

N.Y. Board of Rabbis
10 E. 73rd St.
NY, NY 10021
Attn: Rabbi Harold H. Gordon
Dear Rabbi Gordon,

I am writing in the name of a group of residents of the Amalgamated Warbasse Houses, a cooperative housing development located in the Coney Island area of Brooklyn and sponsored by the Amalgamated Clothing Workers Union and the United Housing Foundations. On August 9, 1965 we requested permission from the Housing Manager to erect a sukkah. We have been stalled by delaying tactics since then, and have not been granted a sukkah.

Housing developments on the Lower East Side under the same sponsorship do have sukkahs. In these instances, permission was denied until Mr. (Jacob) Potofsky, President of the Amalgamated Clothing Workers Union interceded with the housing managements to have permission granted. We believe that similar requests on our behalf by Mr. Potofsky would have favorable results.

I contacted Rabbi Gilbert Klaperman [the founding rabbi of Congregation Beth Sholom in Lawrence, New York][8] for assistance in contacting Mr. Potofsky. Rabbi Klaperman asked that I call you and have you send out a letter to Mr. Potofsky over his signature as chairman of the Religious Observance Committee. I could not reach you, and Mr. Brodsky suggested that I write this letter. I earnestly appeal to you to help us by sending a letter to Mr. Potofsky. I enclose a sheet giving the principal facts in this letter.

***

8   "Rabbi Klaperman," https://www.bethsholomlawrence.org/rabbi_klaperman.

At Henry Mandel's seventieth birthday party held on September 19, 1990, after the revelers sang "Happy Birthday," they began to chant "Speech, Speech!" and he obliged:

> I want to thank you all for coming. I love all of you. And I am sure that you will like me more if I don't make a long speech. I had not planned on making a speech and I will not make a speech. I just want to welcome you and thank you. A few people have said to me "What is the occasion, a seventieth birthday like this?" And I was thinking about it. [Unclear phrase, perhaps "Living through it made me"] think that way. In the Talmud in Tractate *Mo'ed Kattan*, "A Minor Holiday," it tells us that Rabbi Yossi made a party for his sixtieth birthday. And a friend said to him 'Why have a party on a sixtieth birthday? And he said "Now I know that I no longer will be subject to *karet* [excision, early death as a punishment]. I cannot have my life foreshortened and die before my time. And the Gemara in *Shabbat*, there is a *Tosfos*, a commentary, which explains that Rav Yossi, Rav Yosef, had the sixtieth birthday at the time that foreshortening of the life could no longer happen because at that time a life of a man was sixty. And therefore, once he reached his sixtieth birthday, he knew that he was safe. His life would not be foreshortened. Now today, in our time, we have the proverbial "three score" at seventy years. And now I can thank the Lord and praise God now that I know that my life will not be foreshortened. I will not be subject to *karet*. So at least I have passed that milestone. And I am glad to celebrate it and thank the Good Lord for letting me reach this age. And I am very happy that you people have all come down to help me celebrate. And I thank you all for coming and I wish you all a healthy and happy New Year.[9]

According to tradition, excision occurs when one dies before attaining sixty years, which was the usual expected age of death of people in Talmudic times, as is apparent from the Talmud, which states that when Rav Yosef attained age sixty, he threw a big party, because he was no longer subject to excision.[10] Tosfot adds a formal legal ruling based on the Talmudic precedent.[11]

---

9   Henry Mandel seventieth birthday party, September 19, 1990, video tape and transcript in possession of the editor.

10   Talmud Bavli *Mo'ed Kattan* 28a.

11   Talmud Bavli *Shabbat* 25a, Tosfot s.v. "*karet*." Thanks to Rabbi Peretz Chain for locating and explaining the Tosfot.

Chapter 18

Civil Servant and Union Activist

Many a true word hath been spoke in jest.
—Joseph Woodfall Ebsworth

After Mandel returned to the United States, he worked as a tool and die maker and then as a machine shop foreman at the Brooklyn Navy Yard producing arms during the Korean War.[1] In the evenings he taught machine shop practice in New York City High Schools.[2] He then became a civilian industrial specialist for the US Army and the US Department of Defense, where he became an expert in government procurement contracts and received several performance awards.[3] Mandel retired from the federal government in 1970, and left to become a methods analyst for the New York City Department of Health, where he worked for eighteen years.[4] His civil service title was methods analyst, which involved analyzing management procedures, but drawing upon his previous experience with government contracting he served in the in-house title of Director of Procurement. During his years at the Health Department, successive Commissioners decided to alternatively centralize or decentralize services. Mandel, upset with the wastefulness, commented "[i]t would make those of us who had been there for awhile dizzy." But he also sought a way to change the lot of his fellow coworkers. Mandel became a member of the Association of

---

1 "I'd Do It for Free."
2 Mandel Machal questionnaire, AJHS.
3 "I'd Do It for Free."
4 Mandel Machal questionnaire, AJHS.

Methods Analysts, which evolved into the Organization of Staff Analysts (OSA). He helped organize his fellow staff analysts at the Department of Health to choose OSA as their collective bargaining representative. By the time of his retirement from City service in 1990, Mandel had attained the title of Senior Methods Analyst. He then volunteered without pay, at first for one day a week, and then for two, to act as the field representative for union members who had grievances before their agency's labor relations office and arbitrators, initially working from home.[5] After a few years, he was hired by the Union to work three days a week to found its grievance section, which he headed as Chief Grievance Officer until he retired again, at ninety years old.[6]

One of the first laws enacted by the Nazi regime was to eliminate the constitutional protection of the civil service and pension rights of German government workers.[7] Such laws are crucial in a democracy to safeguard individual independence from an arbitrary state. Mandel devoted the happiest years of his life to securing those same types of protection for the members of OSA. Mandel handled complaints about improper wages, unfair discipline, indeed, "just about everything," as he described it when he was interviewed by the *Chief-Leader* in his cubicle-type office at OSA headquarters at East Twenty-Third Street in Manhattan. As a Democratic party voter his entire life, he zestfully battled the Republican Giuliani administration. Mandel told a reporter that "I'm so happy. I would do it for free."[8] Representing upset union members, he liked to say "You have no patience because you are not a doctor." Hank was so pleased with how his decision to continue working for two decades after his official "retirement" kept him engaged and active, that he advised those contemplating retirement to find a new avocation, rather than sitting on a park bench.

On Friday afternoons, he and his wife Libby, who also volunteered at OSA and who had a degree in labor relations, took care of their grandsons when they were released from school early. Sometimes, when prompted, he told stories about his adventures on the *Ben Hecht* on the stoop, interspersed with greetings to pedestrians passing by. As he entered his ninth

---

5   "I'd Do It for Free."
6   Robert J. Croghan, OSA Newsline, March 30, 2015, https://www.osaunion.org/online/mar15/index.html.
7   Anne L. Bloch, "The Law," in *The Black Book: The Nazi Crime against the Jewish People* (New York: The Jewish Black Book Committee, 1946), 85.
8   "I'd Do It for Free."

decade he came to think that he had been rewarded with extra years to compensate for giving up the best years of youth to fight for Israel. Henry Mandel passed away in New York on March 27, 2015.

On March 30, 2015, the following notice appeared on the OSA Newsline:

We had sad news last week. Henry (Hank) Mandel has passed away. Hank Mandel had a long and full life.

In our union office hangs a framed union dues book from his service in the war-torn Atlantic as a merchant seaman. Having survived Nazi submarines, Hank then proceeded to Israel where he was arrested for his work on behalf of that state in formation. A medal dedicated to him from that nation also hangs in our office.

Post-war, Hank worked for the Navy as a federal employee and did so until he retired after a full career. His next step was to take and pass a Methods Analyst exam for New York City. That title was a predecessor to our own title series being created. Hank was on board with the city when our new organization was formed and joined as soon as he heard of it. He became OSA's chapter chairperson for the Department of Health and was very active from the start.

Hank retired from his city job just as OSA was winning the right to represent 650 analysts. He volunteered to use his free time as a retiree to help OSA and he began doing grievances from home. A member would call in a grievance; Hank would go to the member's worksite and fill out the grievance forms there. He would drop the forms off at that agency's labor relations office and would wait for the Step I hearing to be called. He would return on the date of the hearing and get together with the member to prep before the actual hearing.

Hank would follow this procedure through the grievance process, for Step I, Step II and Step III. He would also represent the member at arbitration if the matter went so far.

He did this, week after week, without pay.

Eventually, our union grew large enough to afford an office and Hank now began coming into that office. There, he founded our grievance section and trained other volunteer retirees as the section expanded, year after year.

Hank had attended City College on 23rd street when that street was serviced by the Second Avenue elevated train. He worked for us, on 23rd street, until the city was, for the third time, attempting to build a subway on Second Avenue.

Only after he celebrated his 90th birthday did Hank decide he could no longer keep up with the work as our chief grievance officer.

Many thousands of city employees in the analyst titles have been protected by the fairness built into the system called due process. Hank did his part in making that happen and he did so with all his heart for all his years.

We have lost one of our founders.[9]

---

9   Croghan, OSA Newsline.

Epilogue

At Henry Mandel's funeral, his grandson Joshua Leinwand spoke about how Henry's relationship with his grandmother was his model for a loving marriage. His brother Gabriel Leinwand spoke of how the family had lost its patriarch. His youngest grandson, Benjamin Leinwand, said in his eulogy:

As a child, as my Grandpa Hy and my Grandma Libby took care of me and my brothers and cousins, it was obvious how happy my grandfather was to see all of us and how much he loved us. As I got older, I became smart enough to ask him about his earlier life. He was full of advice and wisdom and support, but he told me all these really fascinating stories about all these different things he'd done and places he'd gone, and it was hard to believe that one man, in one life, could have experienced so many dramatic events and adventures in diverse times and far flung places. Over the years, though, there have been a few times where I was lucky enough to see my grandfather's broader network, outside of family. I've met a few members of his shul, I've gone to an event remembering the *Ben Hecht*, and I worked in his office at the Organization for Staff Analysts (OSA) for a summer. (By the way, he designed the OSA logo.) And in every encounter, each person I met told me how kind my grandfather was, how he was so quick with a joke, and how sweet he was to my grandmother. These were the same things I'd known

1   "Nahmanides," *Encyclopedia Britannica*, https://www.britannica.com/biography/Nahmanides.

my whole life, but it was nice to see that Grandpa treated everyone with the same affection that he had for his family.

My favorite event, though, was my grandfather's ninetieth birthday party. So many people showed up, from all parts of his life, to celebrate Grandpa's many accomplishments, but primarily to talk about what a joy he was to be around. Today, when we're all upset and grieving that Grandpa is gone, and it's hard to find the way to express the depth of our sadness, I feel that that the best way to commemorate him is to think about how happy we felt when all the people he knew were all together, with Grandma and Grandpa at the center of everything.

***

In the years immediately after the October 1973 Yom Kippur War, many yeshivas in Israel faced a fiscal crisis because their supporters had redirected resources towards helping the Israeli government rearm after the devastating losses suffered during the war. When Mandel's daughter Susan was studying in Israel in 1976, Mandel had a dream in which his father rebuked him for allowing the yeshiva of Alter Avrohom's mentor Rabbi Dushinsky, who subsequently became the leader of the Neturai Karta, to flounder. Shaken, Mandel sent his daughter $100 to deliver to the yeshiva run by Rabbi Dushinsky's family. It arrived within three days. The administrator of the program at the Machon Gold seminary where Susan studied unexpectedly announced at the first class that the day's studies were cancelled. Not knowing where to go, Susan got on a nearby random bus in the Ge'ula neighborhood and asked the bus driver what bus to take to that particular street. He answered, "I can take you right there." Once off the bus, in the ultra-orthodox Jerusalem neighborhood of Mea Shearim, she asked directions from another random man, who turned out to be the Principal and administrator at the yeshiva she was trying to find. He told her that the school had just suspended classes due to a lack of funds, and that he was going to retrieve the school mail. With his key in hand he opened the school doors and took the check.

This was not the only dreamt-of request from the grave related to the *Ben Hecht*. Rabbi Aryeh Levine, who had become close to Abraham Stavsky when he was imprisoned in Jerusalem in the early 1930s, had recurring dreams in which Stavsky insisted that Rabbi Levine perform the *chalitzah* ceremony necessary to free his widow from the obligation to marry Stavsky's surviving brother under Jewish law because she and Stavsky did not have children. According to a Talmudic opinion the *chalitzah* rite breaks the marriage bond between a widow and her deceased husband, and in the dream Stavsky was tormented by impending remarriage of his widow while their souls remained bonded. Levine recalled Stavsky pleading with him in a dream "Look, . . . here I am turning from side to side in my grave, unable to rest at all." Troubled, Rabbi Levine inquired and discovered that Stavsky's widow was indeed planning to remarry in the United States. Rabbi Levine arranged for her to travel to Israel so that the supernatural bond that still tethered Stavsky to his widow could be severed.[2]

Mandel was a believer, but he was not superstitious. As an eighty-year-old, while recovering from surgery in a hospital, Mandel lost consciousness and stopped breathing. Thankfully, he was revived. The doctors said he had been medically dead until he was resuscitated. Afterwards, Mandel said that he had expected to be reunited with his father upon death, but he was disappointed to only have seen darkness before returning to life. He also told his daughters he had wiggled his toes in an effort to show them that he was not dead as he heard the doctors proclaim him dead. However, in moments of stress for family members, he sometimes advised to eat a cookie, prefaced with a blessing recited with the person in trouble in mind. When his daughters were young, he cautioned them not to walk backwards, lest their guardian angels be confused. His underlying message may have been that it is important not to look back at the past with regret, but to continue forward with an optimistic spirit.

After his wife Libby passed away in 2011, Mandel, who had been clean shaven his entire life, kept the beard he had grown in the mourning period after her death. He often said thereafter that he saw his father's face in the mirror.

Mandel no doubt knew, in the words of a rabbi with a rationalist bent, that "[w]e hear about . . . coincidences and wonders but not" when "nothing happens at all."[3] But he also knew that we feel the divine, as described by a more mystical scholar, when "we encounter the beauty of nature, the flowers, the ocean, the mountains, the animals, the smiles, the synchronistic

---

2   Simcha Raz, *A Tzaddik in Our Time: The Life of Rabbi Aryeh Levin* (Spring Valley, NY: Feldheim, 1976), 335–337; Talmud Bavli *Yevomot* 107b.

3   Jeremy Rosen, "Magic and Superstition: Then and Now," *Conversations* (Spring 2020/5780): 54.

events that occur beyond all probability," which reminds us "that there is more to this world than our senses."[4]

***

A personal note in conclusion. My grandfather was a man of faith. Prayer was very important to him. He liked to say that when he was young, he read the Hebrew words slowly, and then he got faster, but as he got older he was reading slower again. But he never stopped *davening*, praying. He taught us to take nothing for granted. Sitting in his living room as his life drew to a close, he told my wife Lauren and me to appreciate the sun and the snow he could see through the window, and the floor upon which he walked, and that Hashem protects them and us. Everything comes from Hashem, including both the good and not so good things. "Look forward, not backward" was his philosophy. He passed away on the same date on the Hebrew calendar that his father had died on many years prior, the 7th of Nissan, and on the same secular date that the British announced that he and crewmates would be released from Acre Prison. I trust he would be pleased with these good omens.

---

4   Mel Gottlieb, "Faith and Doubt," *Conversations* (Spring 2020/5780): 74–75.

Acknowledgments

My grandfather Henry Mandel lived through the Great Depression, World War II, and the creation of the State of Israel. He nobly stepped up to the challenges those difficult and tumultuous times presented. I am proud to memorialize his deeds, which stand as examples on how to live a purposeful, impactful, meaningful, and moral life. The core of this book are his words and his lessons. I am most indebted to Florence Shuster, Alyssa Goldschmidt Magid, and Aaron Mandel, Esther Mandel, and Chana Liba Mandel, whose interviews of Mandel are the heart of this book and are presented here almost word for word. My aunt, Bethsheba Mandel, told me that she believed that her father's life merited a book shortly after he passed away, and has remained the most enthusiastic supporter of this project. She also conducted key research of the Machal files at the American Jewish Historical Society, Center for Jewish History, in New York. My mother, Susan Mandel, studied newspaper microfilm at the New York Public Library, edited many drafts as the text slowly solidified, and served as my trusted guide to understanding my Grandpa Hy's viewpoint. My grand-aunt Tziporah Mandel Steinmetz lovingly preserved the eulogy of Moshe Mandel by my grandfather. Ina Cohen, Public Services Librarian of The Jewish Theological Seminary Library, has been unfailingly helpful. The staff of the Israel State Archives and of the Jabotinsky Institute / Metzudat Ze'ev made key archival files available electronically. Jacob Steinmetz succeeded in obtaining a court order to open his uncle's court files, though, alas, the files were not to be found. The comments of Ariel Strauss regarding structure and details alike were generous and keen. Lior Ziv offered acute and logical queries with an eye for the telling detail. My uncle Robert Leinwand, brother Rabbi Keith Flaks, and my cousins Dr. Joshua Leinwand, Dr. Gabriel Leinwand, and Benjamin Leinwand have offered their unique insights into our subject's character. Susan Kaplan Levin generously reviewed the manuscript with a fine-toothed comb (this would be a better book if I had accepted more of her suggestions); and she and Abbie Kaplan shared valuable insights about their father Dr. David Kaplan. The Machal questionnaires and archives collected by the late Dean Ralph L. Lowenstein with great foresight were essential. Dr. Stanley B. Burns graciously granted permission to reproduce *Ben Hecht* photographs, including a photograph he took of my grandfather. Thanks also to Elizabeth A. Burns and The Burns Archive for their assistance. Dr. Rafael Medoff's permission to reproduce photographs, and especially his sage advice, is much appreciated. Stanley K. Shapiro and Dr. Alexandra Harlig of Teaming Sure Entertainment Company gave key aid; special thanks goes to Dr. Harlig, who made insightful suggestions and key editing decisions. Alessandra Anzani and Kate Yanduganova of Academic Studies Press expertly shepherded this book to publication. This book was strengthened by all the above mentioned, though all remaining errors in detail and judgment are my responsibility, especially as I have honored their advice more in the breach than the observance and insisted on an idiosyncratic presentation of the material. This book would not have been completed without my in-laws Charlotte and Perry Schneider taking my family into their home at a time of danger and stress, or my wife Lauren's constant encouragement. The yet to be born great-grandchildren whom Henry Mandel was so eager to greet, including, but not limited to, Stella Leinwand, Henry Leinwand, and Sarah Flaks, provided the motivation.

Selected Bibliography and Works Cited

Acronyms

AJHS—American Jewish Historical Society, New York.
ALFP—American League for a Free Palestine.
Irgun / Etzel—National Military Organization (Israel)
MZ—Jabotinsky Institute / Metzudat Ze'ev, Tel Aviv, Israel.
PRO—Public Record Office, London, England.
USHMM—United States Holocaust Memorial Museum, Washington, D.C.

Articles and Archival Documents

18 US Code § 959.

"3 Pressmen among 21 Detained." *The Palestine Post,* Tuesday, March 11, 1947, 3. Palestine Post Bureau, dateline Haifa, Monday, March 10, 1947.

"20 Indicted for bringing 'Abril.'" *Al Hamishmar,* Tuesday, March 11, 1947. (Hebrew.)

"20 Off the Ben Hecht Will Be Sent to U.S." AP, dateline Washington, March 27, 1947. Found in Newspaper Clippings file, Bob Levitan collection, USHMM.

"599 Abril Immigrants Sent to Island of Deportation." *Al Hamishmar,* Monday, March 10, 1947, 2, dateline Haifa, Sunday, March 9, 1947. (Hebrew.)

"600 Refugees Ship Towed into Haifa." *Palestine Post Bureau*, Sunday, March 9, 1947, front page. Palestine Post Bureau, dateline Haifa, Saturday, March 8, 1947.

"Abril Awarded to Government." *The Palestine Post*, Thursday, December 4, 1947, 3, Palestine Post Bureau, dateline Haifa, Wednesday, morning of December 3, 1947. (Hebrew.)

"'Abril' Immigrants to Cyprus," *Haboker*, Monday, March 10, 1947, front page. (Hebrew.)

"Abril Pressmen to Be Deported." *The Palestine Post*, Wednesday, March 12, 1947, 3, Palestine Post Bureau, dateline Haifa, Tuesday, March 11, 1947.

"Abril Refugees Deported." *The Palestine Post*, Monday, March 10, 1947.

"Albert L. Hirschkoff." New York, Passenger and Crew Lists (including Castle Garden and Ellis Island), 1820–1957. Ancestry.com. Original data: Microfilm Publication M237, 675 rolls, NAI: 6256867, Records of the United States Custom Service, Record Group 36, National Archives at Washington, D.C..

"American Crew Members of Immigrant Ship under Arrest." *PM*, March 10, 1947, 1, 2, and 7. United Press, *PM* reel 53, 3/2–4/30/47, NYPL.

Anonymous [David Kaplan?]. "A M/V BEN HECHT Story." Website of the American Veterans of Israeli conflicts. Illegal Immigration collection, The *Ben Hecht* (*Avril*) file, reference code: K6-5/21, Jabotinsky Institute (MZ) (MZ *Ben Hecht* [*Avril*] Newspaper Clippings file).

Arielli, Nir. "When Are Foreign Volunteers Useful? Israel's Transnational Soldiers in the War of 1948 Re-Examined." *Journal of Military History* 78, no. 2 (April 2014): 703–724.

———. "Recognition, Immigration and Divergent Expectations: The Reception of Foreign Volunteers in Israel during and after the Wars of 1948 and 1967." *Journal of Modern European History / Zeitschrift Für Moderne Europäische Geschichte / Revue D'histoire Européenne Contemporaine* 14, no. 3 (2016): 374–390.

"Arrest of Illegal Immigrant Ship." *Davar*, Sunday, March 9, 1947. (Hebrew.)

"Ashbel, Michael ('Mike')." https://honorisraelsfallen.com/fallen/ashbel-michael-mike/.

"At the Last Moment." *Davar*, Wednesday, March 12, 1947. (Hebrew.)

AVI Newsletter, Spring 2002, in Machal [Mitnadvei Hutz LaAretz] and Aliyah Bet Records, undated, 1930–2010, I-501, American Jewish Historical Society, AJHS Archives, New York, NY.

"Avril, Cytherea—Ben Hecht." http://palmach.org.il/en/history/database/?itemId=5100.

Bar-Yaakov, Ron. "TITLE IN ENGLISH Dégel Nolad Bymia Mavak." https://www.ybz.org.il/_Uploads/dbsArticles/bar_yaacov.pdf. (Hebrew.)

Bar-Zohar, Michael. "David Ben-Gurion." https://www.britannica.com/biography/David-Ben-Gurion.

"'Ben Hecht' Confiscated and the Owner of the Ship Penalized." *Al Hamishmar*, Thursday, December 4, 1947. (Hebrew.)

Ben-Tzur, Tzvi. "The Voyage of the 'Ben Hecht.'" http://www.palyam.org/English/Hahapala/hf/hf_Ben-Hecht.

Bloch, Anne L. "The Law." In *The Black Book: the Nazi Crime against the Jewish People*. New York: Jewish Black Book Committee, 1946.

"Bride Will Wait in Cyprus." *The Palestine Post*, Monday, March 24, 1947, 3. Palestine Post Bureau, dateline, Haifa, Sunday, March 23, 1947.

"British Arrest of Seamen Spurs Crew Recruiting." File 1, Bob Levitan collection, USHMM.

"British Hold 20 U.S. Seamen in Zion Refugee 'Smuggling.'" *New York Post*, Monday, March 10, 1947. AP, dateline Jerusalem, March 10, 1947.

British Public Records Office ADM 116/5648, 1297582, C.M. (46) 107th Conclusions; Minute to Prime Minister, April 30, 1947.

"British will Push Prosecution of Palestine Refugee Ship's U.S. Crew." *PM*, March 10, 1947, 1, 2, and 7. United Press, *PM* reel 53, 3/2–4/30/47, NYPL.

Cable from Stanley B. Kurta to Hyman Robert Levitan. File 5, Bob Levitan collection, USHMM.

Calhoun, Ricky-Dale. "Arming David: The Haganah's Illegal Arms Procurement Network in the United States, 1945–1949." *Journal of Palestine Studies* 36, no. 4 (2007): 22–32. "Came 'Illegally', and Married according to Custom and Law." *Al Hamishmar*, Tuesday, March 25, 1947. (Hebrew.)

Campbell, John L., 1st Lt. Repatriation Movements Officer (Frankfurt), To: Headquarters, Third US Army, APO 403, US Army (Attn: Screening and Repatriation Section, Displaced Persons Branch, G-5 Division), February 18, 1947, signed by C. L. Butler, Major CLC Commanding, 1st. Ind., Displaced Person Branch, G-5 Division, HQ., US Forces, European Theater, APO 757, February 19, 1947, MZ *Ben Hecht* (*Avril*) Newspaper Clippings file.

Cavendish, Anthony. "Inside Intelligence." *Granta* 24 (Summer 1988): 15–78.

"Charlop, Yechiel Michal." https://www.jewishvirtuallibrary.org/charlop-yechiel-michel.

"Court Refuses Bail." *The B'nai B'rith Messenger*, Friday, April 4, 1947.

Criddle, Evan J. "Fiduciary Principles in International Law." In *Oxford Handbook on Fiduciary Law*, edited by Evan J. Criddle, Paul B. Miller, and Robert H. Sitkoff, 347–348. New York: Oxford University Press, 2019.

Croghan, Robert J. OSA Newsline, March 30, 2015, https://www.osaunion.org/online/mar15/index.html.

"Cushenberry, Walter R. 'Rexie.'" http://www.wertheimer.info/family/GRAMPS/Haapalah/ppl/a/3/bce473e1a207e40303a.html.

"Cyprus 'Full' with the Arrival of the 600 Clandestine Immigrants of the 'Abril.'" *Al Hamishmar*, Tuesday, March 11, 1947, front page. (Hebrew.)

The David S. Wyman Institute for Holocaust Studies. The Bergson Group: A History in Photographs: The Bergson Group, Voyage of the *Ben Hecht*.

"Ed Styrak." *AVI Newsletter*, Summer 2013, 10.

Edel, Leon, and James Parlaton. "Ben Hecht Seamen Talk of Dov Gruner." *PM*, Thursday, April 17, 1947.

Einstein, Albert. Letter to Shepard Rifkin, April 10, 1948. https://lettersofnote.com/2010/03/04/when-a-real-and-final-catastrophe-should-befall-us/.

"Eli Freundlich." US World War II Army Enlistment Records, 1938–1946. Ancestry.com. Original data: National Archives and Records Administration, Electronic Army Serial Number Merged File, 1938–1946 [Archival Database] ARC: 1263923, World War II Army Enlistment Records; Records of the National Archives and Records Administration, Record Group 64; National Archives at College Park, College Park, MD.

"Eli Freundlich (1925–2016)." Find A Grave Memorial no. 192035197. Maintained by "wharfrat" (contributor 48079906).

"English Civilian." Readers' Letters, "Legality: British and Jewish." *The Palestine Post*, Monday, August 11, 1947, 4.

"Exiled to America 19 Sailors of the 'Ben Hecht.'" *Haboker*, Monday, March 31, 1947, 4. (Hebrew.)

Finegood, Mike. "Walter 'Heavy' Greaves." American Veterans of Israel Newsletter, April 1993. http://www.machal.org.il/index.php?option=com_content&view=article&id=607&Itemid=980&lang=en.

Forverts, Monday, March 10, 1947. (Yiddish.)

Forverts, Tuesday, March 11, 1947. (Yiddish.)

Fuchs, Sylvia Dershowitz. "Dershowitz Family Centennial." *The Jewish Press*, Friday, April 7, 1989.

Gibson, Lydialyee. "'From Neither Here Nor There': Sociologist Roberto Gonzalez Interprets the Lives of Undocumented Immigrants Growing Up in America." *Harvard Magazine* 122, no. 6 (July/August 2020): 32–36.

Gilligan, Carol. "Make War, Not Nice!" *New York Times*, May 7, 2000.

Golan, Meir, Israeli Defense Ministry. Letter to Henry Mandel. Henry Mandel private papers (in possession of the editor).

Goldstein, Patrick. "Just Win, Baby . . ." *Los Angeles Times*. https://www.google.com/amp/s/www.latimes.com/archives/la-xpm-2001-jun-26-ca-14669-story.html%3f_amp=true.

Gottlieb, Mel. "Faith and Doubt." *Conversations* 35 (Spring 2020/5780): 70–77.

"Government Confiscates 'Ben Hecht.'" *Hamashkif*, Tuesday, July 27, 1948. (Hebrew.)

Gray, Alyssa M. "Reading Tosafot as (Law and) Literature." *Jewish Law Association Studies* 27 (2017): PAGES.

Green, Paul S. "Average Briton Believes 'New York Jews Are behind the Scenes in Palestine.'" *The Sentinel*, July 3, 1947.

Gutmann, David. "Letter." *New York Times Magazine*, June 4, 2000.

Hadjisavvas, Eliana. "Journey through the 'Gate of Zion': British Policy, Jewish Refugees and the La Spezia Affair, 1946." *Social History* 44, no. 4 (2019): 469–493.

Halkenhauser, Ronnie. "Ben Hecht Seamen Tell of Seizure." Bob Levitan collection, USHMM.

Headapohl, Jackie. "Matityahu Shmulevitz Passes Away." *The Jewish News*, December 3, 2018. https://thejewishnews.com/2018/12/03/matityahu-shmulevitz-passes-away/.

"Hecht Sailors Back; British 'Fair,' Says One." *The Daily News*, Thursday, April 17, 1947.

"How Ship's Cook Walter Cushenberry Won His Hand-Cut Olive-Wood Medal." *PM*, March 12, 1947.

Hula, Erich. "The Nationalities Policy of the Soviet Union: Theory and Practice." *Social Research* 11, no. 2 (1944): 168–201.

"Hyman R. Levitan, Tried to Help Jewish Refugees." *Sun-Sentinel*, August 13, 1998, found in Newspaper Clippings file, Bob Levitan collection, USHMM.

"Illegal Immigrant Ship Arrested near Haifa." *Hasapha*, Sunday, March 9, 1947. (Hebrew.)

"Immigrant Ship 'Ben Hecht.'" http://www.palmach.org.il/history/database/?itemId=5100. (Hebrew.)

"Immigrant Ship Captured and Brought to Haifa." *Al Hamishmar*, Sunday, March 9, front page. (Hebrew.)

"The Immigrants Expelled from the Land of Israel." *Haaretz*, March 10, 1947. (Hebrew.)

"In Memory—Hyman Robert Levitan." November 2001. American Veterans of Israel website, November 2001, found in Illegal Immigration collection, The *Ben Hecht* (*Avril*)—Newspaper Items and Publications (including 1949–1953, 1985, 2001, 2007), reference code: K6-5/21, Jabotinsky Institute (MZ) (MZ *Ben Hecht* [*Avril*] Newspaper Clippings file).

"Iowa III, (BB-61)." https://www.history.navy.mil/research/histories/ship-histories/danfs/i/iowa-iii.html.

Irgun, National Military Organization. The Clandestine Immigration and the War. MZ *Ben Hecht* (*Avril*) Newspaper Clippings file.

"It's O.K. to Steal . . . when you're the British Government." ALFP Advertisement, *PM*, December 10, 1946, 19. New York Public Library (NYPL), SASB M1—Periodicals and Microforms Rm 119 *ZY (*PM* daily), November/December 1946.

Jabotinsky, Eri. "Request on the 'Ben Hecht' Transport in France." March 10, 1947, MZ *Ben Hecht* (*Avril*) Newspaper Clippings file.

"Jack Winkler." US Department of Veterans' Affairs BIRLS Death File, 1850–2010. Ancestry.com.

Jeffries, C. J., Colonial Office. Memorandum to J. G. Lange, Esq., CB, labeled "Secret," April 5, 1947. British Public Records Office ADM 116/5648, 1297582, Cabinet 350.

The Jewish Post and Opinion, September 26, 1958.

Johnson, Corey. "Let's Go: A Case for Municipal Control and a Comprehensive Transportation for the Five Boroughs," March 5, 2019, 22, https://council.nyc.gov/news/2019/03/05/soc2019-report/.

Kamp, David. "Monheit Dead! Remembering Spy Magazine's Elegant Blurbist, Messenger, and Nightclubber Extraordinaire." *Vanity Fair*, August 9, 2011.

Kaplan, David. "'This Is the Way It Was': Volunteer from the USA on the 'Ben Hecht.'" http://www.palyam.org/English/Volunteers/13570533.pdf.

Kolatt, Israel. "Religion, Society, and the State during the Period of the National Home." In *Zionism and Religion*, edited by Jehuda Reinharz Shmuel Almog, and Anita Shapira, 292. Hanover, NH: University Press of New England, 1998.

Kovary and Neuhaus families' papers, Finding Aid, accession number 2009.364.15, USHMM, https://collections.ushmm.org/search/catalog/irn714679.

Lange, J. G. Memo to Sir C. J. Jeffries, K.C.M.G, O.B.E, labeled "Top Secret," April 15, 1947. British Public Records Office ADM 116/5648, 1297582.

Liebman, Marvin. "'Ben Hecht' Purser Poses as Refugee, Tells of Life on Cyprus." *PM*, April 20, 1947.

Leiman, Shnayer Z. "R. Abraham Isaac Ha-Kohen Kook: Letter on Ahavat Yisrael." *Tradition: A Journal of Orthodox Jewish Thought* 24, no. 1 (1988): 84–90.

Lev, Yehudah. "The Worm's Eye View." *Direction* (January/February 1987).

Leventhal, Harold, of Ginsburg, Leventhal, and Brown. Memorandum to Ambassador Abba Eban "Re: The Ben Hecht Case: Where do We Stand, and What should be Done," June 6, 1952, labeled "Confidential," 5. File 1816/6, Attorney General, the Ship "Ben Hecht," vol. 1, Israel State Archives (ISA), Jerusalem.

Levitan, Bob. Synagogue lecture notes, 1987. Bob Levitan collection, USHMM.

Levitan, Hyman Robert. Oral History, RG-50.932*0001, accession number 2010.505.2. USHMM.

———. Letter to Mike Finegood. Bob Levitan collection, USHMM.

"Louis Binder." New York, Birth Index, 1910–1965. Ancestry.com.

"Louis Binder." US Department Of Veterans' Affairs BIRLS Death File, 1850–2010. Ancestry. com.

"Louis Brettschneider." School Yearbooks, 1900–1999. Ancestry.com.

"Louis M. Markowitz." New York, Passenger and Crew Lists (including Castle Garden and Ellis Island) 1820–1957. Ancestry.com.

"Louis M. Markowitz." Newspapers.com. Obituary Index, 1800s–current. Ancestry.com.

Maltz, Judy, and Yaniv Kubovich. "What's Killing Israel's Lone Soldiers." *Haaretz*, August 25, 2019. https://www.haaretz.com/world-news/MAGAZINE-israel-army-idf-lone-soldiers-suicide-military-1.7729693.

Mandel, Henry. Aliyah Bet Questionnaire. Machal and Aliyah Bet records, undated, 1930–2011 collection: American Jewish Historical Society, AJHS Archives, New York.

———. Letter to *AVI Newsletter*, dated August 30, 1999. In possession of the editor.

———. Letter to the Israeli Defense Ministry, February 25, 1998. In possession of the editor.

"Maoz" large patrol yacht (1931/1948). http://www.navypedia.org/ships/israel/isr_es_maoz.htm.

"Marvin Liebman, 73, Dies; Conservative for Gay Rights." *The New York Times*, April 3, 1997.

McCombs, Phil. "Revelation from a Right Winger." *Washington Post*, July 9, 1990. https://www.washingtonpost.com/archive/lifestyle/1990/07/09/revelation-from-a-right_winger/f06ffc3c-bf95-4f14-8bf8-905435ca8062/.

Medoff, Rafael. "Sailor's Role in the Birth of Israel." *The Jewish Star*, May 1, 2009 / 7 Iyar 5769.

———. "Special Feature: Ben Hecht's 'A Flag is Born': A Play that Changed History." The David S. Wyman Institute for Holocaust Studies. http://new.wymaninstitute.org/2004/04/special-feature-ben-hechts-a-flag-is-born-a-play-that-changed-history/.

"Military to Mariner." US Department of Transportation, Maritime Administration. https://www.maritime.dot.gov/outreach/military-mariner#My%20title?.

Mizrachi, Yisrael. "Rabbi Eliyahu Rusoff of the Bronx and His Beating on the Subway." July 10, 2014. http://judaicaused.blogspot.com/2014/07/rabbi-eliyahu-rusoff-of-bronx-and-his.html.

"More Ships Are Coming." American League for a Free Palestine's (ALFP) Advertisement, *New York Post,* Thursday, March 13, 1947. Bob Levitan collection, accession number 2010.505.1, United States Holocaust Memorial Museum (USHMM).

"Mrs. Franja Balazs Wed to Louis Binder." *The New York Times,* January 17, 1964.

"Mystery Ship Seen as Exiles' Haven: Ship Built in 1931 Believed Carrying Refugees to Palestine." Bob Levitan collection, USHMM.

The Nationality Act, Seventy-Sixth Congress, Third session, ch. 876, sec. 401, October 14, 1940.

Nicolai, Robert O'Donnell. "I Ran Britain's Palestine Blockade." *Pageant Magazine,* August 1947.

"North Carolina III (BB-55)." https://www.history.navy.mil/content/history/nhhc/research/histories/ship-histories/danfs/n/north-carolina-iii.html.

"Numbers of Illegal Immigrants Full in Cyprus." *Haboker,* Tuesday, March 11, 1947.

"The Pesach Seder in Cyprus Camp." *Al HaMishmar,* Monday, April 14, 1947. (Hebrew.)

"Proceeding to Confiscate 4 Immigration Ships." *Al Hamishmar,* Wednesday, September 3, 1947.

"Proclamation of Independence." *Official Gazette of the Provisional Government of Israel,* no. 1, May 14, 1948 / 5 Iyar 5708. https://www.knesset.gov.il/docs/eng/megilat_eng.htm.

"Prof. Burack, Orthodox Leader, Dies during Synagogue Services." *Jewish Telegraphic Agency Daily Bulletin,* October 10, 1960. https://www.jta.org/1960/10/10/archive/prof-burack-orthodox-leader-dies-during-synagogue-services.

"Rabbi Dr. Gilbert Klaperman z'l." https://www.bethsholomlawrence.org/rabbi_klaperman.

Rice, Judith. "Ben Hecht, An Obscured Tale of Zionist Heroism—The S.S. Ben Hecht, 'The Mandate of Conscience.'" *Jewish Magazine* (June 2010). http://www.jewishmag.com/144mag/ben_hecht/ben_hecht.htm

"Robert Maynard Hutchins." https://president.uchicago.edu/directory/robert-maynard-hutchins.

Rose, Jon, Margaret Huyck, and Jerome Grunes. "David L. Gutmann (1925–2013)." *American Psychologist* 69, no. 5 (July/August 2014): 549.

Rosen, Jeremy. "Magic and Superstition: Then and Now." *Conversations* 35 (Spring 2020/5780): 46–55.

Rothe, Eugenio M. "A Psychotherapy Model for Treating Refugee Children Caught in the Midst of Catastrophic Situations." *The Journal of the American Academy of Psychoanalysis and Dynamic Psychiatry* 36, no. 4 (2008): 625–642.

S.S. *Marine Carp* Manifest, Sailing from Haifa, Palestine Roll T715, 1897–1957, Arriving Port of New York, NY, April 16, 1947, Passenger and Crew Lists (Including Castle Garden and Ellis Island, 1820–1957). Ancestry.com.

Salmon, Helen, and Robert Roth. "Many Sign Here to Man Jews' Ships." Bob Levitan collection, USHMM.

Saperstein, Hilary. "Captain Faced Capture to Rescue Refugees." *Jewish Journal,* Thursday, April 23, 1987. Bob Levitan collection, USHMM.

Seating Chart of "Tribute Dinner Honoring Ben Hecht and Crew of the 'Ben Hecht,'" Grand Ballroom, Hotel Astor, April 21, 1947, Newspaper Clippings file, Bob Levitan collection, USHMM.

"Shepard Rifkin." US Social Security Death Index, 1935–2014. Ancestry.com.

"Shepard Rifkin." School Yearbooks, 1900–1999. Ancestry.com.

"Shoshana Damari." The Jewish Women's Archive.

Silverstone, Paul. "Ben Hecht." http://paulsilverstone.com/ship/ben-hecht/.

Simon, Eliav. "Five Killed in Attack on British Tel Aviv HA." *Sunday News*, March 9, 1947. Bob Levitan collection, USHMM.

Sinclair, Julian. "Ma'apilim." thejc.com. https://www.thejc.com/judaism/jewish-words/ma-apilim-1.6533.

Slonim, Shlomo. "The 1948 American Embargo on Arms to Palestine." *Political Science Quarterly* 94, no. 3 (1979): 495–514.

Steinmetz, Tziporah Mandel. Notes to Samuel Flaks.

Stone, Darla. "Ulanów History." JewishGen, KehilaLinks. https:// kehilalinks.jewishgen.org/kolbuszowa/ulanow/history.html.

Stone, I. F. "Refugees Driven on Cyprus-Bound Ships like Cattle." *PM*, March 10, 1947.

"Suit to Condemn the Ship 'Ben Hecht.'" *Hamashkif*, Wednesday, December 3, 1947. (Hebrew.)

"Three Journalists Came on the Abril." *Al Hamishmar*, Wednesday, March 12, 1947. (Hebrew.)

Tidhar, David. "Rabbi Yosef Tzvi Dushinsky." In *Encyclopedia of the Founders and Builders of Israel*, vol. 4: *1929–1930*. Tel Aviv: Rishonim Library, 1950. http://www.tidhar.tourolib.org/tidhar/view/4/1929. (Hebrew.)

Tyler, Alan. "The View from a 'Brit.'" *AVI Newsletter*, Summer 1999.

"Veterans' Benefits: Eligibility of Merchant Mariners." https://www.everycrsreport.com/reports/R44162.html.

"Voyage of the S.S. Abril, alias the Ben Hecht." http://cosmos.ucc.ie/cs1064/jabowen/IPSC/php/event.php?eid=855.

Walker, Christine. "Hyman R. Levitan, Tried to Help Jewish Refugees." Bob Levitan collection, USHMM.

"Walter Rex Cushenberry." Ancestry.com.

Weiss, Amy. "1948's Forgotten Soldiers?: The Shifting Reception of American Volunteers in Israel's War of Independence." *Israel Studies* 25, no. 1 (2020): 149–173.

"Wild British Shooting Kills-Wounds Innocent Bystanders." Palcor, dateline March 10, 1947.

"Boy Meets Girl in Haifa Jail." *The Palestine Post*, Friday, March 14, 1947, 3. Palestine Post Bureau, dateline Haifa, Thursday, March 13, 1947

Interviews and Oral Histories

HaCohen-Brandes, Yehoshua. Interview by Marsha Feinstein, October 15, 1992, reference code TS5-16. (Hebrew.) Jabotinsky Institute / Metzudat Ze'ev (MZ).

Kaplan, David. Interview by Eliyahu Lankin. July 17, 1987. Parts 1, tape CS-0327, and part 2, tape CS-0328. Jabotinsky Institute / MZ.

Lankin, Eliyahu. Interview by Natan Cohen. Sudat Shlishit Radio program transcript, reference code: TS12-20/1. Jabotinsky Institute / MZ.

Mandel, Henry. Interview by Florence Shuster, June 5, 2000. Conducted at the Museum of Jewish Heritage in New York. Video tape and transcript in possession of the editor.

———. Henry Mandel seventieth birthday party, September 19, 1990. Video tape and transcript in possession of the editor.

———. "I'd Do it for Free." Interview by Della Monica, 1996. *The Chief-Leader*. Newspaper clipping in possession of the editor.

———. *Jewish Week* interview, 1998. Newspaper clipping in possession of the editor.

———. Interview by Alyssa Goldschmidt Magid, December 1, 2006. Audio tape and transcript in possession of the editor.

———. Interview by Aaron Mandel, Esther Mandel, and Chana Liba Mandel, circa 2012. Notes in possession of the editor.

McClure, Stewart E. "Stewart E. McClure: Chief Clerk, Senate Committee on Labor, Education, and Public Welfare (1949–1973)." Interview by Donald A. Ritchie, 1982. Oral History Interviews, Senate Historical Office, Washington, D.C., on the staff of Guy Gillette, interview no. 1.

Monheit, Neil. Interview by Samuel Flaks, 2019. Notes in possession of the editor.

Tyler, Alan. "So I Sat on Deck, Reading the New Year Service to Myself Sitting on Top of an Atom Bomb!" Interview by Mike Stone, September 20, 2017. https://reminiscences. uk/2017/09/20/alan-tyler/.

Books

Arab-Israeli Conflict: The Essential Reference Guide. 2014. Santa Barbara, California: ABC-CLIO.

Aharoni, Reubin. *Leaning Masts: Ships of Jewish Illegal Immigration and Arms after World War II*. Ef'al: Merkaz Toldot Koach Haganah al-shem Yisrael Glili, 1997. (Hebrew.)

Almog, Doron. *ha-Rekhesh be-Artsot-ha-Berit: 1945–1949*. Tel Aviv: Ma'arakhot / Tseva haganah le-Yisra'el. 1987. (Hebrew.)

Andelman, David A. *A Shattered Peace: Versailles 1919 and the Price We Pay Today*. Hoboken, NJ: John Wiley & Sons, 2008.

Barahona, Renato. *The Odyssey of the Ship with Three Names: Smuggling Arms into Israel and the Rescue of Jewish Refugees in the Balkans in 1948*. Reno, NV: Center for Basque Studies / University of Nevada, 2013.

Baumel, Judith Tydor. *The "Bergson Boys" and the Origins of Contemporary Zionist Militancy*. Translated by Dena Ordan. Syracuse, NY: Syracuse University Press, 2005.

Begin, Menachem. *The Revolt*. Rev. ed. Translated by Samuel Katz. London: W. H. Allen, 1979.

Bell, J. Bowyer. *Terror Out of Zion: The Fight for Israeli Independence, 1929–1949*. New York: St. Martin's Press, 1977.

Ben Isaiah, Abraham, and Benjamin Sharfman. *The Pentateuch and Rashi's Commentary: Numbers*. Brooklyn, NY: S.S. & R. Publishing Company, Inc., 1950.

Ben-Ami, Yitshaq. *Years of Wrath, Days of Glory: Memoirs from the Irgun*. New York: Robert Speller & Sons, 1982.

Bercuson, David J. *The Secret Army: The Incredible Story of the Foreign Volunteers who Formed One of the Toughest Modern Armies in the World and Fought for the Establishment of a Jewish State*. Toronto: Lester & Orpen Dennys, 1983.

Bethell, Nicholas. *The Palestine Triangle: The Struggle for the Holy Land, 1935–48*. New York: G.P. Putnam's Sons, 1979.

Boswell, James. *Life of Johnson, Complete and Unabridged in One Volume*. New York: Modern Library, 1955.

Brokow, Tom. *The Greatest Generation*. New York: Random House, 1998.

Bryson, Bill. *One Summer: America, 1927*. New York: Knopf Doubleday Publishing Group, 2013.

Caro, Robert. *The Power Broker: Robert Moses and the Fall of New York*. New York: Alfred A. Knopf, 1974.

Chayes, Abram. *The Cuban Missile Crisis: International Crises and the Role of Law*. New York and London: Oxford University Press, 1974.

Chertoff, Daniel S. *Palestine Posts: An Eyewitness Account of the Birth of Israel Based on the Letters of Mordecai S. Chertoff*. Jerusalem: The Toby Press, 2019.

Cohen, Mark. *Not Bad for Delancey Street: The Rise of Billy Rose*. Waltham, MA: Brandeis University Press, 2018.

Collins, Larry, and Dominique Lapierre. *O Jerusalem!* New York: Simon and Schuster, 1988 [1972].

Daube, David. *Collaboration with Tyranny in Rabbinic Law*. London: Oxford University Press, 1965.

———. *Appeasement or Resistance and Other Essays on New Testament Judaism*. Berkeley, CA: University of California Press, 1987.

Dawidowicz, Lucy S. *From That Place and Time: A Memoir 1938–1947*. New York: Bantam Books, 1991.

———. *The War against the Jews 1933–1945*. New York: Bantam Books, 1978.

Dinnerstein, Leonard. *America and the Survivors of the Holocaust*. New York: Columbia University Press, 1982.

Eban, Abba. *An Autobiography*. New York: Random House, 1977.

———. *Personal Witness: Israel through My Eyes*. New York: G.P. Putnam's Sons, 1992.

Elman, Yaakov. *The Living Nach: Later Prophets. A New Translation Based on Traditional Jewish Sources*. New York / Jerusalem: Moznaim Publishing Company, 1995/5754.

Elon, Amos. *The Israelis: Founders and Sons*. New York: Holt, Rinehart, and Winston, 1971.

Epstein, Kalonymus Kalman, and Aryeh Wineman. *Letters of Light: Passages from Ma'or va-shemesh*. Translated by Aryeh Wineman. Eugene, OR: Pickwick Publications, 2015.

Erbelding, Rebecca. *Rescue Board: the Untold Story of America's Efforts to Save the Jews of Europe*. New York: Doubleday, 2018.

Friedland, Roger, and Richard Hecht. *To Rule Jerusalem*. Santa Barbara, CA: University of California Press, 2000.

Gand, Robert. *Angels in the Sky: How a Band of Volunteer Airmen Saved the New State of Israel*. New York: W. W. Norton & Company, 2017.

Geller, Victor B. *Orthodoxy Awakens: The Belkin Era and Yeshiva University*. Brooklyn, NY: Urim Publications, 2003.

Gershoni, Haim. *Israel: The Way It Was*. Cranbury, NY / London / Mississauga, Ontario: Herzl Press, 1989.

Gitlin, Jan. *The Conquest of Acre Fortress*. Tel Aviv, Israel: Hadar Publishing House, 1982.

Gorbach, Julien. *The Notorious Ben Hecht: Iconoclastic Writer and Militant Zionist*. West Lafayette, IN: Purdue University Press, 2019.

Gould, Robert, and Thomas Bodenheimer. *Rollback! Right-Wing Power in U.S. Foreign Policy*. Boston, MA: South End Press, 1989.

Gurock, Jeffrey S. *The Men and Women of Yeshiva: Higher Education, Orthodoxy and American Judaism*. New York: Columbia University Press, 1988.

Gutmann, Stephanie. *The Other War: Israelis, Palestinians, and the Struggle for Media Supremacy*. San Francisco: Encounter Books, 2005.

Hadari, Ze'ev Venia. *The Mossad L'Aliyah Bet: Operational Logbook—Paris 1947*. Beer-Sheva, Israel: The Ben-Gurion University of the Negev Press, 1991.

———. *Second Exodus: The Full Story of Jewish Illegal Immigration to Palestine, 1945–1948*. London: Vallentine Mitchell, 1991.

Halamish, Aviva. *A Dual Race against Time: Zionist Immigration Policy in the 1930s*. Jerusalem: Yad Izhak Ben Zvi, 2006. (Hebrew.)

———. *The Exodus Affair: Holocaust Survivors and the Struggle for Palestine*. Translated by Ora Cummings. Syracuse: Syracuse University Press, 1998.

Hecht, Ben. *A Child of the Century*. New York: Primus (Donald I. Fine) Plume, 1985. [New York: Simon & Schuster, 1954.]

Hecht, Ben. *A Flag is Born*. New York: American League for a Free Palestine, Inc., 1946.

———. *Perfidy*. New York: Julian Messner, Inc., 1961.

———. *A Guide for the Bedevilled*. Jerusalem: Mila Press, 1996. [New York: Charles Scribner's Sons, 1944.]

Heckelman, A. Joseph. *American Volunteers and Israel's War of Independence*. New York: Ktav Publishing House, Inc., 1974.

Hertz, Joseph J. *The Authorized Daily Prayer Book Revised Edition*. New York: Bloch Publishing Company, 1955/5715.

Hobbs, Stuart D. *The End of the American Avant Garde*. New York: NYU Press, 1997.

Hochstein, Joseph, and Murray S. Greenfield. *The Jews' Secret Fleet: Untold Story of North American Volunteers Who Smashed the British Blockade*. New York: Gefen, 1993.

Hoffman, Adina. *Ben Hecht: Fighting Words, Moving Pictures*. New Haven, CT: Yale University Press, 2019.

Horev, Shai. *Dawning Ships: The Story of the Clandestine Immigrant Ships from "Vilus" to "Ayalon Valley Battle."* Haifa, Israel: Pardes, 2004. (Hebrew.)

Horev, Shaul. *"I Will Gather Them from the Outermost Parts of the Earth": The Revisionism and The Civil Illegal Immigration to Palestine in Mandate Times*. Haifa, Israel: Duhifat Publishers, 2012. (Hebrew.)

Jacobson, Maxine. *Modern Orthodoxy in American Judaism: The Era of Rabbi Leo Jung, Studies in Orthodox Judaism*. Boston: Academic Studies Press, 2016.

Johnson, Paul. *The Quest for God: A Personal Pilgrimage*. New York: HarperCollins, 1996.

Jones, James. *WWII: A Chronicle of Soldiering*. Chicago: University of Chicago Press, 1975.

JPS Hebrew-English Tanakh: The Traditional Hebrew Text and the New JPS Translation. 2nd ed. Philadelphia, PA: The Jewish Publication Society, 2003/5764.

Kaplan, Aryeh. *Meditation and Kabbalah*. York Beach, ME: Samuel Weiser, 1982.

Kennan, George F. *Realities of American Foreign Policy*. New York: W. W. Norton and Company, Inc., 1966 [1954].

Kent, John. *Demise of the British Empire in the Middle East: Britain's Responses to Nationalist Movements, 1943–55*. Edited by Michael Cohen and Martin Kolinsky. Portland, OR / London: Frank Cass, 1998.

Larson, Erik. *The Splendid and the Vile: A Saga of Churchill, Family, and Defiance during the Blitz*. New York: Crown, 2020.

Lazar, Chaim. *Immigration Ship "Ben Hecht."* CITY: Museum of Combatants and Partisans, 1995/1996. (Hebrew.)

Liebman, Marvin. *Coming out Conservative: An Autobiography*. San Francisco: Chronicle Books, 1992.

Liebreich, Fritz. *Britain's Naval and Political Reaction to the Illegal Immigration of Jews to Palestine, 1945–1948*. London / New York: Routledge, 2005.

Livingston, Harold. *No Trophy No Sword: An American Volunteer in the Israeli Air Force during the 1948 War of Independence*. Chicago, Berlin, Tokyo and Moscow: Edition Q, 1994.

Livni, Eitan. *Personal Story of Operations Officer of Etzel*. Tel Aviv, Israel: Idanim Publishing, 1987. (Hebrew.)

Lorch, Natanel. *The Edge of the Sword: Israel's War of Independence 1947–1949*. New York / London: G.P. Putnam's Sons, 1961.

Makower, Batia. *The Power of One: The Story of the Man who Opened the Route to Israel in Sudan for the Ethiopian Jews. Ferede Yazezew Aklum 1949–2009*. Translated by Heidi Gleit. N.p., Israel: Yerusalem Forum, 2019.

Mathews, Anne, Nancy Caldwell Sorel, and Robert J. Spiller, eds. *Reporting World War II: American Journalism 1938–1946*. New York: The Library of America, 2001 [1995].

McDonald, James G. *My Mission to Israel 1948–1951*. New York: Simon and Schuster, 1951.

Medoff, Rafael. *Militant Zionism in America: The Rise and Impact of the Jabotinsky Movement in the United States, 1926-1948*. Tuscaloosa / London: The University of Alabama Press, 2002.

———. *The Jews Should Keep Quiet: Franklin D. Roosevelt, Rabbi Stephen S. Wise, and the Holocaust*. Philadelphia: Jewish Publication Society / University of Nebraska Press, 2019.

———. *The Rabbi of Buchenwald: The Life and Times of Herschel Schacter*. Brooklyn, NY: Ktav, 2021.

Merlin, Samuel. *Millions of Jews to Rescue: A Bergson Group Leader's Account of the Campaign to Save Jews from the Holocaust.* Edited by Rafael Medoff. Washington, D.C.: David S. Wyman Institute for Holocaust Studies, 2011.

Morris, Benny. *1948: The First Arab-Israeli War.* New Haven, CT / London: Yale University Press, 2008.

Méry, Jacques. *1947. Laissez passer mon peuple [Let My People Go]. Préface d'Albert Camus.* Paris: Éditions du Seuil. (French.)

Naor, Mordechai. *Haapala: Clandestine Immigration 1931–1948.* Tel Aviv: Ministry of Defense Publishing House and IDF Museum, 1987.

Penslar, Derek Jonathan. *Jews and the Military: A History.* Princeton, NJ: Princeton University Press, 2013.

Rabinowitz, Jacob. *My Yeshiva College: 75 Years of Memories,* edited by Menachem Butler and Zev Nagel. New York: Yasher Books, 2006.

Rakeffet-Rothkoff, Aaron. *The Silver Era in American Jewish Orthodoxy: Rabbi Eliezer Silver and His Generation.* Jerusalem / New York: Yeshiva University Press / Feldheim, 1981.

———. *From Washington Avenue to Washington Street.* Jerusalem, New York: Gefen / Oxford University Press, 2001.

Rapoport, Louis. *Shake Heaven and Earth: Peter Bergson and the Struggle to Rescue the Jews of Europe.* Jerusalem; New York: Gefen, 1999/5759.

Raz, Simcha. *A Tzaddik in Our Time: The Life of Rabbi Aryeh Levin.* Spring Valley, NY: Feldheim, 1976.

Rechter, David. *The Jews of Vienna and the First World War.* London / Portland, OR: The Littman Library of Jewish Civilization, 2001.

Reynolds, David. *Britannia Overruled: British Policy and World Power in the Twentieth Century.* New York: Pearson Education, 1991.

Rifkin, Shepard. *Desire Island.* New York: Ace Books, 1960.

———. *What Ship? Where Bound?* Knopf: New York, 1961.

Rosen, Doron. *In Quest of the American Treasure: The Israeli Underground (the Haganah) Activity in the United States in 1945–1949.* Jerusalem: Ministry of Defense, 2008. (Hebrew.)

Sachar, Howard M. *Diaspora, An Inquiry into the Contemporary Jewish World.* New York: Harper & Row, 1985.

Sartre, Jean-Paul. *No Exit and Three Other Plays.* New York: Vintage International, 1989.

Schechter, Solomon. *Studies in Judaism.* Philadelphia, PA: Jewish Publication Society of America, 1905 [1896].

Sereny, Gitta. *Into That Darkness: An Examination of Conscience.* London: Andre Deustch, 1974.

Shari, David. *The Cyprus Exile 1945–1949.* Jerusalem: Zionist Library, 1961/1962. (Hebrew.)

Shirer, William L. *The Collapse of the Third Republic: An Inquiry into the Fall of France in 1940.* New York: Simon and Schuster, 1969.

Silverstone, Paul H. *"Our Only Refuge, Open the Gates!": Clandestine Immigration to Palestine 1938–1948.* New York: P. Silverstone, 1999.

Slater, Leonard. *The Pledge.* New York: Simon and Schuster, 1970.

Steinmetz, Sol. *The Little Refugees*. New York: S. Steinmetz, 2011.

Stevens, John Paul. *The Making of a Justice: Reflections on My First 94 Years*. New York: Little, Brown and Company, 2019.

Stone, I. F. *Underground to Palestine and Reflections Thirty Years Later*. New York: Pantheon Books, 1978.

Swarc, Alan. "Illegal Immigration to Palestine 1945–1948: The French Connection." PhD diss., University College London, 2006. https://discovery.ucl.ac.uk/id/eprint/1445118/1/U592432.pdf.

Tal, Eliezer. *Naval Operations in the War of Independence*. Tel Aviv: Ma'arakhot Publishing, 1964. (Hebrew.)

Temko, Ned. *To Win or To Die: A Personal Portrait of Menachem Begin*. New York: William Morrow and Company, Inc., 1987.

Tuchman, Barbara W. *Bible and Sword*. New York: New York University Press, 1968 [1956].

Wandres, J. *The Ablest Navigator: Lieutenant. Paul N. Shulman USN, Israel's Volunteer Admiral*. Annapolis: Naval Institute Press, 2013.

Weiss, Jeffery, and Craig Weiss. *I Am My Brother's Keeper: American Volunteers in Israel's War of Independence 1947–1949*. Algen, PA: Schiffer Military History, 1998.

Wiesel, Elie. *Dawn*. New York: Hill & Wang, 1961.

Wiesel, Elie, and Richard D. Heffner. *Conversations with Elie Wiesel*. New York: Schocken Books, 2003.

Wilde, Oscar. *The Portable Oscar Wilde*. Rev. ed. New York: Penguin Books, 1981.

Williams, Albert. *The Holy City*. New York: Duell, Sloan and Pearce / Boston: Little, Brown and Co., 1954.

Williams, Mason B. *City of Ambition: FDR, LaGuardia, and the Making of Modern New York*. New York: W.W. Norton, 2013.

Wilson, R. Dare. *Cordon and Search, With the 6th Airborne Division in Palestine 1945–48*. Nashville, Tennessee: The Battery Press, 1984.

Wyman, David S., and Rafael Medoff. *A Race against Death: Peter Bergson, America and the Holocaust*. New York: The New Press, 2002.

Zadka, Saul. *Blood in Zion: How the Jewish Guerrillas Drove the British out of Palestine*. London / Washington: Brassey's, 1995.

Zarr, Isaac. *Rescue and Liberation: America's Part in the Birth of Israel*. New York: Bloch Publishing Company, 1954.

Index

1948 Arab-Israeli War, 64n4, 66n13
Abramowitz, Gideon, 112, 132
Acheson, Dean, 162
Achimeir, Abba, 104
Acre (Akko), 54–55
    Acre Fortress (Acre Prison), iv, xii, xiii,
        xvii, 51–55, 57, 149, 152, 158–60,
        165, 167, 181, 184, 2086 241
Agronsky, Daniel, 60
Alexandria, 60, 166
Aliyah Bet, xiv, xv, xvi, xviii, 1, 35, 45, 52,
    59, 89, 105, 111, 112, 140, 173, 177,
    184, 186. *See also* illegal immigration
Altalena, xiii, 45, 171–72, 175, 184
Alvin Theater, 82
Amalgamated Clothing Workers Union,
    198–99
America. *See* United States
American Jewish Historical Society, 209
American Jewish Joint Distribution
    Committee. *See* Joint Distribution
    Committee
American League for a Free Palestine
    (AFLP), xvii, xix, 11, 32, 34–35, 44, 48,
    74, 78–79, 81, 82n64, 83–86, 92–93,
    97–98, 105, 108, 139, 151, 161–62,
    167–69, 172, 241
American Veterans of Israel (AVI), 38, 59,
    83n74, 116n11, 184
antisemitism, 18–19, 39, 80, 97, 107, 119
Arabs, iv, xv, 51, 54, 56, 57, 63, 66, 79, 82,
    88, 90, 132, 145, 153, 159, 188
Ariel, Shmuel, 112–13
Arlosoroff, Chaim, 104–5, 172
Army, xiii, xvi, 5, 15–16, 22, 25, 28–29, 34,
    38, 41, 46, 51, 62–63, 65–67, 69, 73, 79,
    90, 92, 95–96, 113, 117–19, 121, 143,
    156, 163, 172–75, 177, 194
Ashbel, Michael (Mike), 157, 159, 159n23
Assistance aux réfugiés et déportés, 112
Athina, 136
Austria, 3, 16–17, 62–63
Azores, 41, 94, 103

Babe Ruth, 12–13
Balfour, Arthur James, 87, 90
Baltimore, 36, 60, 83, 139
baseball, 12–13, 180
bazooka shell plant, iv, xiii, 64, 67, 173
Beirut, 60, 67
Ben-Ami (Ben Ari), Yitshaq (Mike), xvn14,
    44, 79, 81, 84–85, 110, 112, 137
Ben-Gurion, David, 33, 105
Ben-Nun, Yochai, 176, 177
Begin, Menachem, 44, 85, 106, 153, 156,
    159, 160, 185
Ben Hecht (ship, *also Abril, Argosy, Artheus,*
    Ma'oz, Maria del Mare, and Vita), xii,
    xiii, xiv, xv– xvii, xviin20, xviin21, xviii,
    xix, 17, 31–32, 34–35, 40–41, 43–45,
    47, 49–52, 55, 60–61, 79, 81, 83–87,
    89–95, 97–99, 101–13, 115–23, 126–33,
    135–49, 151–53, 155, 157, 161–72,
    175–76, 181–82, 183n24, 185–88, 202,
    205–6
Bergson, Peter, xii, xiv, 34, 73, 73n2, 74n8,
    180, 184. *See also* Kook, Hillel
    Bergson group, xv, xvn15, xviin20, xix,
        34, 50, 73–86, 90, 96, 98n54,
        105–107, 110, 111, 137, 151,
        171, 181, 185, 187
Berkovitz, Jeno, 61, 99, 135, 148
Berlin, Naftali Zvi Yehuda, xviii
Bernstein, Jack, 40
Betar, xix, 34, 37, 94, 105, 109, 111, 112,
    115, 117, 123, 129, 130–132, 147,
    168, 179
Bethel, Nicholas, 57, 58n25
Bevin, Ernest, 88, 89, 162
Bible, 5, 11, 101, 124
Binder, Franja, 38
Bick, Moshe, Rabbi, 10, 193, 195
Binder, Louis (Lou), 61, 94, 95, 100,
    100n68, 133, 148
Bnei Akiva, 11, 185
Boston cream pie, 27
Bratislava, 3, 6

Bremerhaven, 27
Brenner, Morris, 84
Brettschneider, Louis (Lou), 38, 61, 98n51, 121, 139, 140, 148, 171
Bricha, 41
Britain (British Empire), xii, 49, 57, 66, 77, 80, 85, 87, 88, 90, 91, 125, 133, 139, 160, 163, 186. *See also* England, Great Britain
British Foreign Office, 78, 88
British Navy (Royal Navy), xi-xii, xvii, 32, 97, 125-28, 130, 133, 134, 140, 152, 169, 183, 188
British Royal Marines, 134–136, 138
British Sixth Airborne "Red Devil" Division, 143, 144
Brockman, Yitzhak, 176
Bromfield, Louis, 169
Bronx, xiii, 3–13, 14–16, 29, 62, 63, 96, 98–100, 195
Bundinia, Irina, 146, 147
Brooklyn, vii, xvii, xviii, 10, 15, 29, 32, 36, 52, 84, 86, 92, 93, 95, 96, 110, 163, 173, 199
Brooklyn Navy Yard, xiii, 14, 29, 173, 201. *See also* New York Navy Yard
Buckley, William, 39, 182

Capri, 121
Clay, Robert, Captain, 40, 93, 94, 98, 103, 105, 107, 120, 140
Chan, Henry, 20, 21
Chayl Madda, 65, 67
Chemed, 67, 173
Chertoff, Mordecai, 151
Chevron, 128, 131, 134, 135, 136, 169
Chiang Kai-Shek, 39
Chief-Leader, 11, 202
Chieftain, 128, 131, 133
Child of the Century, 77n33, 112
Coleridge, Samuel Taylor, 20
Chust, 4
City College, 10, 22, 96, 173, 203
Crete, 25
Criminal Investigation Department, 145, 149
Cuba, 37, 83
Cushenberry, Walter Rexie, 58, 61, 97, 98, 99n60, 161, 163, 167, 182, 185
Cyprus, xii, xiv. xvii, 37, 45, 48, 51, 52, 80, 90, 94, 123, 138, 142, 144, 145, 147, 150, 151, 153, 158, 163, 179, 188
    Camp 55, 66, 147, 150
Czechoslovakia, 6, 182, 195, 196

Cunningham, Allan, 132, 149, 151

Depression, xiii, xx, 8, 9, 11, 14, 209. *See also* Great Depression
Dershowitz, Sam, 195
Dershowitz, Zechariah, 195, 196
Dingell, John D., 163
Displaced Persons (DP, DPs), xi, xvii, 59, 67, 80, 91–94, 97, 104, 106, 109, 112, 115, 168-169, 186–188
Dushinsky, Yosef Tzvi, Rabbi, 4, 8, 206
Duvdevan counter-terrorist unit, 185

Eastern Development Company, 64, 65, 173
Eastern Europe, 41, 80
Einstein, Albert, 53, 180
Eisenberg, 108
Elon, Amos, 33n8, 188
Emir Farouk, 175–177
Empire Rest, 144, 146, 150
Empire Shelter, 144, 146, 150
England, xvi, 16, 58, 82, 138, 164, 173. *See also* Britain, Great Britain
Eretz Yisrael, 12
Exodus 1947, xviii, 45, 52, 123, 131, 141, 152, 169, 183

Fast of Esther, 118
FBI, 18, 86, 95
Fédération des sociétés juives de France, 112, 113
Feinstein, Moshe, 102
Fighters of the Ghetto, 169
Forverts (the *Forward*), 161
France, xii, 17, 27, 40–43, 67, 76, 86, 92–94, 104–108, 111–113, 116, 118, 122, 151, 152, 163, 175
Freundlich, Eli, 37, 94–95, 101, 140

Galante, 4
Galicia, 4, 195
Gentile, 18, 58, 78, 119
Germany, 6, 17–19, 31, 35, 57, 75, 77, 80, 83, 87, 92, 94, 96, 106, 112, 114, 121, 152, 183, 188
Germans, 17, 18, 35, 76, 88, 139
Gershoni (Gershenow), Haim, 175, 176
Giladi, Baruch, 112
Gillette, Guy M., xiv, 34, 78, 80
Gilligan, Carol, 188n39
Goldschmidt Magid, Alyssa (AGM), xii-in10, xxi, 32-40, 42-43, 56, 60, 61n36, 198, 209

Gouverneur, New York, 7
Great Britain, 77, 87, 88, 90, 92, 186. *See also* Britain, England
Great Depression, xiii, xx, 9, 209. *See also* Depression
Greaves, Walter ("Heavy"), 38, 40, 50, 51, 59, 61, 94, 96, 99, 139, 140, 148, 171, 181
Greece, 21, 25, 27, 59
Green, Mr., xiii, 33
Grenoble, 52, 113–114
Gruner, Dov, 55, 155–157, 159, 167, 168
Gutmann, Dave L. (Leo), 38, 51, 140, 171, 181
Gutmann, Stephanie, 95n41, 188, 189

HaCohen-Brandes, Yehoshua, 105, 106, 110–112, 132
Haganah, xv, xvi, 38, 44, 45, 48, 52, 64, 65, 67, 85, 89, 108, 112, 127, 137, 140, 152, 153, 171, 173, 174, 181, 188
HaPo'el HaMizrachi, 30, 33
Harrison, Earl, 88
HaShomer HaDati, 11
Hatikvah, 117, 131
Hawaii, 18
Hebrew, xi,, xiv, xvi, 5, 12, 33, 44, 68, 74, 79, 93, 115, 142, 145, 152, 161–166, 168, 172, 195, 208
Hebrew Committee for National Liberation (HCNL), xii, xvii, 44, 74, 78, 81, 115, 142, 146, 162, 170
Hecht, Reuben, 44
Heggie, James, 58, 61, 94, 97, 107
Heinkel, 101, 108
Herminengasse, 6
Hershkowitz, Harry, 98, 107, 111
Hirschkoff, Albert L., 110, 111, 165
Hitler, Adolf, 18, 19, 77, 80
HMS *Chivalrous*, 131
HMS *St. Bride*, 131
Holland, 17
Holocaust, iv, xii, xvi, xvii, xix, xx, xxi, 8, 10, 66, 76, 77, 78, 80, 82, 85, 89, 91, 92, 111, 160, 185, 188, 189, 196
Horowitz, Shmuel Shmelke Halevi, Rabbi of Nikolsburg, 177
House of Commons, 88, 156
House of Representatives, 164
Howe, Robert, 149
Hungary illegal immigration, 6, 17. *See also* Aliyah Bet Jewish illegal immigrant ships

Immigration Act of 1924, 196
Impellitteri, Vincent R., 168
Iowa, 15, 34, 78
Irgun Tzva'i Le'umi (Etzel, ITzL, IZL), xv, 70, 73, 134, 152
Israel, State of, iv, xii, xvi, xix, 64, 66, 69, 168n38, 170, 174, 185, 188, 189
Israel State Archives, 74n6, 209
Israeli Air Force, 173, 179
Israeli Army, xiii, 38, 60, 65, 66, 67, 69, 95, 172, 173, 174, 183
Israeli Defense Forces, xiv, 70, 176, 185
Israeli Defense Ministry, xiv, 32n4, 54n15, 70, 94, 158, 171, 184
Italy, 16, 21, 24, 27, 112
Ivrit, xiv, 11

Jabotinsky, Eri, xii, xvi, 44, 105, 111, 120, 143, 151, 156
Jabotinsky, Vladimir (Ze'ev), xii, xvi, 73
Jabotinsky Institute, 37n13, 45n12, 105n23, 116n11, 186n30, 209. *See also* Metzudat Ze'ev
Japan, 18, 19, 28
Jewish Week, 50n4, 54, 68n23, 173n14
Joint Distribution Committee, 25

Kaiserman, Joseph, 55, 161, 162, 165, 166, 169
Kalonniyot. See British Sixth Airborne "Red Devil" Division
Kaplan, David, 25, 31, 32, 34, 37, 41, 43, 47, 53, 54, 59, 60, 84, 86, 94, 106, 109, 119, 121, 128, 129, 131, 133, 136, 139, 140, 147, 163, 167, 182, 185
Katzir (Katchalski), Efraim, 172
Kimchi, David, xx
Kingsborough College, 21
Klaperman, Gilbert, 199
Kook, Abraham Isaac (Avraham Yitzhak), Rabbi, xv
Kook, Hillel, xv, 45, 73, 93, 110, 180
Kope, Aaron, 162
Krupp, 83
Kurdani, 172

Le Havre, 67, 175
SS *Laconia Victory*, 23
Lakewood, NJ, 29, 95n39
Lankin, Eliyahu, 37n13, 45, 50, 105, 185, 186n30
League of Nations, 36, 49, 50, 87, 88, 90, 138

Leinwand, Benjamin, xx, 185, 197, 205
Leinwand, Gabriel, 197, 205
Leinwand, Joshua (Josh), 197, 205
Lev, Yehudah, 41
Levi, Yehuda, 53
Levin, Aryeh, Rabbi, 55, 206
Levitan, Hyman Robert (Bob), xin1, 40,
    41n29, 91, 180
Licht, Julian, 84
Liebman, Marvin, 39, 46, 61, 92, 116, 117,
    143, 150, 181, 182
    Coming Out Conservative, 39, 40n22,
        116n7, 143n114, 150n150, 181
Liebreich, Fritz, 126
Lilliby, Haakom, 121, 148, 167
Linklater, Captain, 141, 143
Litwin, Wallace, 52, 110, 123, 137, 148, 165,
    234, 235
Livni, Eitan, 153, 157
Lochmai Herut Israel (Lechi), xii, 59, 152,
    157-58, 174, 180-81
Luce, Norman Edward, 61, 148
Lumet, Sidney, 82
Luster, Chaim, 53

ma'apilim, xviii, 50, 112
Machal, 30n20, 59, 69
Malatzky, Menachem, 159
Mandel, Aaron, xiiin10, xxi, 4, 6n10, 209
Mandel, Avrohom (Alter, Abraham), 4–9,
    11, 16, 206
Mandel, Bethsheba, 62, 196, 197
Mandel, Cidelle, 194
Mandel, Dorie (Devorah), 6, 231
Mandel, Esther, xiiin10, xxi, 4n5, 6n10,
    22n11, 118, 209
Mandel, Golda Baila, 7
Mandel, Henry (Chaim, Hank, Hy, Hymie,
    HM), xiii, xivn11, xvii, xx, xxi, 3, 16,
    32, 52, 61, 63, 95, 107, 123, 148, 172,
    184, 187, 193, 195, 200, 203, 205
Mandel, Jacob (Yaakov Tzvi), 5
Mandel, Leo (Yehudah Bezalel), 6
Mandel, Libby Dershowitz, 1
Mandel, Malka Tziporah, 5, 7, 209
Mandel, Moshe, 5, 7, 10, 193, 209
Mandel, Rivkie (Rivkah Esther), 7
Mandel, Susan (Suzy), 196, 197, 206
Manhattan, xiv, 9, 15, 23, 29, 60, 98–100,
    173, 202
Marine Carp, 21, 24, 55, 59–61, 67, 166, 167
Markowitz, Louis, 61, 94
Marseilles, 67, 104, 108, 112, 114, 120, 167

Mayantz, Dr., 194
Matzo, 21, 25, 166
McDonald, James G., 69n27, 75n16,
    175, 184
Mediterranean, 104, 121, 126–128, 131,
    140, 141, 151
Meir, Golda, 123
Metzudat Ze'ev (MZ), 37n13, 186n30. *See
    also* Jabotinsky Institute
Merchant Marine. *See* United States
    Merchant Marine
Merlin, Samuel Méry, Jacques, xv, 110, 123,
    149, 165
Milk, 27
Minyan, 25
Mirabeau, 106
Mitzvah, 102, 116, 185, 197
Moby Dick, 193
Mo'ed Kattan, 200
Monheit, Freddie, 16
Monheit, Frieda, 6, 16
Monheit, Neil Naftali, 16
Monheit, Tuvia, 16
Monheit, Walter, 16
Mossad L'Aliyah Bet (Mossad for Aliyah
    Bet), xvi, 112, 186
Muni, Paul, 82

Naples, 121, 183
National Maritime Union, 34, 98, 193
National Military Organization. *See* Irgun
    Tzva'i Le'umi
naval blockade, iv, xii, xvi
Navy, xi, xii, xiii, xvii, 22, 29, 32, 41, 97,
    125, 203
Navy Yard. *See* Brooklyn Navy Yard
Nazi, 57, 76, 89, 91, 119, 183, 202
Nicolai, Robert O'Donnell, 47, 58, 61, 97,
    103, 109, 117, 137, 148
Neutrality Act, 173, 174
New York, xiii, xiv, xxi, 5, 7, 8, 12, 16, 20,
    24, 29, 52, 59, 60, 63, 67, 75, 84, 89, 93,
    96, 104, 139, 151, 164, 167, 168, 173,
    175, 201, 209
New York Navy Yard. *See* Brooklyn
    Navy Yard
New York Times, 75, 165
New York University, 90n18, 107n27
Nice, 42
North Carolina, 15, 53

O'Dwyer, Paul, 168
O'Dwyer, William, Mayor, 89, 168

Organization of Staff Analysts (OSA), 202-205, 244
Orr, Judge, 169, 170
Orthodox Judaism, xiii, 9, 10, 30, 101, 107, 108

Paducah (Ge'ula), 38, 50, 51, 140, 171, 181
Palestine, xi–xx, 12, 21, 30, 32, 34, 41, 43, 44, 48, 49, 52, 56, 63, 67, 74, 75, 79, 82, 85–113, 115, 119, 121, 128, 130, 138, 141, 151, 156, 157, 159–170, 185, 187, 197
   British Mandatory Palestine, xi, xv, xx
Palestine Post, 60, 90, 145, 165
Panama Canal, 28
Paris, xii, 42, 44, 45, 107, 110, 112, 119, 122, 142, 145, 149
Pearl Harbor, 19, 22
PM, xiin5, 79n43, 92, 149
Po'alei Mizrachi, 11
Poland, 3, 4, 6, 17, 37, 75, 80
Port-de-Bouc, xvii, 40, 42, 43, 48, 104, 105, 107, 114, 116, 120, 152, 167
Purser, 37, 40, 60, 92, 116

Rabbi Elchanan Isaac Theological Seminary (REITS), 10
Rabinowitz, Tzadok ha-Kohen, xviii
Raziel, David, 73
Reisner Mandel, Hedwig (Chana), 6
Reitov, Yaacov, 176
Revel, Bernard, Dr., 9
Revisionist Zionism, xii, xvi, xix, 34, 37, 73, 95, 105-106, 111, 119, 131
Rifkin, Shepard, 43, 61, 85, 96, 101, 149, 180, 181
Romania, 17
Roosevelt, Theodore, President of the United States, 17, 53, 77, 93
Rosenblatt, Zvi, 79, 104, 162
Russia, 17, 33, 136

Sabbath, 3, 8, 22, 70, 101, 116, 117, 178, 183, 195
Salanter Yeshiva (SAR), 8-9, 11, 193
San Remo Conference, 87
Sartre, Jean-Paul, 107
Schatz, Harry Nathan, 51, 61, 182
Scheidman, Alain, 113
Schwartz, Moshe, 109
Shendell, Irving, 84
Shiff, Moshe, 109
Shmulevitz, Matiyahu, 158

Serbia, 17
Sheepshead Bay, 21
Shulchan Arukh, 101, 116
Shuster, Florence (FS), xxi, 11-29, 32, 35, 43, 46-47, 49-51, 56-59, 62-65, 68, 196-97
Sirna, 136
Sokolow, Nahum, 87
Somers, Andrew L., 164
Sorensen, Erling, 61, 121
Spanish Civil War, 174
Spanish John, 37, 39
SS *Coeur D'Alene*, 24
SS *Egg Harbor*, 23, 24
SS *Emma Willard*, 23
SS *Joel Chandler*, 23, 24
SS *New Bern Victory*, 23, 24, 32
Staten Island, 86, 103
Stara, Albert, 44
Stavsky, Abraham (Avraham, Abrasha), xiv, 104, 105, 107, 108, 110, 172, 184, 206, 207
Steinmetz, Sol, 4, 5
Stern Group. *See* Lochmai Herut Israel
Stone, I. F., xiin5, 145, 146, 183
Stoneham, Horace Charles, 12
Stow, Bert, 163
Straits of Gibraltar, 104
Strasbourg, 113
Styrak, Edward R. (Ed), 37, 61, 97, 139, 140, 148, 182

tallis, 25
Talmudical Academy High School (MTA), 9. *See also* Yeshiva University High School for Boys
Tamar, Peleg, 54
Tel Hai day, 118
Teumim, Mota (Motel), 64, 173
tikkun olom, 102
Tradewinds, 169
Trumpeldor, Joseph, 118
Tunisia, 115, 179
Turkey, 21, 90, 121
Tyler, Alan, 126n6, 134, 136, 183
Tyre Shipping Company, 83, 84, 161, 166, 167, 169, 170

Ulanów (Ulonov), 4
Ulua, 127. *See also Haim Arlosoroff*
United Nations Security Council, 179
United States, xiv, xv, xix, 3, 5, 7, 10, 11, 16, 35, 39, 50, 63, 65, 73, 79, 81, 92, 107,

149, 162, 166, 173, 175, 184, 187, 195, 196, 207, *See also* America
United States Merchant Marine, xiii
University of Chicago, 18n9, 38, 181
USS *Cythera, 83*

Vaydat, Claire, 112, 113
Vienna, xiii, 3, 6, 16

War of Independence, xiii, xxi, 173
War Refugee Board, 76, 77, 105, 168
Washington, xiv, 10, 76, 83, 162, 181
Weizmann, Chaim, 74, 75, 87
Willard, Emma, 23
Winkler, Jack, 61, 148
World Jewish Congress, 77
World War I, 5-6, 87, 90, 96

World War II, xiii, xvi, xix, xx, xxi, 1, 6, 23, 29, 33, 52, 66-67, 74-75, 79-80, 88, 91-93, 95-97, 99, 101, 106, 122, 134, 139, 173, 209
World Zionist Congress, 74
Wyman, David S., xviin20, 73n2, 81
    The Abandonment of the Jews, 81

Yeshiva College, xviii, 9–11
Yeshiva University High School for Boys, 9. *See also* Talmudical Academy High School
Yiddish, 3, 4, 6, 8, 11, 12, 15, 64, 106, 135, 143, 161, 195

Zion, Sydney, 81

Illustrations

Geburtsurkunde

ISRAELITISCHE KULTUSGEMEINDE WIEN _____ Nr. 1772/1920)

- - - Heinrich M a n d e l - - - -

ist am 6.9.1920 sechsten September eintausendneunhundertundzwanzig - -

in W i e n., IX, Schulz Stranitzkygasse 6 - - - _____ geboren.

Vater: - - Abraham M a n d e l - - -

- - - - - - - - - - - - - - - -

- - - - - - - - - - - - - - - -

Mutter: - - Hedwig geborene R e i z n e r - -

- - - - - - - - - - - - - - -

- - - - - - - - - - : - - - -

Änderungen der Eintragung:

Wien , den   8. April   19 7?

Der beeidete Matrikenführer

XXXXXXXXXXXXXXXXX

Birth record of Heinrich Mandel.

Avrohom, Chana (Hedwig), Leo, and baby Henry Mandel circa 1920.

Jacob (Yaakov Tzvi) Mandel.

Mandel Family in the early 1930s, probably at Leo's Bar Mitzvah. Top row: Chana and Avrohom Mandel. Middle row: Hymie on left and Leo on right. Bottom row, left to right: Rivky, Moish, Goldie, and Dorie. Tziporah had not been born yet.

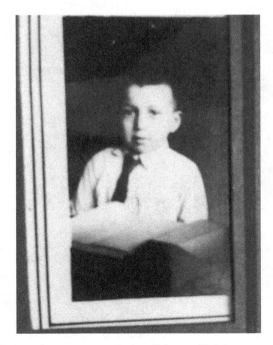

Hymie Mandel as an elementary student at Salanter Yeshiva.

Henry Mandel as a teenager.

Henry Mandel's Merchant Marine identification papers.

Henry Mandel's Engine Department license.

Henry Mandel in Acre Prison, reading on a mattress draped over barbed wire, while wearing the boots he used to pass contraband batteries to an imprisoned Irgun fighter. In the top right corner is David Gutmann and a partially obstructed Harry Nathan Schatz. © Wallace Litwin / Stanley B. Burns, MD & The Burns Archive.

Wallace Litwin on the *Ben Hecht*. © Wallace Litwin / Stanley B. Burns, MD & The Burns Archive.

Photograph of two children refugees with a *Ben Hecht* life preserver taken by Wallace Litwin. © Wallace Litwin / Stanley B. Burns, MD & The Burns Archive.

A wooden medal with a picture of Palestine and Transjordan with an arm holding a rifle and Hebrew lettering: "Only Thus."

Reverse side of medal, which reads: "To a Brave Sailor from His Comrades Members of the 'Irgun Zevai Leumi.' Acre Prison Henry Mandel."

DEPORTED from the Holy Land by the British, American seamen who manned the Jewish Immigration ship "Ben Hecht" arrive here aboard the S. S. Marine Carp. (Story on Page 20.)

The *Ben Hecht* crew, without Mandel, upon arrival in New York. *New York Post,* April 16, 1947.

(NEWS foto by Petersen)

Acting Mayor Vincent R. Impellitteri (right) greets Capt. Hym Robert Levitan on City Hall steps. Grouped around are crew membe

Capt. Hyman Robert Levitan, 7-year-old skipper of the S. S. Ben Hecht, and 20 of the crew members who were jailed by the British for helping to smuggle displaced persons into Palestine, esterday were received at City Hall by acting Mayor Vincent Impellitteri, representing Ma O'Dwyer, who is in Califor Acting as spokesman, Capt. I tan said he and his men w make the trip "again and a despite British threat."

Mandel's copy of the article in the April 19, 1947 edition of the *New York Daily News* describing the City Hall reception of the *Ben Hecht* sailors.

Mandel's Coast Guard identification papers. It reads: "Henry Mandel, [Illegible] 2-580712 D1; Date of Birth 9–6-20, Place of Birth, Austria, Citizenship, USA, Home Address, 1035 Kelly St., Bronx 59, New York," and over "Signature of Mariner," Henry Mandel's signature.

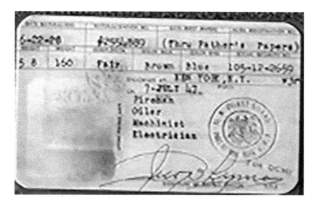

The reverse side of the Coast Guard identification papers.

Henry Mandel's photograph on his passport and his Coast Guard discharge papers, circa 1947.

Nº 80445

Certificate of Substantially Continuous Service
IN THE
UNITED STATES MERCHANT MARINE

This is to certify that _____ Henry Mandel _____

has completed a period of substantially continuous service in the United States Merchant Marine, said period of service having commenced on June 20, 1945 *and terminated on* May 27, 1947 *, within the meaning of the Rules and Regulations prescribed pursuant to Public Law 87, 78th Congress (57 Stat. 162), as amended.*

ATTEST:

A. J. WILLIAMS, *Secretary.*

BY DIRECTION OF THE
UNITED STATES MARITIME COMMISSION

W. W. SMITH, *Chairman.*

Dated _____ May 27, 1947 _____

Mandel's Certificate of Substantially Continuous Service in the United States Merchant Marine, which commenced June 20, 1945 and concluded May 27, 1947 (after returning home from his voyages aboard the *Ben Hecht* and the *Marine Carp*).

Chaim Mandel at the Chemed Israeli arms factory circa December 1948.

AFLP publicity photographs of *Ben Hecht* crewmen David Irving Gutmann, Harry Herschkowitz, Shepard Rifkin, Henry Mandel, Louis Brettschneider, Robert Nicolai, Edward R. Styrak, and David Kaplan.

The *Ben Hecht's* departure from Port de Bouc. © Wallace Litwin / Stanley B. Burns, MD & The Burns Archive.

Profile of the *Ben Hecht*.

"Held by British" newspaper clipping with inset photographs of *Ben Hecht* crewmen. Bottom (left to right): Henry Mandel, David Irving Gutmann, and Shepard Rifkin; top: David Kaplan, Louis Brettschneider, and Harry Herschkowitz.

Photo of the *Ben Hecht* crew upon arrival in New York. *PM*, April 17, 1947.

Henry Mandel at American Veterans of Israel meeting in October 2007. © Stanley B. Burns, MD/The Burns Archive.

Hank Mandel at OSA. OSA website.

Henry (Chaim) Mandel's plaque at Ammunition Hill, Jerusalem.

The deck of the *Ben Hecht* at sea. © Wallace Litwin / Stanley B. Burns, MD & The Burns Archive.

The defiant raising of the Zionist flag aboard the *Ben Hecht*. © Wallace Litwin / Stanley B. Burns, MD & The Burns Archive.

Front of David Kaplan's olive-wood medal awarded him in Acre Prison.

Reverse side of David Kaplan's olive-wood medal.

CPSIA information can be obtained
at www.ICGtesting.com
Printed in the USA
BVHW070527171221
624083BV00003B/12